The Babel Lexicon of

Language

What's the word that describes the process of making supportive noises when you're listening to someone? What is syntax and how does it differ from grammar? Do you know what a morpheme is? And did you know that it's not only an atom that has a nucleus? *The Babel Lexicon of Language* is an entertaining and accessible introduction to the key terminology involved in the study of language. It defines over 500 terms and uses contemporary language examples, explaining complex issues in an easy-to-understand way. Written by the expert editorial team behind *Babel*, the popular language magazine, and assuming no prior knowledge of linguistics, *The Babel Lexicon of Language* is an invaluable resource for students, teachers and anyone with an interest in language.

DAN MCINTYRE is Professor of English Language and Linguistics at the University of Huddersfield. He co-founded *Babel: The Language Magazine* and has published widely on stylistics, corpus linguistics and the history of English. His major publications include the co-authored *Stylistics* (Cambridge University Press 2010) and *Corpus Stylistics* (Edinburgh University Press 2019).

LESLEY JEFFRIES is Professor of English Language and Linguistics at the University of Huddersfield. She co-edits *Babel: The Language Magazine*, co-authored *Stylistics* (Cambridge University Press 2010) and *Keywords in the Press* (Bloomsbury 2017), and has published widely on textual meaning in politics and poetry. She is Chair of the University Council of General and Applied Linguistics.

MATT EVANS is Senior Lecturer in Linguistics at the University of Huddersfield. His research interests are in Critical Discourse Analysis, and his publications include the co-edited *Routledge Handbook of Language and Conflict* (2019). He is Assistant Editor of *Babel: The Language Magazine*.

HAZEL PRICE is an Academic Fellow in English Language at the University of Salford and a Research Affiliate at the University of Huddersfield. Her research interests include corpus linguistics and Critical Discourse Analysis. She is the author of *The Language of Mental Illness* (Cambridge University Press 2021) and is Editorial Assistant for *Babel: The Language Magazine*.

ERICA GOLD is Reader in Forensic Speech Science at the University of Huddersfield. Her research is largely focused on the variability of phonetic parameters within and between speakers, and her research has been cited in court cases worldwide. She compiled WYRED (West Yorkshire Regional English Database), the world's largest forensically relevant database of British English speech.

The Babel Lexicon of
Language

DAN MCINTYRE

University of Huddersfield

LESLEY JEFFRIES

University of Huddersfield

MATT EVANS

University of Huddersfield

HAZEL PRICE

University of Salford

ERICA GOLD

University of Huddersfield

CAMBRIDGE
UNIVERSITY PRESS

University Printing House, Cambridge CB2 8BS, United Kingdom

One Liberty Plaza, 20th Floor, New York, NY 10006, USA

477 Williamstown Road, Port Melbourne, VIC 3207, Australia

314–321, 3rd Floor, Plot 3, Splendor Forum, Jasola District Centre, New Delhi – 110025, India

103 Penang Road, #05–06/07, Visioncrest Commercial, Singapore 238467

Cambridge University Press is part of the University of Cambridge.

It furthers the University's mission by disseminating knowledge in the pursuit of education, learning and research at the highest international levels of excellence.

www.cambridge.org
Information on this title: www.cambridge.org/9781108840453
DOI: 10.1017/9781108886062

First published 2022

A catalogue record for this publication is available from the British Library.

Library of Congress Cataloging-in-Publication Data
Names: McIntyre, Dan, 1975– author. | Jeffries, Lesley, 1956– author. | Evans, Matt, 1986– author. | Price, Hazel, (Linguist) author. | Gold, Erica, 1986– author.
Title: The Babel lexicon of language / Dan McIntyre, Lesley Jeffries, Matt Evans, Hazel Price, Erica Gold.
Description: Cambridge : Cambridge University Press, 2021. | Includes bibliographical references and index.
Identifiers: LCCN 2021024722 (print) | LCCN 2021024723 (ebook) | ISBN 9781108840453 (hardback) | ISBN 9781108886062 (ebook)
Subjects: LCSH: Linguistics – Terminology. | BISAC: LANGUAGE ARTS & DISCIPLINES / Linguistics / General | LANGUAGE ARTS & DISCIPLINES / Linguistics / General | LCGFT: Dictionaries.
Classification: LCC P29.5 .M36 2021 (print) | LCC P29.5 (ebook) | DDC 403–dc23
LC record available at https://lccn.loc.gov/2021024722
LC ebook record available at https://lccn.loc.gov/2021024723

ISBN 978-1-108-84045-3 Hardback
ISBN 978-1-108-81408-9 Paperback

CONTENTS

THE INTERNATIONAL PHONETIC ALPHABET (revised to 2020)

CONSONANTS (PULMONIC)

©⊕® 2020 IPA

	Bilabial	Labiodental	Dental	Alveolar	Postalveolar	Retroflex	Palatal	Velar	Uvular	Pharyngeal	Glottal
Plosive	p b			t d		ʈ ɖ	c ɟ	k ɡ	q ɢ		ʔ
Nasal	m	ɱ		n		ɳ	ɲ	ŋ	N		
Trill	ʙ			r					ʀ		
Tap or Flap		ⱱ		ɾ		ɽ					
Fricative	ɸ β	f v	θ ð	s z	ʃ ʒ	ʂ ʐ	ç ʝ	x ɣ	χ ʁ	ħ ʕ	h ɦ
Lateral fricative				ɬ ɮ							
Approximant		ʋ		ɹ		ɻ	j	ɰ			
Lateral approximant				l		ɭ	ʎ	ʟ			

Symbols to the right in a cell are voiced, to the left are voiceless. Shaded areas denote articulations judged impossible.

CONSONANTS (NON-PULMONIC)

Clicks		Voiced implosives		Ejectives	
ʘ	Bilabial	ɓ	Bilabial	ʼ	Examples:
ǀ	Dental	ɗ	Dental/alveolar	pʼ	Bilabial
ǃ	(Post)alveolar	ʄ	Palatal	tʼ	Dental/alveolar
ǂ	Palatoalveolar	ɠ	Velar	kʼ	Velar
ǁ	Alveolar lateral	ʛ	Uvular	sʼ	Alveolar fricative

OTHER SYMBOLS

ʍ Voiceless labial-velar fricative

w Voiced labial-velar approximant

ɥ Voiced labial-palatal approximant

ʜ Voiceless epiglottal fricative

ʢ Voiced epiglottal fricative

ʡ Epiglottal plosive

ɕ ʑ Alveolo-palatal fricatives

ɺ Voiced alveolar lateral flap

ɧ Simultaneous ʃ and x

Affricates and double articulations can be represented by two symbols joined by a tie bar if necessary.

t͡s k͡p

VOWELS

Where symbols appear in pairs, the one to the right represents a rounded vowel.

SUPRASEGMENTALS

ˈ	Primary stress	ˌfoʊnəˈtɪʃən
ˌ	Secondary stress	
ː	Long	eː
ˑ	Half-long	eˑ
˘	Extra-short	ĕ
ǀ	Minor (foot) group	
ǁ	Major (intonation) group	
.	Syllable break	ɹi.ækt
‿	Linking (absence of a break)	

TONES AND WORD ACCENTS

	LEVEL			CONTOUR	
e̋	or ˥	Extra high	ě	or ˇ	Rising
é	˦	High	ê	ˆ	Falling
ē	˧	Mid	e᷄	ˀ	High rising
è	˨	Low	e᷅	ˀ	Low rising
ȅ	˩	Extra low	e᷈	ˀ	Rising-falling
ꜜ	Downstep		↗	Global rise	
ꜛ	Upstep		↘	Global fall	

DIACRITICS

Some diacritics may be placed above a symbol with a descender, e.g. ŋ̊

̥	Voiceless	n̥ d̥		̤	Breathy voiced	b̤ a̤		̪	Dental	t̪ d̪
̬	Voiced	s̬ t̬		̰	Creaky voiced	b̰ a̰		̺	Apical	t̺ d̺
ʰ	Aspirated	tʰ dʰ		̼	Linguolabial	t̼ d̼		̻	Laminal	t̻ d̻
̹	More rounded	ɔ̹		ʷ	Labialized	tʷ dʷ		̃	Nasalized	ẽ
̜	Less rounded	ɔ̜		ʲ	Palatalized	tʲ dʲ		ⁿ	Nasal release	dⁿ
̟	Advanced	u̟		ˠ	Velarized	tˠ dˠ		ˡ	Lateral release	dˡ
̠	Retracted	e̠		ˤ	Pharyngealized	tˤ dˤ		̚	No audible release	d̚
̈	Centralized	ë		̴	Velarized or pharyngealized	ɫ				
̽	Mid-centralized	e̽		̝	Raised	e̝ (ɹ̝ = voiced alveolar fricative)				
̩	Syllabic	n̩		̞	Lowered	e̞ (β̞ = voiced bilabial approximant)				
̯	Non-syllabic	e̯		̘	Advanced Tongue Root	e̘				
˞	Rhoticity	ɚ a˞		̙	Retracted Tongue Root	e̙				

Typefaces: Doulos SIL (metatext); Doulos SIL, IPA Kiel, IPA LS Uni (symbols)

IPA Chart, www.internationalphoneticassociation.org/content/ipa-chart, available under a Creative Commons Attribution-Sharealike 3.0 Unported License. Copyright © 2020 International Phonetic Association.

PREFACE

Welcome to the Wonderful World of Linguistics!

Do you know the difference between an accent and a dialect? Are you unsure what uptalk is? Have you ever pondered how we produce speech? Perhaps you're confused by creole or perplexed by the passive. If so, then this book is for you. *The Babel Lexicon of Language* is aimed at new linguists and non-linguists and explains over 500 of the most commonly used terms in language study. We hope it will be useful to anyone with an interest in language. If you're studying language at school or college, then it will be of direct benefit in helping you to understand some of the specialist terms used in language study.

Perhaps because most people can speak, write or sign, almost everyone has an opinion about language. But often these opinions are based on mistaken beliefs or half-remembered facts from school. If you really want to know about language, then you need the discipline of linguistics. In fact, the first word you should look up in this book is **linguistics**. Then **linguist**. Linguists study language in the same way that chemists study the composition of matter, and biologists study living organisms. And, like any other academic discipline, linguistics comes with its own specialist terminology. This book will help you to get to grips with it.

Why Babel?

This book is called *The Babel Lexicon of Language*. We have included a definition of the term **Babel** to explain its origins but our reason for including it in the title is that this book is the first offshoot of a magazine that we edit called *Babel: The Language Magazine*. *Babel* is a magazine aimed at introducing linguistics to people who are not necessarily specialists in the field but who are fascinated by language. If you're interested in history or science, for instance, you can buy popular magazines about those subjects; but what we noticed several years ago is that no magazine existed on the topic of linguistics. *Babel* aims to fill that gap in the market. This book began life as a regular feature in the magazine. From 2012 to 2018, each issue included an article called 'The Linguistic Lexicon', in which we defined some of the most common terms used in linguistics. Once we had reached Z, we decided to expand on what we had written and turn the columns into a book, *The Babel Lexicon of Language*. You can find out more about *Babel: The Language Magazine* by visiting our website (babelzine.co.uk) or following us on Twitter (@babelzine).

Conventions

In order to ensure that you get the most out of this book, it will be worth familiarising yourself with the conventions that we use in entries. Entries each begin with a head word or words, indicated in bold type. Cross-references to other entries are also in bold (sometimes the cross-reference may be a plural form while the head word is a singular form; for instance, the cross-reference **verbs** will lead you to the entry for **verb**). Within an entry, any term that does not have its own separate entry is indicated in bold italics. Cited words are in italics. Italics are also used for book titles and, on occasion, for emphasis. In each case, this should be clear from the context. Chapter and article titles are enclosed in single quotation marks, as are example sentences. The entry on the next page demonstrates these conventions.

Underlining is occasionally used in cases where we need to highlight a particular part of an italicised word or phrase (such as, for instance, the **bound morpheme** in *un*happy). One further convention we have followed in the book concerns our use of names in example sentences. We took the decision that to avoid arbitrary and potentially unrepresentative choices of names we would instead use our own (and, in some cases, the names of family members). An example can be seen in the sample entry overleaf ('Hazel is shorter than Dan'). We make no claim as to the truth of such examples, of course!

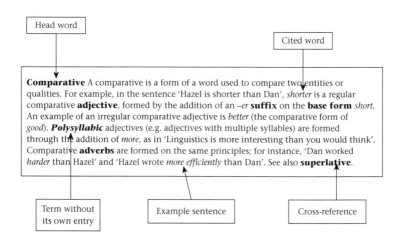

Head word

Cited word

Comparative A comparative is a form of a word used to compare two entities or qualities. For example, in the sentence 'Hazel is shorter than Dan', *shorter* is a regular comparative **adjective**, formed by the addition of an *–er* **suffix** on the **base form** *short*. An example of an irregular comparative adjective is *better* (the comparative form of *good*). **Polysyllabic** adjectives (e.g. adjectives with multiple syllables) are formed through the addition of *more*, as in 'Linguistics is more interesting than you would think'. Comparative **adverbs** are formed on the same principles; for instance, 'Dan worked *harder* than Hazel' and 'Hazel wrote *more efficiently* than Dan'. See also **superlative**.

Term without its own entry

Example sentence

Cross-reference

Transcribing Speech

Obviously enough, a book about language necessarily involves talking about speech. One of the difficulties of describing speech in writing, of course, is explaining what a particular element of speech sounds like. To do this, linguists use what is known as the International Phonetic Alphabet (IPA). This is a set of symbols that makes it possible to represent in writing any sound that you might hear in speech, in any language. For example, there are three sounds (phonemes) in the word *book*: an initial consonant, a vowel, and a final consonant. However, the way you pronounce *book* depends on where you come from. This is where the IPA is useful, as it allows us to describe a pronunciation precisely. For example, in a Standard British English pronunciation, [bʊk], the vowel sound is different from that in the word *goose* (which we would represent as [uː]). But in other varieties (e.g. Lancashire English), the pronunciation of *book* sometimes uses the *goose* vowel, hence [buːk]. In some other varieties of English (e.g. Scottish English, Ulster-based Hiberno-English, Singapore English), these vowels are merged into a single vowel sound which is slightly different from both of the Standard British English ones and can be represented phonetically as either [y] or [ʉ]. The IPA makes it possible to capture these differences of pronunciation in written form. The full International Phonetic Alphabet chart is included at the front of this book and will make more sense when you have read the entries on phonetics in this book (start with **International Phonetic Alphabet**). To help you read the IPA symbols included in the entries, however, listed below are the symbols we most commonly use (these are the phonemes of English), along with examples of words that feature the sounds they represent.

Vowels

Symbol	Southern Standard British English	General American English
iː*	see	see
ɪ	bit	bit
ɛ	bed	bed
a	tap	tap
ɑː*	part	father
ɒ	top	thought
ɔ	law	caught
ʊ	foot	foot
uː*	goose	goose
ʌ	love	love
ɜ(ɹ)**	bird	bird
ə	about	about
eɪ	pay	pay
oʊ	toe	toe
aɪ	like	like
aʊ	cow	cow
ɔɪ	boy	boy
ɪə(ɹ)**	beer	beer
ɛə(ɹ)**	pair	pair
ʊə(ɹ)**	lure	lure

* In the IPA, the colon symbol (ː) is used to mark a vowel (or consonant) with an extended duration.

** General American English includes /ɹ/ after the monophthong/diphthong. Southern Standard British English does not.

Consonants

Symbol	Example
p	<u>p</u>ot
b	<u>b</u>oy
t	<u>t</u>o
d	<u>d</u>og
k	<u>k</u>ill
g	<u>g</u>ive
tʃ	<u>ch</u>urch
dʒ	<u>j</u>udge
s	<u>s</u>ad
z	<u>z</u>ip
ʃ	<u>sh</u>eep
ʒ	lei<u>s</u>ure
h	<u>h</u>op
m	<u>m</u>op
n	<u>n</u>o
ŋ	si<u>ng</u>
f	<u>f</u>ed
v	<u>v</u>an
θ	<u>th</u>ing
ð	<u>th</u>e
l	<u>l</u>it
ɹ	<u>r</u>ip
j	<u>y</u>es
w	<u>w</u>it
ʔ	bu<u>tt</u>er (when pronounced in British English as *bu'er*)

In this book, when we use IPA to transcribe English, unless otherwise specified, the accent that we transcribe is (Southern) Standard British English. You will often notice slash brackets used to enclose the transcription of sounds. Slash brackets indicate what is known as a *phonemic* transcription (see the **phoneme** entry for a more detailed explanation of what this involves). Sometimes, however, you will see square brackets used, as in [ɫ]. Square brackets indicate what is known as *phonetic* transcription, which you can think of as a more detailed type of transcription. For example, while /l/ describes the sounds at both the beginning of the word *light* and the end of the word *seagull*, in some accents these initial and final consonants may be pronounced differently. Square brackets are used to indicate this. For instance, the /l/ at the beginning of *light* may be pronounced [l], while the /l/ at the end of *seagull* may be pronounced [ɫ]. The [ɫ] transcription indicates a sound known as *dark l*, which is pronounced further back in the mouth and is normal at the ends of words in many accents. However, in some accents this sound can occur in an initial position too. Try saying *seagull* and hold your tongue in the position it ends up in. Now, keeping your tongue in the same position, try saying the word *light*. Slash brackets and square brackets, then, indicate phonemic and phonetic transcription, respectively. In cases where linguists wish to indicate (written) letters rather than phonemes, however, angle brackets are used. For example, the word *pterodactyl* begins with the letter <p> but the consonant sound /t/.

A Note on Grammar

People are often not very confident about their grammatical knowledge, and it's not unusual to hear people say that they don't understand grammar. But the term *grammar* refers simply to the set of conventions that govern how acceptable sentences may be formed in a language. If you are a native speaker of a language, then by definition you understand its grammar, otherwise you would not be able to form comprehensible sentences. What people usually mean, then, when they say they don't understand grammar is that they don't have the vocabulary to talk about it. For example, although you might be perfectly able to form sentences in a language, you might not be able to explain what a subordinate clause is or define an adverbial. The entries on grammar in this book will help you to get to grips with some of the most common terms. However, one of the things that should become clear as you read this book is that linguists have many different ideas about how grammar works. Consequently, there are many different grammars, each of which highlight particular aspects of how language is structured. Generative grammar, for instance, proposes that grammar is a system of rules, rather like a computer program, that allows speakers to generate all the sentences that it is possible to form in a given language. Construction grammar, on the other hand, proposes instead that we form sentences by putting together pre-existing chunks of language rather than individual words. In this book, we aim to explain the approach taken by a variety of grammars, but we have also taken the decision to define in more detail the terms associated with a particular descriptive grammar that is sometimes known by an acronym: SPOCA.[1] This stands for 'Subject, Predicator, Object, Complement, Adverbial', all of which are clause elements (all of these terms are defined in this book). A descriptive grammar allows us to describe the structure of a language, and SPOCA is particularly useful for describing English. Throughout the book, entries are illustrated with examples from a variety of languages, but there is inevitably a bias towards English because that is the first language that we as authors all share, and it is the language that we can be sure all our readers will understand. SPOCA uses terms you may be familiar with from school, such as *noun*, *verb phrase*, *subordinate clause*, etc. We took the decision to focus on SPOCA as we think understanding other grammars (such as pattern grammar and generative grammar) is made easier if you first have a basic understanding of a straightforwardly descriptive grammar. Any examples of grammatical analysis in entries that are not primarily focused on grammar (such as **parallelism**, for instance) are based on SPOCA.

Finally ...

... whatever your reason for picking up this book, we hope that it satisfies your curiosity and leaves you feeling enthused about language!

---

[1] Although in general we do not reference other scholarly works in this volume, we do wish to acknowledge the origin of this descriptive grammar of English, which is the influential *Comprehensive Grammar of the English Language* (Longman 1985), co-authored by Randolph Quirk, Sidney Greenbaum, Geoffrey Leech and Jan Svartvik. Often referred to by the shorthand reference *Quirk et al.*, it is one of the great standard reference grammars of English.

ACKNOWLEDGEMENTS

We are grateful to the following members of the *Babel* advisory panel for reading and commenting on the entries in this book: David Crystal, Rob Drummond, Simon Horobin, Tristan Miller, Lynne Murphy, Jeremy Scott, Jane Setter, Peter Trudgill, Lieven Vandelanotte, Katie Wales and Dominic Watt. We are also grateful to Cameron Hartley, Rachel Hatchard, Eszter McIntyre, Jack Wilson and Mao Ye for equally good advice.

Marek Jagucki provided the illustrations for the book, and the fantastic cover art, for which we thank him. We would also like to thank Richard Honey, whose design work on *Babel: The Language Magazine* has been a key part of the magazine's success. Finally, and most importantly, we are grateful to all the contributors to *Babel* over the years, and to all our readers, without whom neither the magazine nor this book would exist.

A

ablaut

This is a process whereby the **base form** of a **word** undergoes an internal **vowel** change, resulting in a change to **function** or **meaning**. It also refers to the outcome of that process. Ablaut originated as a process in **Proto-Indo-European**. As a result, modern **Indo-European** languages have inherited ablauts. If you have ever learned a modern Indo-European language as a second language, you may have had a teacher carefully point out irregular verbs. These irregular verbs are often ones that contain ablauts in certain **forms**. Take the Spanish word *poder* (to be able to). In the first person present form, *poder* becomes *puedo*, where the internal vowel <o> becomes <ue>. An English example is the verb *drink*, whose past **tense** and past participle forms (*drank* and *drunk*) are generated via ablaut, rather than by the addition of an -*ed* **inflection**, which is what happens with regular verbs (e.g. 'She *jumped* the furthest' and 'She has *jumped* the furthest').

accent

Your accent is the way that you pronounce your particular **dialect**. In British English, for instance, the Yorkshire accent differs from the Birmingham accent. Your accent can indicate where you are from, what social class you belong to, how formally educated you might be, what community you wish to identify with, and so on. As a result of this connection to identity, people make value judgements about accents. It used to be the case that newsreaders on the BBC all spoke **Received Pronunciation** (RP), the so-called 'Queen's English'. Nowadays, it's common to hear the news being read in a wide range of accents, from Yorkshire to Geordie to Scouse. But, although it's no longer strange to hear people on TV speaking **Standard English** (dialect) with a regional accent, it would be unusual to hear someone speaking a regional dialect using RP. And, while it is still unfortunately true that people can be judged on the accent they speak, in communicative terms, no accent is any better or worse than any other.

accommodation

This is a term from **sociolinguistics** and refers to the practice of unconsciously (or, on occasion, consciously) adjusting the way we speak in relation to someone else's language variety as a result of spending time with them. Elements of language that may be affected include, for example, *lexis*, pronunciation and **stress** patterns. Reasons why a person's linguistic behaviour may *converge* with the people they are talking to include a desire for approval, recognition of a person's status, and (romantic) attraction. Conversely, a speaker may consciously or unconsciously *diverge* from the linguistic behaviour of people around them, as a means of signalling social distance from them, or to emphasise or reinforce their membership of a different **speech community**. *See also* **upward convergence** and **downward convergence**.

acoustic phonetics

This is a subfield within phonetics that is specifically concerned with the physical properties of sounds. Acoustic phoneticians consider both the **waveform** and the **spectrogram** in their analyses of speech, in order to measure aspects of frequency, intensity and/or temporal domains. Acoustic phonetics has grown tremendously over recent years, largely thanks to the open-access software **Praat**, which allows everyone from the beginner to the seasoned acoustic phonetician the opportunity to explore the physical manifestations of sound.

acrolect

This refers to a version of a language that is seen as the standard variety, or the one that is viewed as the most prestigious. Acrolects are based on socially constructed beliefs that one **form** of language is preferred over others. In Hawaii, Standard American English is seen as the acrolect and superior to Hawaiian Creole. *See also* **basilect**, **creole** and **mesolect**.

acronym

This is the term for a label that is formed from the initial letters of a phrase. This is usually to simplify a complex or long description for ease of communication, though acronyms can also have the effect of excluding or confusing people who don't know their origin. Acronyms are all around us. Many have become so common that people often don't realise they are acronyms at all. **Words** such as *scuba* (self-contained underwater breathing apparatus), *radar* (radio detection and ranging) and *laser* (light amplification by stimulated emission of radiation) are all examples of acronyms that have become commonly used words. One indication of this is the fact that they are now conventionally written in lower-case letters. Acronyms are also commonly used in **linguistics**. *KWIC*, pronounced /kwɪk/, stands for 'key word in context' and is found in **corpus linguistics** (*see also* **concordance**). Databases and software are also often referred to by acronyms – for example, *WYRED* (West Yorkshire Regional English Database) or *CLiC* (Corpus Linguistics in Context). The difference between acronyms and *initialisms* is that acronyms are pronounced as complete words (e.g. *radar* is /reɪda:/) while initialisms are pronounced by articulating each constituent letter (e.g. /ɛs eɪ ɛs/ for *SAS*).

active

Active structures place the **Actor** in a process at the start of the **sentence** in **subject** position, and the **Goal** in **object** position after the verb, e.g. 'The builders mended the roof.' This term is usually applied to transitive structures (where the verb requires an object), which are implicitly paired with **passive** structures.

Actor

This refers to the participant responsible for the process in a clause. Often functioning as the grammatical subject, this is a label associated with **Systemic Functional Linguistics**, which emphasises semantic over syntactic functions. In the sentence 'Matt ran a marathon', Matt is the Actor. But he is also the Actor in 'The department was kept afloat by Matt', a **passive** structure with **Goal** as **subject**.

actuation

This refers to the initiation of a linguistic change. There are numerous explanations for why linguistic changes are initiated. These include ***preserving uniformity, hole-filling, reanalysis, misperception*** and ***expressiveness***. *Preserving uniformity* often involves a move towards regularity; for example, the formation of the plural in English is now largely achieved by adding an *s*-inflection (or related **form** such as *-ies*). This differs from how plurals were formed in **Old English**, where there was a much wider range of plural **inflections** available (some have survived in **words** like *oxen* and *children*). *Hole-filling* is the process of filling a gap in the linguistic system, such as when the pronunciation of a vowel changes, leaving a gap in the vowel space that then needs to be filled by a different vowel (see the **Great Vowel Shift** for more details of this kind of change). *Reanalysis* involves reinterpreting the structure of a particular linguistic form. For example, the constituent morphemes of the word *helicopter* are derived from the Greek words *helix* (spiral) and *pteron* (wing). Reanalysis, however, has led to an understanding of the constituent morphemes as being *heli* and *copter*. As a result of this reanalysis, lexical innovation was made possible, resulting in such terms as *helipad, heliport* and *gyrocopter*. *Misperception*, as you might expect, is the process of linguistic change being initiated by a misunderstanding. It is possible, for instance, that one of the causes of the decline of the Old English inflectional system was the fact that inflections were unstressed and therefore less likely to be heard in conversation than stressed **syllables**. Non-native speakers of Old English (Scandinavian invaders, perhaps) who were attempting to communicate with Anglo-Saxon people may consequently not have produced inflections simply as a result of not having heard them in speech. Finally, *expressiveness* explains the deliberate initiation of a linguistic change. Lexical developments are often the result of expressiveness; consider, for instance, the extension of the word *racist* to function as a censure for any assertion that the hearer doesn't agree with (e.g. Speaker 1: 'Sheffield United are crap.' / Speaker 2: 'That is so racist'). *See also* **propagation**.

adjacency pair

In **Conversation Analysis**, an adjacency pair is a set of speaker turns (*see* **turn**) that fit together functionally; i.e. the first turn usually invites a particular second turn. Adjacency pairs were first discussed by the conversation analysts Emmanuel Schegloff and Harvey Sacks, who found that conversation appeared to be organised in two-turn sequences, in which one person speaks and then another person responds. Some canonical examples of adjacency pairs include questions and answers, greeting pairs, and request / acceptance or rejection pairs. The first turn in an adjacency pair is referred to as the first-pair part and the second is the second-pair part. For example:

First-pair part (question): Will you go out with me?
Second-pair part (answer): No, sorry. I don't fancy you.

Adjacency pairs sometimes occur over several turns, as in cases where clarification is needed before the adjacency pair can be completed. The turns that come between an adjacency pair are called insertion sequences and may take the form of, for example, clarificatory questions within a question–answer pair. For instance:

First-pair part (question 1): Will you go out with me?
Insertion sequence: *Question 2:* Are you rich?
                            Answer 2: No.
Second-pair part (answer 1): No, sorry. I don't fancy you.

Adjacency pairs are a fundamental unit of organisation in conversation and the study of patterns in adjacency pairs allows **linguists** to get a better understanding of how conversations are organised by speakers engaged in interactions.

adjective

Adjectives function either as the head of an **adjective phrase** (e.g. *hungry* in 'I am very *hungry* ') or as modifiers in a **noun phrase** (e.g. *large* and *brown* in 'The *large*, *brown* cows'). Many common adjectives are gradable and have three **forms**: a **base form**, a **comparative** form and a **superlative** form. It's often possible to tell whether a **word** is an adjective by seeing whether you can make a comparative or superlative form from it.

	Base	Comparative	Superlative
Regular	big	bigger	biggest
	slow	slower	slowest
	beautiful	more beautiful	most beautiful
Irregular	good	better	best
	bad	worse	worst

Usually, adjectives specify some quality or property attributed to a **noun**. For example, physical qualities ('The *large, brown* cow'), psychological qualities ('The *fierce* cow'), evaluative qualities ('The *most beautiful* cow'), etc.

adjective phrase

Adjective phrases have an adjective as their **head word** and may include one or more modifying **adverbs**, which are often known as **intensifiers** as they specify the amount or intensity of the quality referred to by the adjective. In the following examples, the adjective phrase is underlined and its head word is italicised:

- The car was bright *green*.
- It was absolutely *hideous*.
- In fact, it was far too *awful*.

Adjective phrases function as a **complement** in a sentence. *See also* **SPOCA**.

advanced

This refers to the **place of articulation** (in the mouth) of the sound being produced. Advanced sounds are produced further forward (i.e. nearer the **lips**) than their expected target (*advanced* can be contrasted with **retracted**). Both **vowels** and **consonants** can be described as advanced, but vowels are more commonly described in this way. There is a specific **diacritic** in the **International Phonetic Alphabet** assigned to the term *advanced*. This is a small plus sign placed under the sound being described. For example, [u̟] describes a [u] that is produced further forward in the mouth.

adverb

Adverbs function as the head of an **adverb phrase**. Sometimes the head is preceded by **modifiers**, which are often adverbs of degree. Here are some examples (the adverb phrase is underlined and the head is in italics):

The professor gesticulated *wildly*.

He spoke exceptionally *loudly*.

The students applauded very *enthusiastically* indeed.

Adverbs can also function as modifiers in adjective phrases (the **adjective phrase** is underlined and the modifying adverb is italicised):

I am *extremely* hungry.

The professor was *very* pleased.

It was *too* hot.

Adverbs in English often end in -*ly* but using this test to determine whether a **word** is an adverb is not a foolproof method, as you will have noticed from the examples above. It's also the case that sometimes what looks like an adverb is actually an adjective – e.g. *friendly*. (For this reason, looking at the function of a word in a sentence is a better indicator of what **word class** it belongs to than what its **form** or **meaning** is.) Some adverbs also have **comparative** and **superlative** forms (e.g. 'He danced *well/better/best*'; 'She danced *gracefully /more gracefully / most gracefully*').

When they are not modifying adjectives (e.g. *really* hot), adverbs modify **verbs**; that is, they give more information about the action, process, state, etc., described in the **verb phrase**. Adverbs can express manner (*quickly, well*), place (*here, there, somewhere*), time (*now, then, last night, six weeks ago*), duration (*constantly, briefly, always*), frequency (*daily, weekly*) and degree (*hardly, rather, quite*).

adverb phrase

Adverb phrases have an **adverb** as their **head word**. In the examples below, the adverb phrase is underlined and the head is in italics:

- Erica writes very *quickly*.
- Matt writes absolutely *spiffingly*.
- Dan writes *worse* than Lesley.

An adverb phrase functions as an **adverbial** in a **clause** or **sentence**. It can also modify an adjective in an **adjective phrase**. *See also* **SPOCA**.

adverbial

An adverbial is a **clause** element in some theories of **grammar** that modifies the **predicator** by providing information about the manner, time or place of the event being described in the **sentence**.

In some frameworks, they may be called **adjuncts**. Here are some examples (underlined):

1. Hazel baked a cake yesterday.
2. She ate it in the evening.
3. That night she felt sick.
4. After taking an indigestion tablet, she felt fine.

Adverbials can be formed from **adverbs** or **adverb phrases** (as in example (1), above), **prepositional phrases** (2), **noun phrases** (3) and **adverb clauses** (4). In contrast to other clause elements, such as the **subject**, **object** or predicator, adverbials in English are relatively flexible in terms of where they can appear in the clause. For example:

- The cat walked to his bowl lazily.
- Lazily, the cat walked to his bowl.
- The cat lazily walked to his bowl.

In principle, a sentence can contain an infinite number of adverbials. A good example of how adverbials can be piled up can be seen in the introductory narration to a classic children's TV programme, *Noggin the Nog*, which was popular in Britain in the 1950s and 1960s (the adverbials are underlined):

> In the lands of the North, where the Black Rocks stand guard against the cold sea, in the dark night that is very long, the Men of the Northlands sit by their great log fires and they tell a tale.

The number of adverbials in this particular sentence also creates a **foregrounding** effect, focusing attention on the final unmodified clause 'they tell a tale'. *See also* **SPOCA** and **complement**.

affix

An affix is a **morpheme** that is added to the **base form** / stem / root of a **word** in order to create a new word or modify the existing base form. An affix placed before the base form is a **prefix**, while one that occurs after it is a **suffix**. For example, we can create the semantic opposite of the word *happy* by adding a prefix: *unhappy*. We can change the **word class** (also known as **part of speech**) of *happy* from adjective to noun by adding a suffix: *happiness*. The question of how the base form changes (if at all) in order to accommodate the affix is something that can be studied in **morphology**. *See also* **infix**.

affricate

This refers to a set of sounds that are classified according to their **manner of articulation**. Affricates begin with a **stop** and are immediately followed by a **fricative**, e.g. /tʃ/ (the pronunciation of <ch> in English). The air in an affricate is first obstructed like a stop, and then released through a constricted channel that causes turbulent **airflow**.

agglutination

This is a process in **morphology** whereby a string of **morphemes** is put together to create a more complex **word**. Turkish and Swahili are two **languages** that use agglutination. An example of agglutination in Turkish is *ev-ler-den*, meaning 'from [the] houses'. Languages that feature high levels of agglutination are known as *agglutinative* languages.

airflow

This refers to the flow of air through the **vocal tract**. In speech, sounds are produced with one of two types of airflow: **egressive** or **ingressive**. Egressive sounds have an airflow that moves out of the vocal tract (through the mouth and/or nose), while an ingressive airflow involves air flowing into the vocal tract. The majority of speech sounds have egressive airflow because it is easier to speak for longer whilst breathing out. Try reciting a rhyme on an egressive and then an ingressive airflow and you will see why. However, it isn't difficult to produce an ingressive sound (think about the ingressive gasp you might make if you are shocked). Ingressive airflow is also used paralinguistically by speakers of Scandinavian languages to signal agreement.

airstream mechanism

This is one of three components (along with **phonation** and *articulation*) that are vital in the production of speech. **Airflow** is needed in order to produce speech, and we rely on three different types of airstream mechanisms to initiate this airflow. The three

types of airstream mechanisms used in producing speech are
pulmonic, glottalic and ***velaric***. Pulmonic sounds require airflow
to be initiated from the **lungs**, and the majority of the world's
sounds are produced pulmonically. The rarer airstream of glottalic
sounds is initiated by the **glottis**, while velaric airstreams are
initiated with the **tongue**.

alliteration

This is a term given to the repetition of the same **consonant** sound
at the start of a series of **words**. Alliteration is a feature of many
famous literary works, including this line from Edgar Allan Poe's
'The Raven' which repeats the word-initial /d/ sound:

Doubting, dreaming dreams no mortal ever dared to dream before.

In addition to the high literature of Poe, alliteration can also be
found in many other text-types, from adverts to comedy sketches.
Here's a nice example from a *Monty Python* comedy sketch ('Bells'),
in which a man is complaining to his wife about the 'religious
racket' of the church bells:

Husband: We don't get Buddhists playing bagpipes in our
        bathroom, or Hindus harmonizing in the hall. The
        Shintoists don't come 'ere shattering sheet glass in the
        shithouse and shouting slogans.

Wife: All right, don't practise your alliteration on me.

allomorph

This is a term in **morphology** that refers to the different ways in
which a single **morpheme** can be produced. Allomorphs are the
morphological equivalent of **allophones** which are variants of one
phoneme. Which allomorph is used depends on either the
phonological or morphological properties of the **word** it is a part of.
An example of allomorphic variation based on morphological
conditions can be seen in the words *vain* and *vanity*, in which adding
the –*ity* **bound morpheme** results in a change in the morpheme
that precedes it.

vain without affixation → /veɪn/
vain plus affixation (-*ity*) → /væn/

Other **base forms** that precede the *-ity* **suffix** also follow this rule, e.g. *sane → sanity, humane → humanity*. Phonological conditioning can be seen in the regular past **tense** in English. There, the last **consonant** of the preceding morpheme determines the allomorph that follows it. For example, while the written version of the words *laughed*, *lived* and *started* all end with the past **tense** <ed> morpheme, the endings are all pronounced differently due to the phoneme immediately before the morpheme:

- *laughed* [lɑːft]

   <ed> is pronounced as [t] because the final consonant in the root is **voiceless**.

- *lived* [lɪvd]

   <ed> is pronounced as [d] because the final consonant in the root is **voiced**.

- *started* [stɑːtɪd]

   <ed> is pronounced as [ɪd] because the final consonant in the root is an **alveolar plosive** and is therefore too similar to the /d/ in the suffix for both to be clearly pronounced. Having a **vowel** in between the /t/ and the /d/ facilitates the pronunciation.

allophone

This refers to a set of different realisations of a **phoneme** in a language. Allophones do not change the **meaning** of a **word**, and often the allophone selected is influenced by the phonetic environment in which it occurs. Allophones are also interesting in that you can sometimes identify someone's **accent** based on their preference for using specific allophones. Take the American English use of /ɾ/ (i.e. a consonant somewhere between a /t/ and a /d/) instead of /t/ in words like *butter* or *flatter*. A Standard British English speaker would use /t/ for these words.

alveolar

Put your **tongue** behind your front teeth. Now move it back slightly. The flattish platform that your tongue is touching is your alveolar ridge. If you run your tongue from your front teeth backwards, you should be able to feel the ***alveolar ridge*** and the slope that takes your tongue further up into your **hard palate** (roof of the mouth). The **alveolar** ridge is the most common place for articulating consonants in English (/t/, /d/, /s/, /z/, /n/, /l/, /r/) and many other languages too. You make use of your alveolar ridge when you produce alveolar sounds like /d/ (as in *dog*) and /t/ (as in *ten*). Try it. You should feel that your tongue is resting or even pressing against your alveolar ridge when you begin to pronounce these **words**. It will move away from the ridge as soon as you've made the /t/ or /d/ sounds. Alveolar **consonants** are produced using the alveolar ridge as an **articulator**. The difference between sounds produced at the same **place of articulation** is that the speaker is doing different things with the tongue and other articulators, i.e. changing the **manner of articulation**.

ambiguity

This is when a linguistic expression has more than one possible interpretation. It can occur at any **level of language**. At the phonological level, imagine hearing the utterance 'The nuthatch is a neckless bird.' It is our knowledge of the world that tells us we cannot be hearing 'the nuthatch is a necklace bird', because on the whole human beings do not wear birds around their necks. This phonological ambiguity arises from the similarity of sounds (not spelling) in the **words** *neckless* and *necklace*. Lexical ambiguity also occurs at the level of the word, with **homonyms** like *bank* and *wave* needing their context to make clear which **meaning** is intended. 'I make my way over to the bank' is likely to imply a river bank if the context is all about a river trip in a boat, but could imply a branch of a financial institution if the context is one of a busy city street. Some ambiguities arise from the **grammar**. **Subordinate clauses** are particularly prone to ambiguity:

'Erica told the girl that Matt was bringing ... '

Here, the ambiguous section is 'the girl that Matt was bringing'. It could be a single element of the **sentence** forming the direct **object** of the verb *told* (i.e. the girl is the person that Matt was bringing to the event), in which case you could replace the whole thing with a single **pronoun**: *her*. The other possibility is that 'the girl' is the indirect object of *told* and 'that Matt was bringing' is the beginning of a subordinate **clause** forming the direct object. The remainder of the sentence is likely to make clear which of these interpretations is the right one:

'Erica told the girl that Matt was bringing to wrap up warm.'
'Erica told the girl that Matt was bringing warm clothes.'

amelioration

In a **linguistics** context, this refers to the upgrading of the **meaning** of a **word**, so that a word with a generally negative **connotation** becomes more positive. In general, amelioration is a less common process than its opposite, **pejoration**. Historically, there have been a number of terms in English that have undergone the process of amelioration – for example, *nice* originally meant foolish, *pretty* used to mean cunning, and *knight* referred to a youth or male servant rather than a nobleman. More recently, we have seen words like *sick*, *wicked*, *ill* and *dope* undergo amelioration in dialects associated with youth or music cultures.

amplitude

This term, typically used in **acoustic phonetics**, refers to the height of a sound wave in a **waveform**. Typically, the louder the sound, the higher the amplitude, and the softer a sound, the lower the amplitude.

analytic language

Analytic languages use **word order** more than **inflections** to convey **sentence meaning**. That is, instead of using a morphological **case** ending to mark, say, the **subject** in a sentence, an analytic language will indicate this by placing the subject in a particular position, typically the first **clause** element in a sentence in many languages. In essence, analytic languages use **words** (or free **morphemes**) to convey meanings that in **synthetic languages** are conveyed by inflections. For example, **Present Day English** uses **prepositions** to express locational relationships between **nouns** whereas Hungarian uses inflections on the nouns themselves. Compare English '<u>in</u> the church' and Hungarian *templom<u>ban</u>* (in the church). An example of a language that has even greater analytical tendencies than English is Mandarin Chinese, where past and plural are marked through **free morphemes** (as opposed to the inflectional **morphology** used in English, e.g. *boys* or *laughed*). The example below shows how Mandarin Chinese uses individual words to convey information about **tense** that in English would be indicated by an inflection on the **verb**:

我	们	吃	饭	了
wɔ	mən	chi	fan	lə
1st person	plural	eat	dinner	past tense
We ate dinner				

anaphora

This describes the practice of referring backwards in language. For example, in the following **sentence**, the **pronouns** *he* and *his* refer anaphorically to the **noun phrase** 'The unhappy linguist':

> 'The unhappy linguist said that he was going to drown his sorrows.'

Anaphora is a form of grammatical **cohesion** and anaphoric reference is a cohesive device that allows the speaker to avoid undue repetition. Most texts will use anaphora to link the sentences together so that readers/listeners know who or what is being referred to by pronouns and other pro-forms. *See also* **cataphora**.

anti-language

'Our pockets were full of deng, so there was no real need from the point of view of crasting any more pretty polly to tolchock some old veck in an alley and viddy him swim in his blood while we counted the takings and divided by four, or to do the ultra-violent on some shivering starry grey-haired ptista in a shop and go smecking off with the till's guts.' This is Nadsat, an anti-language spoken by Alex, the teenage narrator of Anthony Burgess's classic novel *A Clockwork Orange*. Anti-languages are essentially extreme social **dialects** and arise among subcultures as a marker of difference from mainstream society. The term was coined by the **linguist** M. A. K. Halliday. Anti-languages have distinct vocabularies, though are usually based on the **grammar** (i.e. structure) of a parent language. Nadsat is a mixture of English, Russian, some German, cockney rhyming slang and invented **words**, though the grammar is English.

antonym

This refers to a **word** that holds an oppositional **sense relation** with another **lexical item** in a **language**. For example, *light* is the antonym of *dark*, and *soft* is the antonym of *hard*. *Antonym* can be used to refer to all relations of **opposition**, but some linguists restrict its usage to *gradable antonyms*. Many words do not have lexical antonyms, so in order to convey their opposites we may use **morphology** to negate the word in some way, for example by adding the **prefixes** *un-* or *non-* (e.g. *uncomfortable, non-existent*). Some words with negative prefixes have no positive equivalent, and so are 'unpaired'. These include words *nonchalant*, (because English does not have the word *chalant*) and *disambiguate* (because English does not have the word *ambiguate*). Antonymy is a relationship of similarity, where most of the **meaning** is shared between the pair of words, but they are contrasted on a single, important dimension. Many words do not have antonyms: most people would be unable to identify an antonym for the word *squirrel* for example. There are several sub-types of antonyms (although there is some logical overlap between some of these different types) including **complementaries, converses, directional opposites**, gradable antonyms and **relational opposites**.

aperiodic

This is a term used in **acoustic phonetics** to describe irregularity or a non-repeating pattern seen in a **waveform**. Unlike a **periodic** sound, an aperiodic sound will present a random or semi-random pattern in the sound wave, which does not allow for the **fundamental frequency** to be calculated. White noise, such as waterfalls, are aperiodic and to human ears do not have a discernible pitch as a result. In human language, **voiceless** sounds are aperiodic. *See also* **voicing**.

aphasia

This refers to a type of acquired **language** impairment that can affect either language comprehension or language production, or both. Aphasia is caused by some form of brain injury and is most commonly associated with stroke patients. ***Non-fluent aphasia*** is characterised by halting speech with impaired **grammar** but relatively preserved ***lexis***. People with non-fluent aphasia (e.g. **Broca's aphasia**) find it inordinately difficult to produce the **phonemes** needed for speech and cannot form complete **sentences** (they tend to use only **open-class words**, for example). They are also aware of their impairment. People with ***fluent aphasia*** (e.g. **Wernicke's aphasia**), on the other hand, have no problem producing speech sounds and syntactically complete sentences, but encounter lots of difficulties in selecting their words and organising their utterances. They consequently tend to produce speech which is fluent in the sense of free flowing, but which lacks **meaning**. People with fluent aphasia are unlikely to be aware of having such problems. The terms *non-fluent aphasia* and *fluent aphasia* derive from the work of the French physician

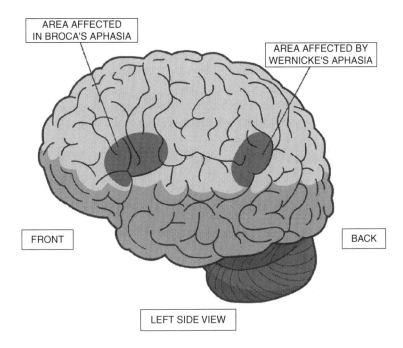

AREA AFFECTED
IN BROCA'S APHASIA

AREA AFFECTED BY
WERNICKE'S APHASIA

FRONT

BACK

LEFT SIDE VIEW

Paul Broca and the German physician Carl Wernicke, respectively. *See also* **jargon aphasia**.

applied linguistics

This is a term that is used to refer to a wide range of sub-areas of **linguistics** and is often defined in slightly different ways by different linguists. The term was originally developed to refer to the type of **language** study that fell outside the mainstream tradition in linguistics where the primary concern was with describing and exploring how the core mechanisms of language work. Some uses of the term applied linguistics suggest that it is the type of linguistics that combines methods and theories from linguistics with other disciplines, such as psychology or sociology. For many people, the dominant meaning of applied linguistics was the application of linguistic insights only to the study of language assessment and teaching, particularly in the English language classroom. Today, applied linguistics has a much broader remit and tends to be used to refer to research that applies linguistic knowledge to some real-world context, such as using methods from **discourse analysis** to improve communication within healthcare settings, or using grammatical analysis to unpack ideology in media texts. In this sense, then, we can think about applied linguistics not as being specific to a sub-discipline or area of linguistics, but as the use of linguistic analysis as a tool in socially motivated research. The range of work in linguistics that falls under the umbrella of applied linguistics is demonstrated by the variety of events hosted under the various associations for applied linguists worldwide, from applications of linguistics in Artificial Intelligence, or the role of language in resolving conflict, to events dedicated to exploring decolonisation in Africa.

apposition

In the UK there is a card game, *Happy Families*, in which the first person to collect a complete set of cards featuring members of the same family is the winner. The game defines the characters on each card by their job (or in the case of the women and children, by their relationship to the man of the family – this is a very old game . . .). So, you have Mr Bones the Butcher, Mrs Chip the Carpenter's Wife, Miss Snip the Barber's Daughter, and so on. The way that these characters are named is known as *apposition*. The term is used to refer to two **words** or phrases (usually, but not always, **noun phrases**) which refer to the same thing or person and have the same grammatical role. So, if a newspaper reports 'Mrs Merton, the town's mayor, arrived at the Town Hall for her inauguration', then the two ways of referring to Mrs Merton / the town's mayor are both the **subject** of the **sentence** and are therefore in apposition to each other. To form a grammatical sentence, you only need one or other of these phrases. The reason for them both being there is usually explanatory – in case readers don't know who Mrs Merton is or who is the town's mayor. Now that you're an expert, spot the apposition in the first sentence of this definition . . .

approximant

This describes a set of **consonant** sounds that are classified according to their **manner of articulation**. Approximants are produced when one **articulator** (i.e. **tongue** or **lips**) comes into close contact with another articulator without making contact. In some ways, approximants are very similar to **vowel** sounds, because the articulators don't touch each other. However, approximants get much closer to each other than they do in the case of vowels. This approximation (i.e. bringing together of the articulators) is almost as close as for a **fricative**, but not quite close enough to cause frication. Examples of approximant sounds include /l/ (*life*), /ɹ/ (*rife*) and /w/ (*wife*).

articulator

Your nose, **lips**, teeth, **tongue**, **alveolar** ridge, **hard palate**, soft palate (**velum**), **uvula**, **glottis**, **pharynx** and **larynx** – these are all articulators. Articulators are ***organs of speech***. We use them to obstruct the flow of air through the **vocal tract**, thereby changing the **manner of articulation** of **consonants** and modifying **vowel** quality.

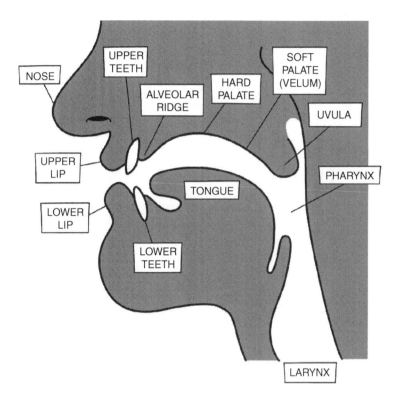

articulatory phonetics

This is the branch of **phonetics** that is related to the production of speech sounds, and is concerned with the movement and use of different anatomical structures.

aspect

This is a grammatical category and is perhaps best understood by contrasting it with **tense**. Tense indicates the position of an action or event in time. For example, the past tense **form** of the verb *drink* in the sentence 'Hazel *drank* a cup of tea' (the **verb phrase** is italicised) indicates that the action occurred at some point in the past. Now consider the **sentence** 'Hazel *was drinking* a cup of tea when her phone rang.' This time, the action described also occurs in the past but, importantly, was in progress when the second event (Hazel's phone ringing) happened. Both sentences have past tense verb phrases but the first is in the simple aspect and the second is in the progressive aspect. Aspect, then, conveys how an action or event ranges over time.

In English, the ***participle*** forms of the verb, combined with **auxiliary verbs**, deliver aspect. For example, *drinking* is a progressive participle (or *–ing* participle), and combines with auxiliary *be* to produce *is drinking*, while *drunk* is a past participle and is used to form what is known as the perfect aspect, combining with auxiliary *have* to produce *has drunk*. Some past participles have a different form from the past tense verb (compare *drank* and *drunk*, for instance) while others use the same form (compare 'I *walked* to work' and 'I *have walked* to work'). The table below explains some of the functions of aspect in English.

Example	Tense	Aspect	Function
Hazel drinks tea every day.	present	simple	Describes habitual actions. However, in some text-types (e.g. sports commentary), it can also be used to describe ongoing actions (*He shoots! He scores!*). In others (e.g. newspaper headlines) it can be used to describe past actions (*Queen dies*).
Hazel is drinking tea right now.	present	progressive	Describes actions ongoing at the time of writing/speaking; can also be used to refer to future time (e.g. *Hazel is walking to work tomorrow*).

Example	Tense	Aspect	Function
Hazel *was drinking* tea when her phone rang.	past	progressive	Describes actions that were ongoing when something else happened.
Hazel *has drunk* seven cups of tea so probably needs the loo right now!	present	perfect	Describes actions that occurred in the recent past.
Hazel *had drunk* seven cups of tea by the time Erica arrived.	past	perfect	Describes actions that occurred in the past *before* a second action.
Hazel *has been drinking* tea for years.	present	perfect progressive	Describes an action that has been ongoing over a period of time.
Hazel *had been drinking* seven cups of tea a day for years before she realised it was probably bad for her.	past	perfect progressive	Describes an action that had been ongoing over a period of time before a second action occurred.

Not all **languages** convey aspect in the same way. Mandarin Chinese has separate aspect markers, for example, while German does not make aspectual distinctions. And aspect functions differently too. In Italian, for example, the structure that in English conveys present perfect aspect (i.e. *have* + past participle) is often used to convey the simple past. For example, *Io ho scritto un libro* (literally, 'I have written a book') may be translated as 'I wrote a book.' *See also* **tense**.

aspiration

This refers to the expulsion of air from the mouth or the nose when we pronounce certain sounds. We can see this happen with **plosive** sounds such as /k/. If you say the **word** *kill*, you should notice a puff of air after you pronounce the /k/ sound. Try putting your hand or a strip of paper in front of your mouth as you say it. However, if you say the word *skill*, you should not notice a puff of air after you produce the /k/ sound. See **unaspirated** for more on the /k/ in *skill*.

assimilation

This is a phonological process whereby one aspect of a **segment** is changed to make it more similar to another segment. Often the segment that assimilates is affected by the segment that directly precedes or follows it. A common example of assimilation is that a **vowel** following a **nasal** segment commonly becomes [+nasal], i.e. more nasal-like. Contrast the /ɛ/ in /aːmɛn/ (*amen*), for example, with the /ɛ/ in /ɛksɪt/ (*exit*). Another common assimilation is when two **consonants** occur in sequence and the first takes on the **place of articulation** of the second. Thus, the **word** *handbag* is usually pronounced as /hæmbæg/ because the /d/ disappears in such a dense consonant cluster, leaving behind /m/ + /b/ where the nasal becomes **bilabial** to match the /b/.

auditory phonetics

This is a branch of **phonetics** focused on the hearing and perception of speech sounds.

authorship attribution

This is a type of analysis carried out in **forensic linguistics**. It involves trying to work out the most likely author of a *disputed text* (that is, a text whose authorship is either unknown or contested). The disputed text is also known as the *questioned document* (QD). This is compared against a *distractor set* of texts written by authors who are suspected of possibly having written the QD. Numerous tests can be carried out in order to determine the likelihood of one of the authors in the distractor set also being the author of the questioned document. Some of these methods nay be quantitative in nature (see **quantitative research**). For example, the forensic linguist may investigate which author's **n-grams** (sequences of **words** or letters) most closely match those of the QD. Average word-length is another measure that can be used, as is **lexical richness**. Quantitative authorship attribution is also known as *stylometry* or *stylometrics*. Other methods may be qualitative (see **qualitative research**), such as looking at spelling conventions or uses of abbreviations. Whatever the methods used, authorship attribution proceeds on the assumption that an author's writing is indicative of their **idiolect**. Methods of authorship attribution are used in criminal cases but have also been used to answer more scholarly questions, such as whether Shakespeare really was the author of all those plays (the consensus among stylometrists is that yes, he was). More recently, authorship attribution was used to reveal that the novels of the crime writer Robert Galbraith were, in fact, written by J. K. Rowling, the author of the Harry Potter series.

auxiliary verb

This refers to a special sub-type of **verb** which is used to add grammatical information, such as **tense** and **aspect**, to a **clause**. In many **languages**, this information would be added by **inflection** rather than being carried by a separate **word**. There are three primary auxiliary verbs in English and nine **modal auxiliary verbs**. The primary auxiliaries are *be*, *have* and *do*. The modal auxiliaries are *can*, *could*, *shall*, *should*, *may*, *might*, *will*, *would* and *must*. Historically, *dare*, *need* and *ought (to)* were also modal verbs, but they have gradually been moving towards the behaviour of full *lexical verbs* and are often known as *semi-auxiliaries* as a result.

In contrast to lexical verbs, auxiliary verbs are **closed class**, which means that the auxiliary verb category has a much more stable membership than **open class** categories such as **noun** or verb (though note that the semi-auxiliaries are gradually leaving the category). Closed-class words are also often known as **grammatical words** or **function words**. Lexical verbs, by contrast, are open class; consequently, new lexical verbs appear in English all the time – for example, *to Google* or *to Whatsapp*.

Note also that the primary auxiliary verbs in English share their **form** (but not their function or **meaning**) with three lexical verbs, *be*, *have* and *do*. Although this can seem confusing, you can tell when they are acting as lexical verbs because there is no other verb in the clause. For example, in the **sentence** 'Hazel is a baker', *is* functions as a lexical verb as it is the only verb present, whereas in the sentence 'Hazel is baking', it is an auxiliary adding tense and aspect to the main verb *baking.*

The verbal element in an English clause (also sometimes known as the **predicator**) can take up to four auxiliaries in a strict order before the main (lexical) verb. The lexical verb is always the last verb in the verbal element, if there are auxiliary verbs present. When a sentence contains a modal auxiliary verb, it comes first in the **verb phrase**; if the sentence also contains other auxiliary verbs then they come after the modal auxiliary in the following order:

	Verb	phrase					
Hazel	*might*	*have*	*been*	*being*	*beaten*	*by*	*Matt*
	modal	perfective	progressive	passive	main		
	auxiliary	auxiliary	auxiliary	auxiliary	verb		

Linguists have developed tests for identifying whether a verb is functioning as an auxiliary. One test (or diagnostic) to work out whether a sentence has an auxiliary verb is the subject–auxiliary inversion test. The subject–auxiliary test is when you reorder the sentence (in the case of the example below, a **declarative** sentence) to make a **yes/no question**. If the sentence or clause is grammatical (as in example A below), then it contains an auxiliary verb. If the sentence is not grammatical, the sentence does not have an auxiliary verb (as in example B below). When a clause or sentence is deemed **ungrammatical** in **syntax**, linguists mark it with an asterisk:

(A) 'Hazel is a good baker. ' (declarative)
     Is Hazel a good baker? (yes/no question, grammatical →
     auxiliary verb present, functioning as a lexical verb)
(B) 'Hazel runs in the park.' (declarative)
     *Runs Hazel in the park. (ungrammatical → auxiliary verb not
     present)

In addition to carrying the question function (by being fronted in this way), auxiliary verbs also carry emphasis (*You SHALL go to the party!*) and negation (*I won't be at the party.*) Where there is no auxiliary to perform these functions, the **dummy auxiliary**, *do*, is used (*I don't care. I DON'T want any cake. Do you understand me?*).

B

babbling

This is the stage at which babies start to make linguistic noises (in addition to the crying and 'cooing' – sounds like *aaaa* and *eeee* – that they do earlier on). Babbling combines **vowel** and **consonant** sounds, usually in open **syllables**, which is where you have an initial consonant and a vowel, but no closing consonant – such as *ma* or *da*. You can see how easy it is for adults hearing these utterances to interpret the syllables as first **words** such as *mama* or *dada*! Speech sounds may be interspersed with more general playing such as gurgling (**velar** trills) and blowing bubbles (**bilabial** trills). Early babbling contains a great deal of repetition (*babababa*); later on, babies combine different consonants and vowels (*badadida*). Babies quickly home in on the sounds that are significant in the language(s) they are learning – the **phonemes** of their languages – and limit their use to these sounds in their babbling. The babbling usually begins before, but overlaps with, the **holophrastic** (i.e. one-word) stage of development.

Babel

This was the name of the biblical city whose inhabitants supposedly constructed a tower to reach the heavens. This work was said to have been made easier by the single common **language** shared by all the people of the world. On seeing their work, and realising that if they could manage this task then his authority was at risk, God decided to destroy their single common language by breaking it up into myriad different languages. A drastic solution, perhaps, but who are we to argue with omnipotence? So, the story of the tower of Babel is an origin myth to explain the number of different languages in the world. It is also an excellent title for a magazine about language and a **lexicon** of **linguistics**.

baby talk

Sometimes referred to as *caretaker speech*, *motherese* or *child-directed speech*, this is the name given to the speech directed at babies and young children by older people. Baby talk is thought to be a *universal language feature*, leading some researchers to believe that baby talk is a species-typical trait. Baby talk exhibits some interesting linguistic properties and shows clear patterns. For example, in English, baby talk is often categorised as being very musical in its rhythmic properties. Baby talk is typically repetitive and slower than standard speech, e.g. *bot bot* for bottle or *nom nom* for food. Another feature of baby talk is the addition of diminutive **suffixes** such as the /i/ or /ɪ/ vowel sound on the end of nouns in English, as in *doggy* (*dog*) and *horsey* (*horse*). In addition to changes in specific **words**, the **syntax**, or structure, of baby talk **utterances** deviates from the adult norm; for example, **function words** such as **prepositions** and *articles* may be omitted in utterances such as 'Lucy give Mummy dummy'. Some **linguists** have suggested that baby talk plays a role in **language acquisition** by being clearly addressed to the baby through exaggerated intonation patterns and higher base-level pitch. Speech to young children provides a changing curriculum, leading them towards the adult **forms** through a set of simplified forms, such as using the third person to refer to the speaker ('Mummy is going upstairs') instead of the shifting **deixis** of **pronouns**, or by focusing on the immediate context (e.g. 'Look at the doggy!') which helps children to match **lexical items** with **meanings**.

back-channelling

This is the process of making supportive noises in a conversation to demonstrate to your **interlocutor** that you are following what they're saying. Examples include *hmm, right, yes, uh huh, really?* To see the importance of back-channelling for smooth communication, try missing it out next time you're having a conversation with someone. They'll soon notice.

back-formation

This is a way of forming **words** by removing an apparent **affix** from an existing word, to create an underlying **form** that did not exist before. For example, the **verb** *televise* was created by removing a familiar form, which is an affix in many other words (*-ion*) from *television* (unlike *depletion, production* where the words are formed by the addition of the *-ion* morpheme). Similarly, *burgle* comes from *burglary* (unlike *butchery, carpentry* where the *-y* is added to an existing word) and *laze* from *lazy* (unlike *hazy, curly* where the *-y* is added to existing **nouns**). Notice that the affix deleted by back-formation may not match the spelling in other words because this process is based largely on how things sound.

backslang

As the term suggests, this is a type of slang in which **words** are written or spoken in reverse, or in which the order of **syllables** in a word are reversed, in order to restrict an out-group (the opposite of an in-group) from knowing what is being discussed. Backslang has been documented as a method of communication used by the so-called 'criminal underworld' – historically, for example, by prisoners in order to converse without prison warders understanding what was being discussed. Common backslang usages included *esclop* for police and *yennep* for penny. One example of backslang that remains in English today is *yob* for boy. Similarly, the word *fika* (to get coffee) in Swedish is a backslang formation, taken from the Swedish word *kaffi* (coffee). Researchers have reported a decline in the use of backslang in English, although the French argot *Verlan*, in which the sounds of syllables are inverted, is still well used. Backslang formed a minor plotline in the 'New Kids on the Block' episode of the American animated sitcom, *The Simpsons*. In the episode, Bart, together with Nelson, Milhouse and Ralph, form a band called 'The Party Posse' and release the hit single 'Drop Da Bomb' which features the line 'Yvan eht Nioj'. Bart's sister Lisa later discovers that the song's chorus is a subliminal message to join the navy.

base form

This is a term in **morphology** that refers to a **word** that has undergone no morphological process, and thus has no **prefixes**, **suffixes** or **infixes**. The base **form** of a word is sometimes referred to as the **stem** or **root word**. For example, the base form of the word *uncontrollable* is *control* once the bound prefix *un-* and suffix *-able* are taken away. A key feature of any **morpheme**, including base forms, is that it cannot be divided into smaller meaningful units. In some cases, the base form can look very different from its related inflected forms (*see* **inflection**). For example, *bad* is the base form of the **comparative** and **superlative** forms *worse* and *worst*, and *go* is the base form of *goes*, *went*, *going* and *gone*.

basilect

This refers to the least prestigious **variety** of a **creole** or post-creole language. In comparison, **acrolect** is the most prestigious variety of a creole or post-creole language. In Jamaica, for example, the higher-prestige variety (the variety that is used in official language arenas such as education) is Jamaican English, and the basilect is Jamaican patois, or *patwa*. Patois is spoken by many Jamaicans as their **native language**. The use of *basilect* or *acrolect* is usually determined by the context, and users have a command of both varieties. *See also* **mesolect**.

Bernoulli Principle

The Bernoulli Principle is an aerodynamic principle that is very important in explaining the production of speech, specifically the movement of the **vocal folds**. The principle explains how the vocal folds open and close as a result of competing air pressures. As air pressure from the **lungs** forces the vocal folds open from one side, the high velocity air causes pressure on the other side of the vocal folds, and the vocal folds are consequently brought back together. In this respect, speech shares something in common with aeroplanes, as the same principle that is responsible for the opening and closing of the vocal folds also helps ensure that aeroplanes can achieve lift and take off. Aeroplane wings are shaped such that air will flow faster over the top of the wings and slower underneath the wings. As a result, this causes a higher air pressure from underneath the wings, which in turn pushes an aeroplane up rather than dragging it down.

bidialectalism

This refers to the ability of a speaker of a **language** to use two different **varieties** of a language. These two varieties may be the national standard, e.g. British **Standard English**, and a regional variety, e.g. Yorkshire **dialect**. If a speaker of a language can use both varieties of the language with equal proficiency, they are said to be bidialectal. In English, it is often the case that the high status of standard forms of the language causes the standard language to overshadow the less prestigious varieties, which are judged not to be varieties as a result. However, this judgement is based on subjective, sociohistorical criteria rather than objective linguistic ones. No dialect is intrinsically more correct or incorrect than any other, even if dialects may diverge widely in terms of their perceived social status. For **linguists**, whose interest is in the description of language, dialects are a rich and fascinating source of sociolinguistic language variation. Here are some examples of different dialects:

- *Geordie (North East) dialect*: I had went to the shop (I had gone to the shop)
- *Yorkshire dialect*: I'm supping baht ale (I'm drinking without beer) [i.e. I've finished my beer and am waiting for you to buy me another!]
- *Multicultural London English*: Why you going there for? [Why are you going there?]

bilabial

Bilabial sounds are made by the **lips** coming together to make a full or partial closure and, as a result, restricting **airflow**. The most common bilabial sounds are the **voiced** and **voiceless plosives** /p/ and /b/ respectively, and the bilabial **nasal** /m/, though some languages also use the bilabial **fricatives**, the IPA symbols for which are [ɸ] for voiceless and [β] for voiced. *See also* **place of articulation**.

bilingual

This refers to people who speak two **languages** at the level of proficiency of first language speakers. They may both be *native languages* (for example, where children have parents with different first languages, or the parents have a different first language from the community they live in). But *bilingual* can also be applied to speakers of learned languages if the level of competence is high. Of course, most of the world's population is bilingual or **multilingual**, which means that the idea of a monolingual speaker being the norm is rather out of touch with reality.

birdsong

This is a type of vocalisation in birds. It has garnered some interest in **linguistics** as it is believed that not only do birds have distinct calls for different predators and food sources, but some bird calls, specifically those of Japanese Great Tits, exhibit **combinatorial structure**. Combinatorial structure refers to the combination of a finite set of **words** or sounds, just like the combination of words to make **sentences**. The combination of syntactic units (such as sounds or words) was previously thought to be uniquely human (*see* **design features**). Due to their complex calls, birds and their song provide a fascinating area of potential exploration within the field of animal communication.

blade

This is the name given to the upper part of the front of the **tongue**, just behind the tip of the tongue. One way you can identify the blade of your tongue is to close your mouth and place your tongue in a resting position. The blade of the tongue sits just under the **alveolar** ridge. The sounds that are produced using the blade of the tongue to obstruct air passage are called *laminal* sounds to contrast with apical sounds which use the tip of the tongue. Most languages do not use this distinction in their phonological systems. Keep your tongue in the position and trying *sah*. The *s* sound that you produce will be a laminal.

blending

This is a method of **word** formation. Blends, also known as *portmanteau* words, are formed by taking elements from two existing words and combining them to form a new word – in effect, blending two existing words together. For example, *netiquette*, a blend of *(inter)net* and *etiquette*, was used for a while to refer to appropriate linguistic behaviour when communicating online. Not all blends make it into common usage but some do get absorbed into everyday **language**. In **Standard English**, we find *pixel (picture + element)*, *vitamin (vita + amine)*, *Brexit (Britain + exit)* and *fortnight (fourteen + night)*. In **Early Modern English**, the now obsolete *se'night (seven + night)* was a blend that meant *week*. Blends whose source words are a little more obvious include *moobs (man + boobs)*, *Twitterverse (Twitter + universe)* and *bromance (brother + romance)*. *Boxercise (box + exercise)* as the name of a sport now appears to be fairly common, and has perhaps become well established because it accurately symbolises the blend of two activities using a blend of the names of these activities. Blending is found in other languages too. *Teuro*, for instance, is a German blend of *teuer* (expensive) + *euro*, while *zargat* (to disturb) is a Hungarian blend of *zavar* (to bother) and *kerget* (to chase). A popular blend in 1920s Japan was *moga* (*modern + girl*). This one is particularly interesting since it is formed by blending elements from a **calque** (look up this entry to find out more).

borrowing

Lexical borrowing is a term used to describe the process by which a **word** from one **language** starts to become used in another language. Words that are 'borrowed' from a language are termed **loanwords.** The terms *loanword* and *borrowing* are not very fitting, however, as loanwords that are borrowed are never given back! Often, words that are borrowed into a language were not borrowed directly. For example, the word *charter* was a **Middle English** loanword from Old French (*charter*), which itself was borrowed from Latin (*charta*). Borrowing has been a productive source of bringing new words into English during its history, ranging from the Latin words borrowed into **Old English** to contemporary loanwords such as *karaoke* from Japanese.

boulomaic modality

Also sometimes known as ***bouletic modality***, this is a sub-category of **modality** that refers to the expression of desire (e.g. 'I wish the weather was good!'). Some **linguists** view boulomaic modality as being a sub-category of **deontic modality**, which is to do with permission and obligation. *See also* **auxiliary verb**.

bound morphemes

Bound morphemes (as opposed to ***free morphomes***) are **morphemes** that cannot occur on their own but have to be linked to other morphemes. For example, **verb suffixes** such as -*ing*, -*ed*, -*en* and the **comparative** (-*er*) and **superlative** (-*est*) endings on gradable **adjectives** are all bound morphemes because they cannot stand alone. (You'd never just say -*en* to someone.) These examples are grammatical **inflections**, but **derivational affixes** are also bound morphemes: *in*-, *de*-, -*tion* and -*ment* are all derivational bound morphemes that can be attached to free morphemes, as in *indirect, decontaminate, production* and *abandonment*.

Braille

This is a system of raised dots on paper that can be 'read' through touch by visually impaired people. There is a code for every character (and number, punctuation mark and even musical notes), and these codes use different combinations of the six potential dots

of the Braille system, which are ⠒⠒ For example, <a> is indicated by
⠒⠒ while <b> is indicated by ⠆⠒

There are simplified codes for common **words** and symbols that
aid the speed of reading Braille, and it is increasingly easy to obtain
printed materials of all kinds in Braille form as the technology for
producing Braille improves. Louis Braille, the inventor of this
system, tried a form of raised alphabetic letters before he developed
Braille. It was much harder to read than the dots. Unlike, for
example, **sign language**, which has developed as a separate
linguistic system in different geographical areas (see, for example,
American Sign Language or British Sign Language), Braille is
entirely reflective of the **language** it represents (e.g. English,
French, German), though some of its contracted **forms** are unique
to Braille.

British National Corpus

The British National Corpus, or BNC for short, is a 100-million-word
corpus of British English released in 1994. Approximately 90 per
cent of the BNC is composed of written texts. Most of these were
published between 1985 and 1993, though some date back to 1960.
The other 10 per cent is made up of spoken language, some of which
is naturally occurring conversation and some context-governed
speech (such as classroom interaction, news reports and business
meetings). The BNC has been widely used as a reference corpus (i.e. a
corpus against which other corpora are compared) of British English.
Work has begun on a new BNC, known as BNC 2014. The spoken
component, consisting of approximately 10 million words of
conversation, was released in 2017. The written component is
currently being compiled.

Broca's aphasia

Also commonly called *expressive aphasia*, this is the label for
language impairment linked to one of the two main language
areas in the brain (Broca's and Wernicke's). The term is named after
the French physician Paul Broca, who described the symptoms of a
patient who suddenly lost the ability to speak. Broca later
identified the damage to the patient's brain as being in the left
posterior frontal lobe. Recent research has shown that other areas

of the brain (e.g. the medial insular cortex) connected with motor functions are also affected. This type of **aphasia** is characterised by non-fluency, few **words** and short **sentences** (often with disturbed **grammar**). Despite these expressive difficulties, patients with Broca's aphasia often have good comprehension. Broca's aphasia is often considered to be synonymous with the term ***non-fluent aphasia***.

C

C-unit

This refers to a grammatical unit of conversational speech. C-units can be clausal or non-clausal. In very basic terms, a clausal C-unit is the spoken equivalent of a **sentence** in writing. It is often preferred by **linguists** to the term *sentence* because the **grammar** of conversation is substantially different from the grammar of written **language**. Here, for example, is an extract from the spoken section of the **British National Corpus**:

> He's, he's already come in for one form put it he's obviously filled one form in he came up and he said can I have an application form for that job in the window so I gave him one and he went, oh well I've just filled one in (File KC6)

By the terms of written grammar, this looks like an **ungrammatical** sentence. However, **spoken grammar** operates differently from written grammar, so it makes little sense to analyse utterances in the same way that we would analyse units of written language. This is where the concept of a C-unit comes in. First, we can segment the above example into finite **clause**-like units, indicated by vertical lines:

> | He's, he's already come in for one form | put it | he's obviously filled one form in | he came up | and he said | can I have an application form for that job in the window | so I gave him one | and he went | oh well I've just filled one in (File KC6)

But what we can also notice is that some of these units can stand on their own and do not have any syntactic connection to the units that come before or after them. These are indicated with double vertical lines:

> || He's, he's already come in for one form || put it || he's obviously filled one form in || he came up | and he said | can I have an

application form for that job in the window I so I gave him one I and he went I oh well I've just filled one in II (File KC6)

The double vertical lines indicate clausal C-units. A clausal C-unit is composed of an independent clause and any dependent clauses it contains. Non-clausal C-units, on the other hand, are segments which are not part of clausal units and do not contain clausal structure. Non-clausal C-units are indicated by three vertical lines in the example below, which continues the conversation from the example above:

A: II So he sto II do you know I where the two tills are downstairs I do you? II

B: III Yeah III

A: II They were on the erm I the main one we use II

B: III Yeah III

A: II just by the step in he was stood resting on the erm perspex thing II

(File KC6)

Non-clausal C-units include **interjections**, greetings and **discourse markers**, among other non-clausal elements of speech.

calque

A calque is a **loanword** or **phrase** from another **language** that has been translated (almost) literally from that language. For example, *beer garden* is a calque of German *biergarten*, while *rest in peace* is a calque of Latin *requiescat in pace*. Calquing is common as a process of **word** formation in many languages. Hebrew *gan yeladim*, for instance, is a calque of German *kindergarten*, and Japanese *moga* is a blend which comes from the English phrase *modern girl*, which was calqued into Japanese as *modan gāru* in the 1920s (see **blending** for more details).

cardinal vowels

These were first defined by Daniel Jones (1881–1967) as a set of reference **vowels**. There are eight primary cardinal vowels [i e ɛ a ɑ ɔ o u] and eight secondary cardinal vowels [y ø œ ɶ ɒ ʌ ɤ ɯ]. The first five primary vowels are articulated with 'spread' **lips** (i.e. no lip-rounding) and the last three have rounded and protruding lips. The secondary vowels reverse this pattern with the first five in the list having lip-rounding and the final three having spread lips. Vowels from all **languages** can be described in relation to the cardinal vowels. These vowels exist at the extremes of the space available in the mouth for producing vowel sounds, and rarely occur in real human languages in their pure form. It is instructive to try and produce the cardinal vowels yourself (with some help from the recordings available online). As well as making the vowel sounds in order and noting how your jaw drops for the more open ones and closes for the close vowels, you can also try alternating between cardinals 1 and 9, by pronouncing a long [i:] sound and then pushing the lips forward to produce [y]. This will demonstrate how, for example, the secondary vowel in French *tu* is pronounced.

case

This is a grammatical **category** in some languages where **inflections** (i.e. **bound morphemes**) are added to **base forms** to indicate the grammatical or semantic functions of **nouns** (and other items such as **pronouns**, **adjectives** and numerals which function as nouns) in **sentences**. For example, in **Old English**, a noun could be in the *nominative* case, *accusative* case, **genitive** case or *dative* case. The nominative case marks the **subject** of a sentence. The accusative case marks the direct **object**. The genitive case marks (among other things) possession, and the dative case marks the recipient of an action (often the indirect object). Other languages have many more cases (see the entries for genitive, **locative** and **vocative** for some examples, though there are more besides these). Case is usually marked by the addition of an inflection to a noun. Here are some examples from Hungarian to show how this works:

Example	Translation	Case	Case function
A *tanár* hangosan beszélt.	The *teacher* spoke loudly.	nominative	Indicates the subject.
A diák megcsodálta a *tanárt*.	The student admired the *teacher*.	accusative	Indicates the object.
A diák adta az almát a *tanárnak*.	The student gave an apple to the *teacher*.	dative	Indicates the indirect object.

Case languages generally have a less rigid **word order** than non-case languages as the role of the **words** is already clear from their case (see **analytic language** and **synthetic language**). While Old English was a case language, **Present Day English** (PDE) is not, though the remnants of the old case system can be seen in personal pronouns, which change their **form** according to their function in the sentence. Compare, for instance, the two forms of the first person singular, *I* and *me*. The first is the subject form (the nominative) and the second is the object form (the accusative). The possessive apostrophe in Present Day English is a remnant of the genitive case inflection, though PDE is primarily an analytic language rather than the synthetic language it used to be in the Old English period.

cataphora

This – also known as cataphoric reference – is a cohesive device (*see* **cohesion**), and the opposite of **anaphora**. The normal way that **language** refers to things and people is to introduce them first in detail and then refer backwards to this first mention by using **pronouns** ('Erica was a doctor. *She* was tall and imposing'). Cataphora, however, uses a pronoun to refer forwards to a fuller **noun phrase**. In this extract from a newspaper article, cataphora is used to pique the reader's interest. That is, you have to keep reading in order to find out the referents of *they* in the first line, which is specified first by a generic noun phrase (*two D-day veterans*) and only later by the names of the people in question:

Seventy-five years ago, <u>they</u> jumped into the unknown, landing noiselessly in Normandy's fields in the inky dark and pumped with adrenalin over what horrors might await them. Now in their nineties, <u>two D-day veterans</u> made the same landing on Wednesday, this time to loud applause as part of a spectacular Red Devils display with flags and signature red smoke before a cheering crowd. <u>Harry Read</u>, 95, a retired Salvation Army officer, was a 20-year-old wireless operator with the Royal Signals when he was pushed out of his plane in the early hours of 6 June 1944. <u>John 'Jock' Hutton</u>, 94, from Larkfield, Kent, was 19, and serving with the 13th Lancashire Parachute regiment when he descended over the famous Pegasus Bridge.

('D-day veterans in their 90s parachute into Normandy once more', *The Guardian*, 5 June 2019)

categorical assertion

Also known as *categorical statement*, this term only really makes sense in contrast to **modality**. Whilst modal statements introduce doubt (in the form of questioning the factuality or desirability of something) into a text, a categorical statement is one that has no modality at all and therefore asserts the **proposition** with confidence. Compare, for example, 'Erica might know the answer' with 'Erica knows the answer.' The latter is categorical and makes no reference to the opinion of the speaker, whereas the former implies that it is only the speaker's assessment and not necessarily true.

categories

Linguistics needs categories at all levels of its descriptive apparatus (from **phonetics** to **pragmatics**) in order to provide information about **language** that can be measured, compared and discussed accurately. However, in most cases, the categories we appear to use (e.g. **vowel, noun, speech act**) are in fact more like reference points on a continuum, or **prototypes**. Thus, for example, an actual vowel produced by a speaker and analysed by a phonetician will be nearer or further from one of the **cardinal vowels** and described in relation to these hypothetical configurations of the mouth. In British English, the vowel in the **word** *big* is usually transcribed as /ɪ/ and yet it is usually pronounced somewhere between cardinal vowels 1 and 2. In **grammar**, a category we usually label *noun* is actually a prototype category, rather than having clear boundaries. A prototypical noun has a certain kind of **form** (in English, it normally has a plural) and a certain range of functions (it is usually the head of a phrase acting as a **subject**, **object** or **complement**). However, some items that we may want to call nouns will challenge some of these characteristics (e.g. *sheep* doesn't have a plural, and *house* is not acting prototypically when it modifies another noun, as in the phrase *house cat*). Although this makes the idea of a linguistic category look like no more than a convenient fiction to help the analyst, in fact, there is some evidence that the prototypical categories at least have some psychological reality for speakers.

catenative verbs

Most lexical **verbs** can combine only with **auxiliary verbs** that add information about extent (*was running*) or completion (*had run*) or **modality** (*might run*). However, there is a small group of verbs, called catenative verbs, which can *concatenate* (combine in a sequence) with other lexical verbs. They include verbs like *try* (*try running*), *avoid* (*avoid running*) and *want* (*want to run*), and can be linked together into fairly long 'chains' of verbs, e.g. 'The government agreed to try to decide to stop running the train company.' Some **linguists** define catenatives as verbs that take other verbs (in either **infinitive** or *-ing* participle **form**) as **objects**, but this implies that each verb in a catenative string is in a separate **subordinate clause**. However, it seems counter-intuitive to suggest that the example **sentence** given above has four levels of subordination. Catenative verbs, then, present something of a puzzle for grammatical description.

clause

A clause is a unit of syntactic structure that expresses a complete **proposition** and contains some evidence of structure, usually showing how the **predicator (verb phrase)** links the participants (**subject, object**, etc.) together. Although many **simple sentences** are composed of just one clause, e.g. 'No-one saw the intruder in the kitchen', clauses are not the same as **sentences**, which can be made up of more than one clause. See **compound sentence** and **complex sentence** for descriptions of sentences with multiple clauses. *See also* **SPOCA**.

cleft sentence

This is a term used to describe structures which focus on one element of an assumed underlying simple **clause** by dividing (i.e. cleaving) the original clause into two and producing a **complex sentence** instead. So, for example, if the presumed basic clause is 'Dan made the cheese and onion pie on Sunday', it has a **subject + predicator + object + adverbial** (SPOA) structure. The default focus in a simple clause would be on the last of the obligatory clause elements, which is the object here, because the time adverbial ('on Sunday') is grammatically optional. If the speaker wants to emphasise or focus on one of the other participants in the clause, the option is there for them to use a cleft sentence structure, where the S is an empty indefinite **pronoun** ('it'); the main **verb** is the **copula** *be*, and the rest of the information is included as a subordinate clause in the **complement** position, resulting in a main clause structure 'It is/was X.' Once the cleft sentence structure is in place, all that is needed is to revise the remaining information to fit grammatically. If the focus is to be on the original S, the result is: 'It was Dan that made the cheese and onion pie on Sunday.' For a focus on the O, you would have: 'It was the cheese and onion pie that Dan made on Sunday.' And a focus on the A would result in: 'It was on Sunday that Dan made the cheese and onion pie.' Note that the only clause element in the base clause that cannot be made the focus of a cleft sentence is the P (i.e. the verbal element). This would result in an **ungrammatical sentence**: *'It was making that Dan did to the cheese and onion pie on Sunday'. Practise using cleft sentences to focus on different parts of this sentence: 'The teacher sent the children into the forest to collect leaves.'

clipping

This is a **word** formation process in which a new word is formed by shortening an existing one. Examples include *lab* from *laboratory* and *prof* from *professor*. *Advertisement* is a word that has been clipped twice, to *advert* and to *ad*. Some clipped **forms** are now more common than their full versions; for example, *taxi* is from *taximeter cabriolet*, *wig* is from *periwig*, and *pram* is from *perambulator*. Note with the last example how the reduced **vowel** – the **schwa** – in the full form impacts on the spelling (and pronunciation) of the clipped form; i.e. *pram* rather than *peram*. Clipping differs from **back-formation** in that it does not change the **word class** – or the **referent** – of the original word.

closed class

This refers to the type of **word** (and **word class**) that has a largely grammatical function, rather than introducing **semantic** content into the **text**. So, for example, the **pronoun** system in English has a number of members (*I, we, my, our, you, your, he, him, his, she, her, her, they, them, their, it, its*) which identify **referents** in the real world or in the surrounding text and not much more than this. There is some semantic information (e.g. **gender** and **number**) but the main function of a pronoun is to identify a referent grammatically. The reason for calling these word classes *closed* is to acknowledge that they form a system which is relatively stable and has internal structure. So, for instance, there is very little change in a pronoun system over time, and when a change happens, it takes a very long time. The gradual loss of the second person singular familiar/ respectful pronoun, *thou* (and its object and possessive **forms** *thee* and *thy*) in English is an example of a closed-class change and had the effect of altering the **meaning** of the other second person pronoun (*you*) which had previously only been used for plural second person and to show social distance. Current social changes in gender identity are beginning to affect pronoun meaning again, but these processes are slow. Words belonging to closed-class categories are known as **grammatical words**. *See also* **open class**.

co-text

This is the term sometimes used to refer to the textual surroundings of an item or extract, to distinguish it from the situational (or wider social) context. *Context* is also sometimes used to refer to *co-text*, though it can be confusing as *context* also refers to the situation in which **language** is used.

coda

This is used to refer to the final part of a **syllable** following the **nucleus**, and is made up of one or more **consonants**. Generally speaking, **languages** tend to favour the open syllable shape, with an **onset** and a nucleus, but no coda. The following **sentence** is made up of only open syllables: *The blue bee flew by*. Although in English there are many open-syllable words, English codas may be made up of as many as four consonants, e.g. *sixths* /sɪksθs/ and *twelfths* /twɛlfθs/, though these are often reduced to three in anything but the most careful pronunciation: /sɪkθs/ and /twɛlfs/.

code-switching

When speakers have more than one **language** or **dialect** in their repertoire, they often switch rapidly and repeatedly between them in situations where both languages or dialects are being spoken. This is called *code-switching* and it happens particularly with **multilingual** speakers, though it can also occur with second language speakers. Code-switching can be a way of acknowledging other participants' linguistic identity and ability, and it also helps speakers to express concepts in cases where **vocabulary** might not be entirely overlapping in the two codes. *Code-shifting* and *code-mixing* are related terms which are sometimes preferred in order to move away from the idea that the languages in question are entirely separate.

cognate

A cognate **word** is one that has a common etymological origin with a word from another **language**. For example, English *false* and German *falsch* are cognates as they both trace their **etymology** to Latin *falsus*.

cognitive linguistics

This is an area of **linguistics** that examines the structure and function of **language**. Where it differs from other areas that do this (such as **corpus linguistics**) is in its assumption that the structure of language reflects the way that we conceptualise the world (that is, language use is indicative of patterns of thought). Cognitive **linguists**, therefore, are interested in what language might reveal about our conceptual system. **Conceptual metaphor theory** is a cognitive linguistic theory precisely because it argues that metaphor is not simply a matter of language but a matter of thought. In essence, conceptual metaphor theory accepts at least a weak version of the **Sapir–Whorf hypothesis** that language affects our conception of reality. For example, when we discuss difference in language, we often use the conceptual metaphor of DIFFERENCE IS DISTANCE. For example, we might describe two opposing views as being 'poles apart'. Conceptual metaphor theory argues that the linguistic metaphors we use when we talk about difference are indicative of how we actually conceptualise the notion of difference based on the underlying conceptual metaphor.

coherence

This is a property of **texts**. Texts that are coherent can be interpreted as meaningful. Coherence is dependent on the reader's schematic knowledge, which helps them to understand the text. **Cohesion** (which links sentences together) often helps a text to be coherent but it is also possible for a text to be coherent but not cohesive, as this example shows:

Linguistics Research Seminar
Wednesday 17 December. 3.30pm.

Dr Kevin Harvey (University of Nottingham)
'A multimodal approach to health communication'

This was a poster in a university **linguistics** department, advertising a talk by a visiting academic. There are no formal cohesive links between the **phrases**. Nonetheless, if you understand what 'Linguistics Research Seminar' means, then you can infer that this is an advertisement for a lecture, particularly if you were to see the text on a noticeboard in a university building, or were to receive it by email from an academic email address.

cohesion

This refers to the linguistic links between **sentences** and between **clauses**. Cohesion can be achieved lexically – through substitution, for instance. Here is an example, in which B's response involves replacing the name *Mr Brown* with a **noun phrase**:

A: What do you think of Mr Brown?
B: I can't stand the sexist old dinosaur.

Cohesion can also be achieved grammatically, via **anaphora** and **cataphora**. Anaphoric reference involves using a **pronoun** to refer back to a previous noun phrase, as in the following example:

Dan said that he was going to drown his sorrows in Guinness.

Cataphora, by contrast, involves referring *forwards* in the text, so that the reader/listener comes across a mysterious person or thing first, often introduced by a pronoun. Only later on is the reader enlightened about who or what is being referred to ('*He* was quiet and enigmatic. His name was Matt.').

It is possible for a **text** to be cohesive but not **coherent**. For example, here is a text used in a **psycholinguistic** experiment in 1972 by the **linguists** John D. Bransford and Marcia K. Johnson:

The procedure is actually quite simple. First you arrange items into different groups. Of course one pile may be sufficient depending on how much there is to do. If you have to go somewhere else due to lack of facilities that is the next step; otherwise, you are pretty well set. It is important not to overdo things. That is, it is better to do few things at once than too many. In the short run it may not seem important but complications can easily arise. A mistake can be expensive as well. At first, the whole procedure may seem complicated. Soon, however, it will become just another facet of life. It is difficult to foresee any end to the necessity of this task in the near future, but then, one can never tell. After the procedure is completed one arranges the material into different groups again. Then they can be put into their appropriate places. Eventually they will be used once more and the whole cycle will have to be repeated. However, that is part of life.

Although there are cohesive relations between its sentences, the text is very difficult to make sense of. Bransford and Johnson used it to demonstrate that understanding texts requires schematic knowledge (see **schema theory**) as well as grammatical knowledge. Once you know that the title of this text is 'Washing clothes', you should find the text much more coherent.

collocation

J. R. Firth (1890–1960), the UK's first Professor of General Linguistics, famously said 'You shall know a word by the company it keeps' (Firth, *A Synopsis of Linguistic Theory*, Studies in Linguistic Analysis, Oxford: Blackwell, 11). Firth had observed that **words** have a tendency to cluster together. That is, when we use a particular word, it is likely that it will be preceded or followed by certain other words. Think about the incomplete **phrase** *fish and*, for example. It's highly likely that if British English is your first language, you will expect the word *chips* to follow. We can therefore say that *chips* is a **collocate** of *fish*. Or, to put it another way, when we encounter the word *fish*, there is a high chance that *chips* will be co-located (hence, *collocation*) nearby. Collocation extends beyond the immediate vicinity of a word. We can observe collocation happening up to approximately five words to the left and five words to the right of the particular word we are interested in. **Corpus linguistics** offers a means of systematically searching for the collocates of any given word. Searching the **British National Corpus (BNC)**, for example, shows that frequent collocates of the word *job* include *unenviable*, *thankless* and *back-breaking*. Collocates of *career*, on the other hand, include *illustrious*, *high-flying* and *distinguished*. That is, whenever the words *job* and *career* are used, it is statistically likely that these different sets of words will be found somewhere in the surrounding context. The corpus linguist John Sinclair maintained that **meaning** is best seen as a property of words in combination. This is nicely illustrated in the *job* and *career* examples, where the collocates of the words generate the respective negative and positive **connotations** associated with them. These findings suggest that we do not have entirely free choice when it comes to our decision on which words to use in a **sentence** or **utterance** (see **idiom principle**). That is, if we use the word *job*, we are likely to find ourselves (often subconsciously) also using more negatively evaluative **adjectives** than when we use the word *career*. This practice can give rise to what corpus linguists call **semantic prosody**. There are two ways of measuring collocation: **collocational frequency** or **collocational strength**. The first approach refers to how many times a word collocates with our chosen word. The second refers to the probability that the collocate will appear with the other word. For example, the most frequent adjective collocate of *incompetence* in the BNC is *economic*. However, the strongest adjective collocate is *know-nothing*. That is, *know-nothing* collocates with *incompetence* more than it collocates with any other word. *Economic*, on the other hand, collocates with *incompetence* but with lots of other words too. Collocational strength can be measured using statistical tests, such as the Mutual Information (MI) test.

combinatorial structure

This is a universal feature of human **language** and refers to the combination of different, finite linguistic building blocks such as **morphemes** or **phonemes** to make larger meaningful units. For example, the forty-four phonemes in English may be combined in many different ways to create **words** in the spoken mode. Combinatorial structure is thought to be unique to human language; however, recent studies have found preliminary evidence to suggest that some species of birds exhibit combinatorial structure in their **birdsong**. *See also* **hierarchical structure**.

comparative

A comparative is a **form** of a **word** used to compare two entities or qualities. For example, in the **sentence** 'Hazel is shorter than Dan', *shorter* is a regular comparative **adjective**, formed by the addition of an -*er* **suffix** on the **base form** *short*. An example of an irregular comparative adjective is *better* (the comparative form of *good*). **Polysyllabic** adjectives (e.g. adjectives with multiple **syllables**) are usually combined with a separate **adverb**, *more*, to produce comparative forms. For example: 'Linguistics is more interesting than you would think'. Comparative adverbs are formed on the same principle – for instance, 'Dan worked *harder* than Hazel' and 'Hazel wrote *more efficiently* than Dan.' *See also* **superlative**.

competence

This is a term that was introduced by the **linguist** Noam Chomsky and refers to the tacit knowledge you have about your first **language**, or any language which you speak to a high level. Your linguistic competence enables you to decide whether a **sentence** is grammatically acceptable or not. Competence can be affected by **performance**. Chomsky's view was that linguistic competence was what linguists ought to concentrate on studying. Many linguists disagree, arguing that performance is just as central to developing our understanding of how language works. The concept of competence derives from the concept of **langue** introduced by the Swiss linguist Ferdinand de Saussure (1857–1913). See also *I-language*.

complement

A complement is a unit of **clause** structure that has the same **referent** as either the **subject** or **object** in a **sentence**. For example, in the sentence *Dan is a drummer*, the **noun phrase** *a drummer* provides additional information about the subject, *Dan*. This is an example of a subject complement. An object complement provides additional information about the object in a sentence, as in 'My university degree made me a linguist.' Here, the complement is *a linguist* and refers back to the object *me*. In English, complements follow a special group of **copular** verbs (e.g. *be, seem, know, feel, become, sound*) and can be single **words** ('Dan is *great*'), **phrases** ('Dan is *a terrible drummer*') or clauses ('Dan is *not what I would describe as a genius*'). *See also* **SPOCA**, **predicator** and **adverbial**.

complementaries

These are pairs of **lexical items** (usually individual **words**, but they could be **phrases**), which are conventionally seen as opposites in a **language**. Unlike **gradable antonyms** which label the extremes of a range (e.g. *big–small; tall–short*), complementaries divide up the conceptual field into two mutually exclusive halves. So, *dead* and *alive* are complementary terms because the language treats them as being mutually exclusive. If you are not *dead*, therefore, you must be *alive*. There are some complementaries (e.g. *male–female*) where the reality of the world may challenge the mutually exclusive binary. However, the language may remain binary at least until it catches up with social change. Note also that some sets of words (e.g. colour terms in English) can be seen as treating other continua as though they were made up of discrete **categories**, though in this case they are not binary, but multiple. See **opposition** for details of other types of opposites.

complementary distribution

This is a term commonly used in **phonology** and **morphology** to describe the relationship between two elements. Specifically, these two different elements are of the same kind; however, one element is always found in certain environments and the other element is found in different environments. Most importantly, these two elements are never found in the *same* environment. As a result, this indicates that the two superficially different elements are actually the same linguistic unit at a deeper level. If this sounds confusing, think about Superman. Under this alias, the DC Comics superhero fights crime and foils the dastardly plots of evil super-villains. But, as his alter ego Clark Kent, he is a simple reporter at the *Daily Planet* newspaper. The reader (or viewer) knows that Clark Kent and Superman are the same person, yet you never see Superman working at the *Daily Planet*, or Clark Kent saving people falling from buildings – a perfect example of complementary distribution! Now back to how this works in **language**. An example in English is the relationship between *clear l* and *dark l*. In many **accents**, speakers use clear l at the beginnings of **words** (e.g. *light*) and dark l, where the /l/ sound is pronounced further back in the mouth (i.e. velarised), at the ends of words (e.g. *full*). Both of these pronunciations count as /l/ in English, though they are affected by their surroundings. Interestingly, these sounds can be contrastive in other languages (e.g. Russian).

complex sentence

A complex sentence contains a main **clause** and one or more **subordinate clauses**. The following **sentence** has two subordinate clauses in addition to the main clause: 'Although I was tired, I waited until after supper, which arrived soon after.' The first subordinate clause (before the comma) acts adverbially in the sentence as a whole, and the second one (from *which* to the end) is a **relative clause** modifying *supper* within the **noun phrase**. Many subordinate clauses are linked by a subordinator such as *when*, *if* or *although*, and they would not make sense on their own. Now you can have fun counting the clauses in this sentence from *The Last Good Kiss* by James Crumley: 'When I finally caught up with Abraham Trahearne, he was drinking beer with an alcoholic bulldog named Fireball Roberts in a ramshackle joint just outside of Sonoma, California, drinking the heart right out of a fine spring afternoon.' *See also* **SPOCA**.

components

These are the building blocks of **language**, both structurally and semantically. In **syntax**, a component at one level (e.g. **phrase** structure) is made up of items at the lower level (e.g. **words**) and contributes to the structure as a unit at the higher level (e.g. **clause**). So, for example, *the mattress*, in the **sentence** 'The mattress was comfortable' is a component, because it takes up the whole of the **subject** position and can be replaced by a single **pronoun** (*it*). In the sentence 'The mattress that I bought was comfortable', the same two words (*the mattress*) cannot be seen as a component because they are linked to the **relative clause** (*that I bought*), and only together can they be replaced by a single pronoun (*it*). In **semantics**, components are normally seen as the basic building blocks of **meaning**. Componential analysis is the division of lexical meaning into semantic components which occur in more than one word's definition. So, for example, *boy* and *man* would share the component [+male] whereas *girl* and *woman* will share [+female]. Only certain areas of **vocabulary** are amenable to neat binary features of this kind, however (e.g. how could one easily define *lope* versus *amble*?), and the ambition to define meaning in all human languages by a single universal set of components is so far not realised.

compound sentence

This refers to a **sentence** which is made up of two or more **clauses**, neither (none) of which is more important than the other(s) and which can exist independently. This is achieved by the use of coordinating **conjunctions** (*and*, *but*, *or*) or semicolons. Examples would include 'Erica had a daughter but Lesley had a son'; 'Hazel bakes cakes and Matt runs marathons'; 'Lesley played her trumpet; Dan played his drums.' George Orwell's dystopian novel *1984* opens with a compound sentence: 'It was a bright cold day in April, and the clocks were striking thirteen.' In some descriptions, these could also be called *coordinated clauses*. *See also* **SPOCA**.

compound word

A compound word is a **neologism** created through the combination of two existing **words**. Compounds can be formed from two existing words of the same **word class**, as in *headhunter* (from the **nouns** *head* and *hunter*), or from words from different classes, such as *humblebrag* (from the **adjective** *humble* and the noun/**verb** *brag*).

Sometimes, you can see compounding happen gradually over time: in older **texts**, for instance, you may see *no body*, in later ones *nobody*, and in more contemporary ones *nobody* (this is a process of **lexicalisation**). Compounding is different to **blending** in that the pre-existing words are joined together in their entirety.

conceptual metaphor theory

Traditionally, metaphors were seen as a linguistic phenomenon particularly common in literature. But research in **cognitive linguistics** has demonstrated that metaphor is likely to be structuring how we think, given that we use metaphor all the time in communication and not just in literary composition. Conceptual metaphor theory proposes the existence of conceptual metaphors, which are cognitive structures that conceptualise one domain of life in terms of another. They underlie the **language** we use and can therefore be expressed linguistically in many different ways. One particularly common conceptual metaphor, for instance, is LIFE IS A JOURNEY (conceptual metaphors are conventionally written in small capitals). Here, the **target domain** LIFE is described in terms of the **source domain** JOURNEY; that is, we conceptualise the abstract concept of life as if it is a physical journey that we take. We use this conceptual metaphor all the time; for example, when we say things like 'He's on the road to ruin', 'You've come a long way since you started school', 'I'm stuck in a rut' and 'There's a long road ahead of us.' Conceptual metaphors work by taking a concept from the source domain and mapping this onto the concept denoted by the target domain. In the examples above, for instance, *rut* is a term from the JOURNEY domain (meaning a groove worn into a path which is difficult to get your wheels out of) and is mapped onto the target domain, where we understand it to mean an impediment to our progress. Similarly, 'you've come a long way' maps the concept of distance onto the notion of progress. Other common conceptual metaphors are ARGUMENT IS WAR ('The MP defended himself against criticism'; 'The author attacked her critics'), UP IS GOOD ('She was on cloud nine', 'I think you've come out on top', 'We've raised our expectations), THE ECONOMY IS A PLANT ('The British economy continued to grow') and TIME IS MONEY ('Don't waste my time!', 'Spend your time doing things you love'). The 2011 movie, *In Time*, is set in a world in which time is the actual currency in which people are paid, making the conceptual metaphor literal (and, by so doing, foregrounding our metaphorical usage). This leads to the following complaint about prices from one character: 'Four minutes for a cup of coffee?!'

concord

This is a grammatical term that refers to *agreement* – that is, the requirement that a particular **word** change its **form** to agree grammatically with neighbouring words. For example, in English the form of the **verb** *to be* depends on the **pronoun** that precedes it. We say *he is* and *she is* but *they are*. That is, there must be concord or agreement between the pronoun and the verb.

concordance

This is a term from **corpus linguistics**. A concordance is a list of all the instances of a particular search term in a **corpus**. On the next page, for example, is a partial concordance of the word *tend* in the **British National Corpus** (taken from BYU Corpora, available at w ww.english-corpora.org/bnc).

Concordances are useful because they allow us to see patterns in how **lexical items** are used. For instance, in the example opposite we can see that *tend* is usually followed by an **infinitive clause**. This sort of information can be particularly useful to people trying to learn a second **language**. It is also useful to **linguists** writing **grammars** or dictionaries of a language, as corpora allow us to see how language is really used. Consequently, linguists no longer have to rely on their own intuitions about language use. And, since corpora are ready sources of examples of how language is used, there is less of a need to invent examples which can result in unnatural-sounding **sentences**.

conjugation

A grammatical conjugation modifies the base (**infinitive**) **form** of a **verb** into another form through **inflection**. A verb is conjugated in order to provide context (or more information) about the situation in which the process is taking place. Most speakers do not realise that they are conjugating verbs in their native **language** as it becomes so automatic. It is often only when you are in school and

British National Corpus (BNC)

FIND SAMPLE: 100 200 500 1000
PAGE: < < 1/61 > >>

CLICK FOR MORE CONTEXT

		A	B	C	[?] SHOW DUPLICATES
1	D95	A	B	C	er. (SP-D95PS001) No you just contribute mm. (SP-D95PS004) Erm, you've got that to **tend** with and erm on top of that erm, you can't ware of (unclear)
2	D95	A	B	C	correct differential between right and (unclear) whatever that means, and that the charter might **tend** to induce our views as defenders, instead of. (SP-D95PSUNK)
3	D95	A	B	C	Council we don't have, it's not organised like that. Department's **tend**, eh, the actual service department are very much what I would call practitioner
4	D97	A	B	C	'm, I'm, I'm only going on the fact that I I **tend** to do everything on the cheap so I tend to get (pause) if I can
5	D97	A	B	C	on the fact I I tend to do everything on the cheap so I **tend** to get (pause) if I can find somebody who does photocopying I can (unclear) do
6	DCH	A	B	C	get interested and then, then it'll, it'll carry on otherwise they **tend** to drop. Right, now we've come I think to future events.
7	DCH	A	B	C	I know you're not very keen on that idea and it, it does **tend** to remove information from the ordinary membersm if, if you have a
8	F7A	A	B	C	cinema er (pause) because people don't go abroad so much in America. They **tend** to er summer in America (pause) and go to the cinema whether they're on
9	F7E	A	B	C	Some (SP-PS1LT) A-- (SP-PS1LU) of them, do you think it'll (SP-F7EPS000) I I tend (SP-PS1LU) create problems (SP-F7EPS000) I **tend** to sa-- sa-- to say right (pause) yo
10	F7E	A	B	C	, do you think it'll (SP-F7EPS000) I I tend (SP-PS1LU) create problems (SP-F7EPS000) I **tend** sa-- sa-- to say right (pause) you know, one A and one B
11	F7F	A	B	C	know. (SP-F7FPS000) Does seem (unclear). (SP-F7FPSUNK) Andrew? (SP-F7FPS002) I would, I would **tend** to say the majority aren't, aren't interested in their, in the
12	F7G	A	B	C	as Marian that says (SP-PS1M7) What er (SP-PS1MA) (unclear) (SP-PS1M7) that (SP-PS1M6) But filing cabinets **tend** to put people off. (SP-PS1M9) No! We we will ask
13	F7J	A	B	C	regard to education er (pause) issues and time off for them, erm (pause) they **tend** to be let's say reasonable (pause) er about it (pause) er but that's
14	F86	A	B	C	the church lives which make common confession of faith particularly difficult er today. We **tend** to conceive er generally of faith very much in personal terms, we s
15	F86	A	B	C	to recall (pause) oh sorry, the convenor, yes indeed. (pause) (SP-F86PSUNK) I **tend**, Moderator, to Professor (-----)'s view that this complicates the issue and
16	F86	A	B	C	report makes the point that er (pause) when (pause) legal proceedings are entered into they **tend** to create further barriers and make it m-- less and less likely that
17	F86	A	B	C	town really doesn't it. I mean (pause) (SP-PS1R8) Yes. (SP-PS1RA) postal towns **tend** to be the place where the council is. (SP-PS1R8) Yeah. (SP-PS1RA) So if I
18	FLS	A	B	C	if he (pause) he's on a twelve hour shift (pause) and, those meetings **tend** to (pause) have been around the same sort of time, then obviously

being taught a new language that you become aware of how verbs need to conjugate in order to fit grammatically. If a verb was to be left in its infinitive form, a listener may be able to have a general understanding about what is intended by the speaker, but details about the context (e.g. **tense**, **person**, **mood**) may be lost in the communication. Here is an example of the verb *to be* in English being conjugated in the present tense:

- I *am* a linguist.
- You *are* a linguist.
- Linguistics *is* awesome.
- We *are* linguists.
- All linguists *are* cool.

conjunction

This refers to a small **closed class** of **grammatical words** which are used to link units at the same level of structure. In English, the list contains just five: *and, but, or, yet, nor*. They can coordinate **morphemes** (*pre-* *and* *post-natal*), **words** (*dazed* *but* *manic*), **phrases** (*red shoes* *and* *blue socks*) or **clauses** (*she wanted a pizza* *but* *he wanted a pie*). Some grammatical descriptions also call **subordinators** (e.g. *because*) a kind of subordinating conjunction, but that is potentially confusing as the term appears to be contradictory. Both word classes link units but conjunctions link them as equals.

connected speech

This refers to the continuous sequence of sounds we produce when we speak naturally. The way we speak in natural conversation is different from the way we speak when, for instance, we carefully read a **text** aloud. For example, all **words** are accented (i.e. emphasised) when pronounced in isolation. But in naturally occurring speech, both grammatical (**closed-class**) and lexical (**open-class**) words are pronounced differently. **Grammatical words** are often de-accented, and these reduced **forms** are known as **weak forms**. For example, the **definite article**, *the*, in English, is normally pronounced with an unstressed **schwa vowel** as /ðə/ in connected speech, though, in isolation, we may well pronounce it with a full vowel as /ði:/. Some unaccented grammatical words become **clitics**. Clitics are treated like the unaccented **syllables** of

lexical words and are consequently attached to a leading or trailing syllable. Compare, for example, the pronunciation of the **sentence** 'We are listening' in isolation (1), and in naturally occurring conversation (2), where the pronunciation of the **auxiliary verb** *are* is de-accented:

1. /wiː ɑ lɪsənɪŋ/
2. /wəlɪsnɪŋ/

What we can observe here is vowel reduction; that is, the long vowel /iː/ is reduced to the mid-central vowel schwa /ə/. H-dropping is another common feature of connected speech. In naturally occurring conversation, /h/ is pronounced only at the beginning of an accented syllable, as in *humbug* /hʌmbug/ and *heart* /hɑːt/. Conversely, grammatical words that begin with /h/ but which are not accented syllables have weak forms. Again, compare the pronunciation of 'Has he hurt himself?' in isolation (3) and in context (4):

3. /hæz hiː hɜːt hɪmsɛlf/
4. [əzɪˈɜːtɪmsɛlf]

Note that the transcription (4) would only apply to a variety of English that permits /h/-dropping in **content words** as well as **function words** (e.g. Yorkshire English). No-one is immune from the effects of connected speech, despite what they might claim. It would sound very odd if people spoke with equally stressed and full vowels in every syllable. *See also* **assimilation**, **elision** and **hiatus**.

connotation

This refers to the **semantic** associations that a **word** has. For example, while the denotational **meanings** (*see* **denotation**) of *doggy* and *canine* are the same, the former might sound like a cuter or more domesticated animal than the latter, or be associated with the kind of **language** used to children rather than by scientists. Another well-known example concerns the differences in meaning that many people perceive between *bachelor* and *spinster*. In terms of denotative meaning, these words have identical meaning except for the **gender** of the person being referred to ('an unmarried male' or 'an unmarried female'). The differences that we note are to do with the connotations of the words, established over years of culture and usage – while *bachelor* has generally positive connotative associations (young, handsome, eligible?), *spinster* has generally negative connotations (old, beyond marriage, excessively fond of cats?). We may not see any truth in these connotations, and they are not accounted for by denotational meaning, but many English speakers will recognise them as being attached to these words by association.

consonant

While most people will think of consonants in terms of written **language**, the reason for distinguishing between consonants and **vowels** is that they differ phonetically. The air that we breathe out is used to form speech sounds as it passes by, through and over the **articulators**, i.e. the parts of the oral and nasal cavities that shape the sounds we use to speak. In broad terms, consonants are those sounds that obstruct or significantly impede the passage of exhaled air from the **lungs** to the outside of the body via the mouth or the nose. There are different levels of obstruction that form groups of sounds sharing the same **manner of articulation**. These include, for example, the **plosive** consonants, such as /p/ and /t/, which create a complete closure somewhere in the mouth. When the air builds up significantly behind the closure, it explodes the articulators apart, causing a sound. Try preparing to say /p/ and stop with your **lips** closed. You may find that it is difficult to stop them from bursting apart as the pressure builds up. While this definition of a consonant is broadly accurate, there are exceptions. Some classes of consonants do not involve obstruction – **approximants**, for example. In fact, some approximants are very similar to vowels in articulation, and [j] and [w] are sometimes referred to as *semivowels* for this reason. So, while it is basically true that consonants block the air and vowels do not, sometimes the distinction is more to do with what a sound is doing linguistically. For example, if an articulation involves the front of the **tongue** being raised towards the **hard palate**, it is a consonant in a word like *yet* and a vowel in a word like *tea*. Some languages allow some very 'consonantal' things to be vowels, like Chinese allowing **alveolar fricatives** as vowels.

consonant cluster

This refers to a sequence of **consonants** with no intervening **vowels**. Phonetically, this sequence can occur at the beginning (*spry* /spɹaɪ/) or end (*acts* /akts/) of **syllables**, or across syllable boundaries where two clusters meet (*matchbox* /matʃbɒks/). In some cases, where the consonant clusters become unwieldy, there will be cluster reduction in order to keep the pronunciation manageable. For example, *sandcastle* may be pronounced with a three-consonant cluster in careful speech – /saŋdkasl/ – but in most cases of **connected speech** it would lose the **plosive** /d/ and the **nasal** /n/ would then assimilate to the **velar** positioning of /k/, resulting in the pronunciation [saŋkasl]. Consonant cluster reduction is a common phenomenon in spontaneous speech, where certain consonants within a cluster are not pronounced. Another English example is how speakers often reduce *gifts* to [gɪfs], where the /t/ is dropped.

constative

This is a term established by the **language** philosopher J. L. Austin for a piece of language that makes a statement. Examples include 'I am the resurrection', 'Papa was a rolling stone' and 'Heaven is a place on Earth'. Note that, in theory, with enough information, each of these statements could be proved to be either true or false. This is in contrast to **performatives** which have no truth value.

construction grammar

In **generative grammars**, **language** is seen as consisting of **words** (i.e. a **lexicon**) and a system of **rules** for combining them (i.e. a **grammar**). But there are numerous examples of expressions that cannot easily be explained by such grammars. Idiomatic **phrases** such as *kick the bucket* and *It's raining cats and dogs*, for example, would seem to be complete chunks of language with predefined **meanings** rather than strings of individual words that have been combined. In particular, the meaning of these idiomatic expressions cannot be deduced from the meanings of their constituent words. The same is true of expressions like *all of a sudden*, *in the end*, *by and large* and *to be honest*. Traditional grammars treat such expressions as anomalies. That is, they are considered as exceptions to the rules of the grammar. Construction grammar states that this explanation is unsatisfactory and that a grammar must be able to account for all instances of language use, not just the prototypical. To do this, construction grammar posits that the building blocks of language are not words but *constructions*, and that we acquire these when we learn language. A construction is a grammatical structure paired with its meaning (which may be **semantic** or **pragmatic**). Constructions can be fixed and unvarying (e.g. *by and large, all of a sudden*) or they can be flexible (e.g. *hit the road, hits the road, hitting the road*). They can also be entirely schematic (e.g. N + *s* = plural **noun**, **verb** stem + *ed* = past **tense**, **infinitive** verb = command). Despite its name, there is no single, unified construction grammar. Different **linguists** have different views about the nature of constructions. Consequently, numerous different types of construction grammar have been posited and the term *construction grammar* is best understood as an umbrella term for a group of grammatical theories that share basic underlying principles. Construction grammar has similarities with **corpus**-derived **pattern grammar**.

content word

This is an alternative term for **lexical word**. Examples of content words include **nouns**, lexical **verbs**, **adjectives** and **adverbs**. *See also* **open class**.

Conversation Analysis

This is a method of investigating social interaction by studying the structure of naturally occurring conversation. Pioneered by the sociologist Harvey Sacks in the early 1970s, Conversation Analysis (CA) takes as its starting point the fact that conversation involves **turn-taking** – that is, in conversation people take it in turns to speak. Of course, sometimes the turn-taking system breaks down, but Sacks was clear that conversation is structured and rule-governed, and set out to determine what those **rules** were. Turns are made up of *turn-constructional units*, which are complete grammatical units such as a **clause** (or, in **spoken grammar**, a **C-unit**). In a normal conversation, participants take it in turns to hold the **floor** (which we can define as the right to speak and be listened to). Turn-taking is governed by the ***turn-allocational component*** and the ***turn-constructional component***. The first controls how turns change (that is, how turns are allocated between speakers), and the second governs the length and complexity of the turn. Turn allocation happens at a ***transition relevance place*** (TRP) in the conversation, and at that point a change of speakers can happen via one of a number of methods. The current speaker can select the next speaker (perhaps by directing a question at one person in particular), or the next speaker can self-select (for example, by disagreeing with the previous speaker's point). Alternatively, the turn can ***lapse***, leading to a pause in the conversation. At this point, the current speaker might choose to incorporate that pause into their turn and continue speaking until the next TRP. Any overlap in turns that does not occur at a TRP constitutes an interruption. Turn length is managed through the turn-constructional component. For example, if it looks like someone is about to start interrupting you, you might raise your voice. You might even make a metalinguistic comment like 'Let me finish!' These aspects of Conversation Analysis focus on the production of talk. But talk is also interactive and so it is important to understand how turns relate to one another. Here, the study of **adjacency pairs** is important.

converse

This refers to a type of **opposition** and so it is one of the **sense relations** that can hold between **lexical items** in a **language**. The relationship of converseness is between concepts (or objects) that are mutually dependent, such as *parent/child* or *borrow/lend*. In each case, if one exists (e.g. *parent*) or is happening (e.g. *borrowing*), then, by definition, the other also exists (e.g. *child*) or is happening (e.g. *lending*). Many converse pairs, such as *borrow/lend, buy/sell, give/take* are transactional verbs and they simply provide a perspective on the transaction from one or other of the participants' points of view. There are also some converse relationships amongst the **grammatical words** in a language, such as the **prepositions**. So, for example, if a bridge goes *over* a river, then, by definition, the river goes *under* the bridge.

conversion

This is a **word** formation process that involves taking an existing word and using it as a different **part of speech** (i.e. *converting* it from one part of speech to another). For example, the **verb** *ask* ('Can I *ask* you a question?') can be converted to a **noun** ('That's a big *ask*').

Cooperative Principle

The Cooperative Principle (CP) is a highly influential account of how speakers convey implied **meaning** – that is, how we manage to understand each other when we so very rarely say exactly what we mean. Put forward by the philosopher H. P. Grice in 1975, the CP proposes that we make certain assumptions whenever we engage in conversational interaction. These assumptions are summarised by Grice in a series of four maxims. These are the maxims of **quantity**, **quality**, **relation** and **manner**. Rather unfortunately, the maxims are formulated as **imperatives**, which has led some people to mistakenly think that they are instructions for communication. This is not the case and we should instead think of them as assumptions or expectations. For example, the maxim of quality says 'Do not say what you believe to be false.' What this means is that, whenever we have a conversation with someone, we assume that what they say to us will be the truth (at least, as they believe it to be). Of course, people do not always observe the Gricean maxims, and it is in breaking them that interesting effects are created. The maxims can be broken in a number of ways: by violation, **flout** or infringement. For example, a well-known example of a violation of the maxim of quality is the former US President Bill Clinton's assertion, in reference to accusations that he had had sex with a young White House intern, Monica Lewinsky, that 'I did not have sexual relations with that woman.' Violating a maxim involves breaking it intentionally with the hope that your hearer will not realise you have broken it. Interestingly, it is only when a lie is uncovered that we can say for sure that the maxim of quality has been violated, since, if the lie had been successful, we would never have known for sure. Flouting a maxim also involves breaking it intentionally, but the difference between this and violating is that flouts are intended to be recognised as such by the hearer. For example, if someone were to say 'The motorway was empty – I literally flew home', we would not for a moment assume that they had suddenly gained the power of flight. In this respect, the speaker cannot possibly have violated the maxim of quality, since it is obvious to the hearer that what they have said is patently not true. This, then, is not a violation but a flout. And what is important about a flout is that it creates **implicature**, or implied meaning. In the case of this example, the implicature is likely to be that the speaker was able to drive home very quickly. Finally, infringing a maxim means breaking it unintentionally. If you are asked for directions, for instance, and you mistakenly send your interlocutor off in the wrong direction, you have not violated the maxim of quality so long as the information you conveyed was given in good faith: you believed you were telling the truth. In certain circumstances, speakers may also choose to *opt out* of the Cooperative Principle. For example, when a politician replies 'No comment' to a journalist's question, they are in effect opting out of the typical expectations of a conversational exchange. The problem with doing this, of course, is that it is often difficult to avoid hearers making inferences on the basis of this. 'No comment' in response to a question like 'Did you make fraudulent expenses claims?' is inevitably likely to be interpreted as an admission of guilt. Similarly, if you post a picture on Twitter, accompanied with the words 'Posted without comment', viewers of your tweet are highly likely to infer an implicature, even if you claim there isn't one (there must be – otherwise, why would you have tweeted in the first place?). Finally, there are certain contexts or text-types in which we might assume the CP not to be in place. For instance, poetry is often deliberately obtuse, thereby flouting the maxim of manner. But, generally speaking, we expect poetry to do this. In this respect, then, our normal assumption is not to expect clarity but to presume the opposite. And as an example of how the CP may be suspended contextually, consider what happens in a job interview situation. Here we might expect the maxim of quantity ('Do not make your contribution more informative than is required') to be relaxed, as the interview candidate does their best to persuade the interview panel that they are the best person for the job. The Cooperative Principle is a contribution to the area of **linguistics** known as **pragmatics**.

copular verb

A copula (*copula* is the noun, *copular* is the adjective) is a **verb** that links the **subject** of a **sentence** to a **complement** (subject complements provide additional information about the subject in a **clause**). For example, in the sentence 'Erica is a phonetician', *Erica* is the subject, *is* is the copula and *a phonetician* is the complement. The primary copular verb in English is *be*. Other copular verbs include *appear* ('Lesley appeared tired'), *feel* ('Matt felt on top of the world') and *become* ('Hazel became rich'). *See also* **verb phrase**.

corpus

The term *corpus* (plural ***corpora***) comes from the Latin for *body*, and in **linguistics** refers to a database of **language** (a 'body' of data) that aims to represent a particular language **variety**. Although early corpora were not digital, they are always electronic in format these days. The first electronic corpus to be produced was the Brown corpus (named after Brown University in the USA, where it was compiled), which consists of 1 million words of written American English from the 1960s. The constituent **texts** of the corpus are drawn from many different genres (newspapers, government documents, fiction, etc.). The corpus as a whole is intended to be a representative sample of general written American English of the early 1960s. The representativeness of corpora is important, as it is this factor that enables corpus **linguists** to be confident that what they observe in the corpus is also likely to be true for the language (or some subset of the language, e.g. that within a **speech community** or genre) as a whole. The creation of the Brown corpus sparked a wave of corpus-building which continues to this day. For instance, there is now a Brown 'family' of corpora, consisting of 1-million-word databases of written British English from the 1930s, 1960s, 1990s, and 2000s, as well as equivalent corpora for written American English. This makes it possible to carry out comparative studies of how British and American English have developed over time. The size of corpora has also increased in line with technological developments. The **British National Corpus** (BNC), for instance, is a 100-million-word corpus of written and spoken British English, primarily from the 1990s. This has recently been supplemented by the spoken British National Corpus 2014, an 11.5-million-word corpus of British English speech recorded between 2012 and 2016. Similarly, there exists a wide range of national corpora for a broad variety of languages, including the **Corpus of Contemporary American English** (COCA), the Hungarian National Corpus and the Czech National Corpus. In addition to these, there are a number of other so-called 'megacorpora', including the 1.9-billion-word GloWbE (Global Web-based English) and the 14-billion-word iWeb corpus. Some corpora consist simply of raw (i.e. unannotated) text, while others include further linguistic and metalinguistic information (*see* **metalanguage**) about the corpus text. For example, ICE-GB (the British component of the International Corpus of English) consists of a million words of spoken and written English which have been annotated for **parts of speech** and information about syntactic structure. If you want to explore a range of commercially available corpora (including the British National Corpus and Corpus of Contemporary American English), try Mark Davies's English Corpora website: english-corpora.org. *See also* **corpus linguistics**.

corpus linguistics

This involves the use of computational techniques to analyse large databases of **language** (corpora). The corpus **linguist** John Sinclair (1933–2007) famously said 'The language looks rather different when you look at a lot of it at once.' By this, Sinclair meant that it is possible to see patterns in large corpora that would be impossible to detect in small samples of language. For example, by analysing corpora it is possible to detect **semantic prosody**. The **phrase** *build up of*, for instance, is usually used in the context of something negative. Examples from the **British National Corpus** include *build up of fumes*, *build up of toxic gases* and *build up of blackheads around the nose*. *Build up a*, on the other hand, tends to be used in positive contexts. Examples include 'build up a family nest egg', 'build up a life for themselves' and 'build up a certain degree of credibility'. What this means is that, if we use *build up of* in a positive context (e.g. 'There has been a build up of goodwill towards the government'), we are likely to be interpreted as being either ironic or insincere. These are insights that could only have been gained through studying corpora. Other corpus linguists have studied the changing frequency of particular **lexical items** or syntactic structures. For example, Geoffrey Leech (1936–2014) demonstrated that **modal verbs** in British English have declined in usage since the 1960s. Corpus linguistics is seen by some linguists as simply a methodology for studying language. Others consider it to constitute a sub-discipline of **linguistics** in its own right, on the grounds that it has revealed insights into **grammar** and **meaning** that would have otherwise remained undiscovered. There are a number of analytical techniques that are commonly used in corpus linguistics. These include analyses of *frequency*, **keyness** and **collocation**. Corpus linguistics has revolutionised many areas of language study, including *child language acquisition*, **historical linguistics**, **syntax** and *lexicography*.

Corpus of Contemporary American English

The Corpus of Contemporary American English (COCA) is a collection of 560 million words of spoken and written American English. The corpus spans the years 1990 to 2017, and includes approximately 20 million words from each year. COCA is freely available via the English Corpora website: english-corpora.org. The English Corpora site offers access to a wide variety of other corpora too.

countable noun

Known also as a *count noun*, this is a **noun** that can be pluralised by the addition of the plural **morpheme** *s* or its **allomorphs** *es* and *ies*. Examples include *cats*, *boxes* and *baddies*. Countable nouns can be modified by cardinal numbers and general ordinals (*see* **enumerator**), e.g. *two* cats, *three* boxes and *other* baddies. *See also* **mass noun**.

covert prestige

This describes **prestige** that is attached to elements of **accent** or **dialect** that are often stigmatised as being nonstandard. For example, speakers of British English with a South Yorkshire accent would pronounce the word *right* as [rɛjʔ]. This is a regional pronunciation that in certain social situations would mark the speaker out as using a nonstandard **variety**. And it may well be the case that in such situations the speaker would be judged negatively as a result of their use of this nonstandard **form** (note that these negative evaluations would constitute a form of **prescriptivism**). Despite this, research in **sociolinguistics** has found that some speakers use such forms, even when they are aware of the negative associations that they can convey. This is because such forms act as markers of in-group identity and show that a speaker belongs to a particular social group. For example, the British sociolinguist Peter Trudgill found that working-class men in Norwich saw the use of nonstandard forms as a marker of status within their **speech community**. That is, speakers conferred upon these forms *covert prestige*. *See also* **overt prestige**.

creak

In Stanley Kubrick's horror film *The Shining*, Danny, the son of the central character Jack Torrance, has an imaginary friend called Tony. To give the effect of Tony speaking, Danny raises his index finger and moves it up and down while speaking in what phoneticians would describe as a *creaky voice*. Creaky voice is a particular kind of sound produced by regulating the passage of air through the **vocal folds** (commonly known as the vocal cords). Air passes between the folds when we speak. The vocal folds are attached to the arytenoid cartilages, which form part of the **larynx** and enable the vocal folds to move. If the arytenoid cartilages are pulled together, the vocal folds become compressed. In such an instance, the **airflow** between the folds is limited and air passes through at a slower rate than usual. The vocal folds consequently vibrate below the frequency used during normal speech. Creaky voice is a distinctive feature of some **languages** (e.g. Jalapa Mazatec and San Lucas Quiavini Zapotec, both spoken in Mexico). But it's never been used to creepier effect than in *The Shining*. *See also* **glottis**.

creole

A creole is a **pidgin** that has acquired **native speakers**. If a child grows up speaking a pidgin as their first **language**, then at that stage the pidgin can be considered a creole. For example, Jamaican Creole is a creole that developed from a pidgin formed from various **varieties** of British English and the West African Akan language (along with other linguistic influences from West Africa).

Critical Discourse Analysis

This is often shortened to CDA and refers to a field of research that has now developed a wide range of approaches to the study of linguistic data (i.e. **texts**), usually in relation to their context of production and reception. Originating as a practice known as **critical linguistics**, which applied linguistic analysis to the study of ideological naturalisation and manipulation in texts, CDA became ever more interested in the contextual aspects of the way in which texts replicate and spread ideologies – particularly those often characterised as right-wing. Influenced and inspired by theoretical Marxism, many early (and, indeed, more recent) CDA scholars are explicitly working in a tradition of critiquing the mainstream and dominant ideologies found embedded in public texts, including political and news texts. This political motivation on the part of the researchers is often acknowledged openly by an assertion that there is no such thing as truly objective research, so that you should acknowledge your inherent biases in order for the reader to take these into account in looking at the results of your work. Some scholars reject this defeatist attitude to the aim of objectivity and point out that there are two dangers with this approach. First, simply giving way to your prejudices may mean that you see what you expect to see in the text you are investigating and miss some of the ideation and ideologies that do not match these expectations. Second, there is some evidence that ideological **meaning** can be truly textual (*see* **critical stylistics**), in being traceable through textual features that can be recognised by a reader, irrespective of whether they agree with the implied ideology. This, it is argued, is true of all texts, irrespective of their political leanings and origin. It may thus be entirely possible, and indeed desirable, to at least aim for objectivity in the process of analysing such texts. The interpretation, including the contribution of an individual reader's own views and/or the influence of contexts of production (such as the power of the mass media), can be separately considered, with the analysis itself intact as a rigorous and quasi-objective account of the textual meaning.

critical linguistics

This refers to the earliest development of **linguistics** towards an overtly political aim, to expose and critique ideologies in powerful

texts (such as the mass media) through linguistic analysis. The term has now largely been replaced by **Critical Discourse Analysis** and, to a lesser extent, also by **critical stylistics**.

critical period hypothesis

The critical period hypothesis claims that there is a limited period of time during which children can learn **language**. If a child is not given sufficient exposure to language during this period, then they will struggle to acquire language at a later age. Some **linguists** take cases such as that of **Genie**, who did not benefit from normal human interaction for the first thirteen years of her life, as evidence that there is a point beyond which children will struggle, or be unable, to acquire a language. Different linguists place the critical period at different points – Genie's is an extreme case, and children without language who have been discovered at an earlier age have become competent with language. Some also argue that *critical* overstates the case – even Genie, who never gained a high degree of competence, was nevertheless able to communicate with others.

critical stylistics

This is the name given to an offshoot of **Critical Discourse Analysis**, aimed at reinstating some of the rigour and objectivity that CDA explicitly set aside. In this case, a framework for the analysis of textual **meaning** is based partly on the features deriving from **Systemic Functional Linguistics** that were taken up by, first, **critical linguistics**, and then CDA. It also adds a number of other textual features (e.g. **negation**, **opposition**) which have not previously been explicitly connected to textual meaning. This framework is then used to provide systematic accounts of the meaning of a **text**, including its ideation and ideologies, with the aim of drawing conclusions about the effect of these features in the context of reception.

D

declarative

This is one of the terms used in **grammar** to indicate a **sentence** which makes a statement or an assertion, such as 'This butter is rancid.' This contrasts with other types of sentence which, for example, ask a question, as in 'Is that butter rancid?' (**interrogative**), or instruct the hearer to do something, as in 'Eat that rancid butter' (**imperative**).

definite article

The definite article is a type of **determiner**. In English, the definite article *the* appears before a **noun phrase** and usually signals that the **referent** being discussed has already been introduced. For example, compare the use of the definite article with the **indefinite article** in the following examples: *the language magazine* and *a language magazine*. We have a sense of knowing what is being referred to in the first case but not in the second. In English, the definite article is not marked for **gender, case** or **number**, but in some **languages** it is. For example, the definite article in French has both a masculine (*le*) and feminine (*la*) as well as a plural (*les*) **form**. This is also the case in many other Romance languages, such as Italian and Portuguese.

deixis

This refers to the capacity of human **language** to shift the reference of certain **words** and **phrases** according to the point of view and/or position (in time and space) of the speaker. Thus, in English, the **adverb** *there* refers to a place that is distant (***distal***) from the speaker, and *here* refers to the speaker's location (***proximal***). *Then* and *now* work similarly for time. The **pronouns** work similarly by identifying the speaker (*I*) and the addressee (*you*). In a conversation, then, the identity of these pronouns changes with each speaker change. This is difficult for young children when they first begin to use language, so we instinctively use the third person to get around the deixis of first and second person pronouns by saying things like 'Mummy is just going upstairs for a moment' or 'Does Emma want a cuddle?' It is sometimes claimed that deixis is either the result of – or the cause of – the capacity of human beings for empathy. Because we can literally put ourselves in the place of others (for example, giving directions over the phone and imagining ourselves in the place of the hearer), then we also seem to be able, in a metaphorical sense, to imagine ourselves in their shoes. The **adjective** related to *deixis* is *deictic*.

demonstrative

This is the name given to a set of deictic **lexical items** that (in English, at least) can be used as **determiners** before a **noun**, or can be used on their own as **pronouns**. Thus, we see the determiner use in proximal <u>*this*</u> *chair* and <u>*these*</u> *cupboards*, and the distal <u>*that*</u> *carpet* and <u>*those*</u> *flowers*. Notice that physical distance might be less important in their meaning than metaphorical (usually emotional) distance. The pronoun use makes this emotional distance clear when you compare, for example, 'Look at *this*' and 'Look at *that*', the latter potentially sounding more indignant than the former.

denotation

This is the term used for the set of **referents** of a **word** or **phrase** in a **language**. It captures the notion that language links to the real world by a process of labelling, though this is clearly not the whole story, as much of language links not to the world but to itself (*see* **structuralism**). The denotation of the word *dog*, for example, is the whole class in the real world of what we would label *dog*. *Denotative meaning*, therefore, is the kind of semantic information that we find about a word in a dictionary definition – the stable and conventional **meaning** of a word. If you know the denotative meaning of a word, then you know what it can and cannot be used to refer to. For instance, if you know the socially accepted denotative meaning of the word *book*, then you know that a newspaper cannot be called *a book*, while a novel or a dictionary can. As children are learning language, they might have a shaky grasp on a word's denotative meaning, and use *book* to refer to a newspaper. ***Connotative meaning*** and **social meaning** are other kinds of meanings that words and phrases can communicate. *See also* **connotation**.

dental

Dental sounds are those that involve some kind of contact between **tongue** and teeth. In English, the only dental sounds are those known as **interdental consonants**, which happen also to be **fricatives**. These consonants involve the tongue sticking out slightly between the teeth, and the result is that there is bound to be an escape of air – this is what makes the sounds fricative. There are two such sounds – the **voiced** version [ð] that you find at the start of *this*, and the **voiceless** version [θ] that is the first sound in *thing* (both represented in English spelling by <th>). In other **languages**, there are dental sounds that are **plosive** in their **manner of articulation** (involving a full closure between the tongue and the teeth and a subsequent explosive pulling apart). These include, for example, the French and Italian versions of <t>, which in English is not dental but **alveolar** (the tongue against the alveolar ridge, which is just behind the teeth). In the case of dental plosives, the tongue is held tight up against the back of the teeth until the air pressure builds up to cause the plosive sound, such as the initial /t/ sound in *tout*.

deontic modality

This refers to one particular type of **meaning** produced by modal items (**modal verbs, adjectives, adverbs, verbs**, etc.). Deontic modality produces the understanding that the speaker or writer thinks that something ought to happen, so that, for example, 'Hazel *should* make us some cakes' indicates that the speaker thinks Hazel is under some obligation to make the cakes. Modal verbs (*ought, should, can, could*, etc.) usually have the capacity to be understood as either deontic (as above) or **epistemic**. In the latter case, we would understand the same sentence as meaning that it is probable (but not certain) that Hazel will make the cakes. Usually, the context will make clear which of these interpretations is intended ('Hazel should make us some cakes, but if she doesn't, we can always buy some').

derivation

This is a **word** formation process that involves adding derivational **morphemes** to an existing word. For example, *im + pertinent = impertinent, joy + less = joyless, beautiful + ly = beautifully*. By adding derivational morphemes to a word, we can generate a new word that differs in terms of **semantics** from its source word (e.g. *unhappy* is semantically different from *happy*). This is different from adding inflectional morphemes, which simply form grammatical variants of the same word. For instance, *chairs* is simply the plural of *chair*, while *jumped* is simply the past **tense** of *jump*; the inflectional morphemes do not change the semantic **meaning** of *chair* or *jump*.

descriptivism

This is the opposite of **prescriptivism** (*see also* **proscriptivism**) and is the approach that **linguistics** takes to its appointed task. Traditionally, grammarians, publishers, educators, lexicographers and other gatekeepers to **language** thought that there should be a 'correct' form of the language which should be adhered to, but, with the advent of modern linguistics in the early part of the twentieth century, there was a realisation that language change is inevitable and harmless, so our task is to describe linguistic usage rather than prescribe how people should use language.

design features

These are features of human **language** that distinguish it from the communication systems used by other animals (e.g. **birdsong**, the so-called *wagging dance* of bees, and the calls that gibbons use). Proposed by the **linguist** and anthropologist Charles Hockett (1916–2000) and developed over several years, Hockett's final list comprises the following sixteen features:

- *duality*, i.e. the fact that meaningful **utterances** are composed of smaller units in combination (*see* **combinatorial structure** and **hierarchical structure**).
- *productivity*, i.e the capacity for creating new, never-heard-before utterances from the rules of the language.
- *arbitrariness*, i.e. the fact that the relationship between a linguistic sign and its **meaning** is entirely arbitrary. For example,

in English there is no logical requirement for the **phoneme** combination /kat/ to mean 'small furry mammal that miaows'; we could choose any other combination of phonemes to do the same job, so long as all speakers in a **speech community** are in agreement about this.

- *interchangeability*, i.e. the capacity of language users to function as both producer and hearer.
- *specialisation*, i.e. the fact that speech is intentional (as opposed to instinctive).
- *displacement*, i.e. the ability to talk about things that do not relate to your immediate surroundings. For example, humans are able to talk about things that happened in the past, or plan events that will happen in the future.
- *cultural transmission*, i.e. the fact that the **rules** and conventions of language are conveyed culturally (e.g. through teaching and learning), rather than genetically.
- *vocal–auditory channel*, i.e. the notion that language is conveyed and received through speaking and hearing.
- *broadcast transmission and directional reception*, i.e. the fact that when we speak, our utterance may be heard by anyone within earshot; hearers, however, focus on a particular message, despite the fact that lots of people may be talking at once.
- *rapid fading*, i.e. the fact that once sound is made, it quickly disappears.
- *total feedback*, i.e. the fact that speakers can hear the message they are conveying (compare, for example, fish whose changing eye colour conveys a message – the fish conveying the message are, of course, unable to see what their eyes are doing).
- *semanticity*, i.e. the fact that specific elements of an utterance have particular meanings.
- *discreteness*, i.e. the notion that language is produced from discrete units (such as phonemes) and that if we change one of those units, we change the meaning of the message.
- *prevarication*, i.e. the capacity for messages to be false or meaningless.

- **reflexiveness**, i.e. the capacity for discussing language via **metalanguage**.
- **learnability**, i.e. the ability of the speaker to learn another language.

Hockett's point is that while some animal languages may have some of these features, only human language has them all. Hockett's design features are indicative of his underlying views about the nature of language. For instance, Hockett disagreed vehemently with the concept of **Universal Grammar** (UG), as is indicated by his concept of cultural transmission, which is at odds with UG. The concept of design features is a useful starting point for defining human language. However, evolutionary linguists (i.e. linguists interested in tracing the origins of language) have pointed out that if we consider the features as necessary conditions for the definition of human language (that is, if we accept the **Uniformitarian Principle**), then it becomes very difficult to trace the emergence of language in humans.

determiners

These are **words** that introduce **noun phrases** in English and other similar **languages**. They constitute a syntactic class because they cannot co-occur. That is, they form a **paradigmatic** set. This means that they are alternatives in the structure – i.e. you can only choose one of them. In English, the determiner class includes the **definite** and **indefinite articles** (*the, a/an*), the possessive **adjectives** (*my, our, his, her, its, their, your*) and the **demonstrative** adjectives (*this, these, that, those*). You can say *my house* or *the house* but not **my the house*.

deviation

This is a term from **stylistics** that describes any linguistic movement away from a perceived norm that therefore results in unexpected irregularity. Deviation can happen at every **level of language**: *lexis*, **phonology** and **grammar**. For example, in James Fenton's poem 'A German Requiem', the speaker says it would be nice to join with others occasionally and 'forget' the old times. This is lexical deviation, since *forget* doesn't usually **collocate** with *old times*; instead, we'd expect *remember* or *reminisce about*. There is evidence from **psycholinguistics** that deviation results in **foregrounding**, i.e. linguistic deviations stand out and readers spend longer interpreting their significance.

diachronic

This is an **adjective** that refers to **language** change over time. Diachronic analysis can be contrasted with **synchronic** analysis, which looks at a snapshot of language at a specific point in time. Diachronic analysis is used in many subfields of **linguistics**. For instance, the sociolinguist William Labov carried out a diachronic study of **words** for *sandwich* (e.g. *hoagie*) used by the people of Philadelphia, Pennsylvania, over a 100-year period.

diacritic

In **phonetics**, a diacritic is a mark or character that is added to a phonetic symbol to alter the basic value of that symbol. A diacritic can be placed above a phonetic symbol (e.g. [ŋ̊]), below it (e.g. [ɛ̞]), at its upper right corner (e.g. [xʷ]), or even through it (e.g. [ɫ]). There are thirty-one different diacritics listed in the **International Phonetic Alphabet**, and diacritics can be extremely helpful when making accurate transcriptions of speech. It may help to think of diacritics as being like the decorations that go on a Christmas tree. A tree without lights or ornaments is still symbolic of the holiday or the season, but once decorations are added the Christmas tree takes on a more unique identity. That identity will reflect the family or person who has decorated it. Diacritics work in much the same way. A phoneme without any diacritics is still representative of a sound. However, once you add diacritics that symbol takes on a unique identity that records the nuance of what was actually spoken.

The term *diacritic* is also used to refer to an accent placed over a particular **grapheme** to indicate a particular pronunciation. For example, the accents over the letter <a> in the Hungarian **word** *viszontlátásra* (goodbye) indicate the pronunciation /æ/. By contrast, unaccented <a> in Hungarian is pronounced /ɒ/, as in *mascka* (cat).

dialect

This is used to refer to any **variety** of a **language** based on a **speech community** that could be geographically delineated (e.g. Yorkshire dialect) or socially defined (e.g. teenage dialects). In line with recent developments in **sociolinguistics**, dialect is increasingly also used to refer to varieties that are used by communities defined by identity (e.g. **gender**, sexual orientation, ethnicity, etc.), but there are also other terms (e.g. **register**) that can be used for specific types of contextualised language (e.g. language of the law courts) without being necessarily a full dialect. The terms **accent** and *dialect* are often used interchangeably; however, *dialect* is more appropriately used to discuss varieties of a language with respect to lexical and grammatical choices. *Accent* on the other hand, is more appropriately used to describe differences in the pronunciation and production of **words**.

diglossia

This refers to a linguistic situation in which two **language** varieties are routinely used by the members of a particular **speech community**. Each **variety** has a different function, and one of the varieties will always have more **prestige** than the other. The variety with more prestige is typically referred to as the H (i.e. high) variety, while the less prestigious one is the L (i.e. low) variety. A case in point is German, of which there are various H and L varieties. In Switzerland, where German is one of four official languages,

Standard German is the H variety while Swiss German is the L variety. Swiss German is used primarily in speech while the H variety is found primarily in written **texts**. Such is the difference between the H and L varieties that native speakers of Standard German can have problems comprehending the L variety, Swiss German, if it is not a **vernacular** language for them (e.g. if they grew up in Germany, rather than Switzerland). Some sociolinguists argue that *diglossia* can also be used to refer to situations in which speakers routinely switch between different **styles** and **registers**, not just dialectal varieties.

diphthong

This is a phonetic term that refers to the combination of two adjacent **vowel** sounds that are within the same **syllable**. A diphthong, unlike a **monophthong**, has two different intentional vowel targets. It begins with one vowel sound and ends with a different one. An example is the /aʊ/ diphthong in the word *flout*. Diphthongs can be produced with many different **tongue** movements – for example: front to back, back to front, low to high, or central to back. Diphthongs do not have to contain a large tongue position movement, as you can have diphthongs that move only slightly, such as the /eɪ/ in *wait*. **Spectrograms** are great tools for identifying diphthongs visually – you will see movements in the first or second **formant** (i.e. it does not remain completely stable) as the diphthong is being produced.

directional opposite

A directional opposite is one kind of oppositional **sense relation** between **words** or **phrases** in a **language** (sometimes used interchangeably with *reversive opposition*). The pairs of terms in a directional relationship reverse each other's direction, so that, for example, the prepositions *to* and *from* indicate related directions that each denote the opposite direction of the other. A similar relation holds between other pairs, such as *up* and *down*. See **opposition** for other types of opposite.

discourse

This is a **word** that is so overused nowadays that it has almost lost impact. When it was first used in **linguistics**, it referred to structures (**texts** and conversations) larger than the **sentence**, which for many years had been the largest unit in **language** to be analysed. That is, *discourse* was seen as the largest unit in the hierarchical structure of language. When researchers started realising that there were patterns of linguistic behaviour that operated across longer stretches of text, they started investigating these patterns, often considering their meaning in relation to the context in which the text was used. This secondary meaning of *discourse*, which includes the text, but also places it in context, has since been very widely appropriated by disciplines outside linguistics, including literary and cultural studies, politics, sociology and so on. In many cases, where the research is not being carried out by **linguists**, the analysis of text has been largely abandoned in favour of the analysis of context. It is therefore important, when using terms such as **Discourse Analysis** and **Critical Discourse Analysis**, to be certain what is meant by the term *discourse*.

Discourse Analysis

This has become a very wide (or, some might say, 'vague') term for a range of approaches to studying **language** in context. Originally, the term referred to the investigation of language in **texts** longer than a **sentence** (see **discourse**), whereby the links between and structures of sentences in a text were the focus of systematic study (*see* **cohesion, coherence**). Many early studies were concerned not just with the wider **co-text**, but also with context (often in the school classroom) and this meant that there was some tendency to study not just the sentences of one speaker, but of exchanges between speakers (such as teachers and children in a classroom). At the same time, a focus on both the ideological (**critical linguistics**) and applied aspects of studying longer stretches of language meant that scholars from other disciplines became interested in being able to characterise what was going on in the language relating to their discipline or field of work. As this became more common, the term *Discourse Analysis* started to become associated with examination of texts from a wide range of perspectives, to the point where some of them are barely informed any longer by **linguistics**. There are insights from all of these, of course, but there is also the danger of losing the strengths of linguistics, not least the awareness that the meaning of language is not transparent.

discourse marker

This is a term coined by the **linguists** William Labov and David Fanshel, and later developed substantially by Deborah Schiffrin. A discourse marker is a **lexical item** that helps organise **discourse** in some way. That is, discourse markers signal the relationship between an **utterance** and whatever discourse has gone before it. Here, for example, are instances of the discourse markers *well*, *however* and *so* from the **British National Corpus**, along with an explanation of their functions:

- 'Okay, what are the disadvantages of this technique? *Well* first of all, as I've just mentioned, you can't control the internal medium' (File J8K) [*Well* indicates that what follows is an elaboration of the previous point]
- 'Conservative Ministers have explained this by saying that the questions are loaded. *However*, the newspaper asked a simple straight-forward question' (File J9G) [*However* functions to contradict the previous point]
- 'immunity to that one factor can lead to immunity (pause) er (pause) to the disease as a whole. (pause) *So*, I've gone through (pause) a series of examples (pause) of exotoxins' (File F8S) [*So* indicates that the following **proposition** is a consequence of the previous point]

Discourse markers are typically **conjunctions** (e.g. *so, however*), prepositional **phrases** (e.g. *on the other hand, after all*) and **adverbials** (e.g. *you know, then*). Discourse markers are sometimes also referred to as *discourse connectives, pragmatic connectives* and *discourse operators*.

downward convergence

Part of the bigger *communication accommodation theory* (CAT), downward convergence (also called *divergence*) is a strategy that speakers adopt (mostly subconsciously) in certain social settings in order to accentuate the differences between their speech and the speech used by their **interlocutor(s)**. For example, when in front of her friends, a teenager may purposely speak differently from her parents in order to disaffiliate herself from them. *See also* **accommodation** and **upward convergence.**

dummy auxiliary

In English, there is a range of **auxiliary verbs** (modals, **passive**, continuous, perfective) which precede the main **verb** in **declarative clause** structures. The auxiliary is also the carrier of **interrogative**, negative or emphatic meaning, by being fronted ('Is he coming?'), having the negative particle added ('She wasn't running fast') or being stressed ('They are eating my chocolates!'), respectively. When there is no auxiliary to perform these functions, English uses the ***do operator***, also known as the dummy auxiliary, instead. The **sentences** 'Does he go to school yet?', 'Erica doesn't have a cat' and 'You don't need all those sweets!' illustrate the dummy auxiliary carrying interrogative, negative and emphatic functions in turn.

E

E-language

This is a term introduced by Noam Chomsky that contrasts with
I-language. The two terms are similar to Chomsky's earlier terms
performance and **competence**, though there are subtle
differences, primarily concerning the distinction between E-
language and performance. Your linguistic competence is your tacit
knowledge about the **rules** of forming grammatical **sentences** in
your first **language**. Your linguistic performance is the result of
applying these rules in speech. *Performance* therefore refers to the
externalisation of linguistic competence. *E-language*, by contrast,
refers to anything language-related that is not I-language. This
includes linguistic performance but also encompasses, for instance,
the shared knowledge in a **speech community** of the
sociolinguistic value attached to particular **forms** of speech (see, for
example, **covert prestige**). The *E* in *E-language* may be thought of as
referring to *external* language, though to properly grasp the
difference between I-language and E-language, it may also be useful
to think of the *E* as meaning *everything* language-related that is not I-
language. *See also* **Universal Grammar**.

Early Modern English

Early Modern English (EModE) refers to the English used between
approximately 1500 and 1750. This period is notable for the
development of the first written standard form of the **language**
since the West Saxon standard of the **Old English** period (in contrast
to EModE, the earlier **Middle English** period was characterised in
part by the absence of a standard form). The standard **variety** came
about as a result of the increase in publishing and literacy that
followed Caxton's introduction of the printing press to Britain in
1476 (the printing press made use of movable type, an innovation

introduced by the German printer Johannes Gutenberg in 1439). But **standardisation** is not the only marker of difference between Early Modern English and its precursor Middle English. The **Great Vowel Shift** also helps us to differentiate the two periods, as its influence on pronunciation makes Early Modern English markedly different from Middle English. So, too, does the regularisation of spelling and the simplification of the **pronoun** system (there were many more forms of the personal pronoun in Early Modern English than there are in **Present Day English**). The Early Modern period also saw the first significant spread of English beyond the British Isles, initially to the American colonies and later even farther afield. Arguably, the most famous exponent of Early Modern English is Shakespeare, and most modern readers will feel that the English in which he wrote his plays is generally recognisable and comprehensible, even though there may be elements that are difficult to grasp. By contrast, Middle English requires significantly more specialist knowledge to read and understand.

egressive

Egressive sounds are those sounds in human speech that are created when we push air out through the mouth or nose. In English, the vast majority of speech sounds that we make are egressive. **Plosive** sounds are good for demonstrating this; try holding your hand in front of your mouth while making a *p* sound, and you should feel a burst of air from your mouth. **Nasal** sounds are also egressive; hold your finger under your nose and make a long *mmm* sound, and you will feel the passage of air through your nostrils. *See also* **air flow**.

ejective

An ejective is a type of **consonant** sound that is produced with a glottalic **egressive** airstream, which means that the air travelling out of the mouth originates not in the **lungs** but above the vocal cords in the **glottis**. Ejective consonants are easily identifiable in the **International Phonetic Alphabet** as they are transcribed with an apostrophe after the main symbol for the consonant being produced, e.g. [p']. Ejective consonants are necessarily **voiceless** because the vocal cords are clamped shut until the release of air. In some languages, they are known to contrast with similar aspirated or

voiced consonants. Ejectives can be found in **languages** like Georgian, Chechen, Hausa and Gumuz.

electropalatography

This is a technique that allows researchers to analyse patterns of contact between the **tongue** and the **alveolar** ridge or the **hard palate**. The term is often abbreviated to EPG. An artificial palate – which looks a lot like a retainer (i.e. an orthodontic brace) – is created to fit the mouth of a speaker and fitted against their hard palate. This retainer-like device contains many pressure-sensitive electrodes. The electrodes are connected to wires that are curved around the artificial palate and hang out of the speaker's mouth. When the tongue comes into contact with an electrode, that sensor is activated and a recording is made of all of the electrodes that are contacted during an articulation. As electropalatography can record the details of tongue activity in speech, it can be a powerful tool for providing articulatory information that can be used in speech therapy. Electropalatography is not just used effectively in speech therapy; it is also used more generally in **phonetics** research as it allows researchers to study the physiology of articulations that involve the tongue and palate and consider the size and shape of certain oral constrictions. One down-side to electropalatography is that each speaker who is analysed needs their own unique palate made for them (we all have differently shaped palates – and this is not something you'd want to borrow from someone else!).

elision

Elision (also referred to as *deletion*) is the omission of one or more sounds in a single **word** or a **phrase**. You can elide **vowels**, **consonants** or even an entire **syllable**. Elision is extremely common in spontaneous, natural speech. Elision is easily spotted in the contracted form of English words we produce, such as *haven't* for *have not*, or *couldn't* for *could not*. Elision can also appear in many other places – not just contractions. In English, elision commonly occurs in the following words and phrases:

Laboratory → *lab-ratory*
Going to → *gonna*
Don't know → *dunno*

ellipsis

This refers to the omission of certain **words** or **phrases**, particularly in repeated structures, where the item omitted is entirely predictable (*recoverable*) from the co-text. Thus, the **verb** in the second **clause** of the **sentence** 'Dan ate a pear and Hazel an apple' can be missed out because it is clear that it is the same as the verb in the first clause (*ate*). Ellipsis can happen at the phrasal level too, so that, for example, the coordinated **noun phrase** *my blue coat and hat* would normally be taken to mean that both the coat and the hat were blue, though the **adjective** only appears once. Theoretically, of course, it is ambiguous between the elided version, which is a summary of *my blue coat and my blue hat*, and the *non*-elided version in which *my blue coat* is one item and *my hat* is another (with no colour specified). Grammars of the **language** are expected to be able to explain these **surface** ambiguities and usually do so by hypothesising a **deep** level of structure in which the ambiguity is erased. Note in this case that the possessive **determiner** (*my*) does not recur either, but this ellipsis is the only possible interpretation of the phrase, where the possession of both items can be made explicit (*my coat and my hat*) but the elision of the second determiner (*my coat and hat*) is not ambiguous and cannot mean *my coat and someone else's hat*).

embedded clauses

These take a number of different forms, including those that entirely replace one of the higher-level **clause** elements, such as the **subject**: 'Swimming in cold water is not a pleasant experience.' Here, the subject of the **verb** *is* consists of the whole clause 'swimming in cold water', which is made up in turn of a **verb** (*swimming*) and an **adverbial prepositional phrase** (*in cold water*). Together, even though they make up a clause, they perform the role of a **noun** in the higher-level **sentence**, which can be demonstrated by replacing the whole embedded clause with a **pronoun**: 'It is not a pleasant experience.' Other embedded clauses take the role of other clause elements in the higher structure, but in the case of **relative clauses** they form only part of a clause element in **noun phrases**, as they postmodify (or qualify) the **head noun**: *your son, whom I saw in the pub last week*. This ability for **language** structures to be embedded within each other is known as **recursion**, and it allows for structures to become long and complex with no absolute limit on the levels of embedding that are possible, beyond the human capacity for comprehension. Children's stories are often based on recursive structures of this kind. One famous example is 'The House that Jack Built', which produces a new focal item in the sentence each time, and backgrounds the previous information into a string of relative clauses which grows by one on each repetition: 'This is the cat that caught the rat that ate the malt that lay in the house that Jack built.'

embedding

This is a term often used by grammarians to refer to **phrases** and **clauses** occurring inside other phrases and clauses. Embedding can also be called *subordination*, as in **subordinate clause**. However, it can be a more helpful, general term, which refers to smaller embedded items. So, the **noun phrase** *car seat*, which can perform a normal clause function such as **subject** ('My car seat is broken') may also appear as a **modifier** before a different **noun** and therefore be classed as 'embedded' within the larger noun phrase, as in *my fluffy car seat cover*. In this case, the possessive **determiner** (*my*) refers not to the seat itself, but to the cover. Thus, the whole noun phrase *car seat* is at a lower level of grammatical structure. *See also* **recursion**.

endophoric reference

Endophoric reference and **exophoric reference** refer to the two different ways in which human **language** can refer (*see* **reference**). On the one hand, language does make some contact with the non-linguistic ('real') world, so that there is a link between, for example, the word *car* and the kinds of things in the world that we feel comfortable calling a 'car'. This is known as an exophoric reference. Endophoric reference, on the other hand, draws on the idea that language is (mostly) a closed system of internally structured communication, so that any links outside that system (*ex-* implies 'outside') will be distinct from the relationships that items in linguistic **texts** may have with each other. In the case of the word *car*, then, its exophoric reference may be all the things in the world that we might call a 'car'. Its endophoric reference, on the other hand, would be seen in the context of other linguistic structures, as in the following passage:

There was a blue car coming in the other direction. The car was carrying a large surfboard on top, which looked as though it might fall off at any moment. It was not going to stop, though I flashed my lights at it. The blue car screeched to a halt just as the surfboard slid onto the road beside my car.

Here, the five references to the same vehicle are highlighted. In the first instance, as we have not yet encountered the car in the story, it is preceded by an **indefinite article** (*a*). The second instance uses what is known as **anaphora** to refer backwards to the earlier mention, using the **definite article** to indicate familiarity (not just any car, *the* car). The third and fourth mentions could also be seen as anaphoric, but it is not immediately clear whether *it* refers to the car or the surfboard. In these cases, you could therefore see *it* as having cataphoric reference (*see* **cataphora**), which indicates that it refers forwards in the text rather than backwards. The final mention of the car completes the reference of *it* by making the **referent** very clearly *the blue car*.

entailment

This is a logical phenomenon that refers to the relationship between two **propositions**. If proposition A entails proposition B, then, if A is true, B must also be true. Below is an example:

Proposition A: The president was assassinated.

entails that

Proposition B: The president is dead.

An entailed **sentence** (B) is a logical consequence of an entailing sentence (A); if sentence A is the case, then it is impossible for sentence B to not also be the case. If two propositions entail each other, they are logical paraphrases.

enumeration

This is the listing of members of a **category** (differing in one vital respect from **exemplification**). For example, the packaging on a pack of biscuits will enumerate the ingredients. With enumeration, we often assume that what we are given is the full list of the phenomena concerned. We would hope, when reading the list of possible side effects on a bottle of medicine, that the producers have enumerated all and not just some of the potential consequences of taking the drug. Note that, when we hear or see a list like this, whether it is an example of exemplification or enumeration, we assume that there must be some sort of connection between the items listed. In the example above, the connection is easy to see. However, sometimes such lists are surprising by virtue of incorporating **foregrounding**, forcing us to search for a **meaning** relation between the enumerated elements. A good example is David Bowie's recollection of how he dabbled 'with Satanism, Christianity and pottery'.

enumerator

In some **grammars**, an enumerator is a **part of speech** (alternatively, **word class**). There are three types: cardinal, ordinal and general. Here are some examples:

cardinal numbers   *one, two, three*, etc.
ordinal numbers   *first, second, third*, etc.
general ordinals   *next, last, further, other*, etc.

epiglottis

This is the flap of cartilage that sits at the base of the **tongue** and covers the entrance to the **glottis** (where the **vocal folds** are). It deflects food down the oesophagus and into the intestine. It prevents us from choking by stopping food from being able to go down the *trachea* (windpipe). When food 'goes down the wrong way', it is because some particles of food have managed to get past the epiglottis. *See also* **glottis**.

epistemic modality

This refers to the use of certain **words** and **phrases** to indicate the speaker's certainty or uncertainty about the events and actions being referred to in a **clause**. There are **modal auxiliary verbs** in English (*may, might, can*, etc.), which are the most obvious way to produce the epistemic effect, but similar effects can be produced by **adjectives** (*possible, certain, likely*) and **adverbs** (*possibly, certainly, definitely*) or even by non-verbal cues (doubt might be indicated by a shrug, for example). Non-modal **utterances** are known as **categorical assertions** and they can be much more persuasive ('John broke the window') than modalised utterances where even certainty ('It was <u>definitely</u> John that broke the window') can draw attention to the fact that it is the speaker's opinion and, by doing so, undermine the confidence of the assertion. Small children (and adults, too) often forget this when they are trying hard to persuade others ('It <u>really</u> <u>really</u> wasn't me').

ethnography

This is a method used in **linguistics** to collect data about people and their cultural practices within a given social group, from the point of view of somebody involved within that social group. **Linguists** engaged in ethnographic fieldwork, for a given period of time, become members of the group that they are documenting. This means that the data collected will more closely resemble the natural **language** that would occur should the linguist not be present, and avoid the problem of the ***observer's paradox***. Ethnographic research therefore provides the opportunity for linguists to observe the **language** used by a social group in more natural and realistic settings than under lab conditions. Compare for example, the difference in the type of data collected by asking people questions about how they use language, in a laboratory setting, vs observing those people interacting in their homes and communities. Ethnographic research takes into account the settings in which language occurs – for example, geographical features of the area or the group dynamics of speakers engaged in interaction, all of which may affect how people speak, or the things that people refer to in their interactions. In documenting these traditionally non-linguistic elements of interaction, the linguist has a better understanding of some of the motivations speakers may have for speaking in a certain way. For example, the sociolinguist and ethnographer Penelope Eckert spent time in secondary schools in Detroit in the USA to explore how teens used language to identify as part of different friendship groups. Eckert documented a wide range of characteristics of the students she observed, ranging from the clothing choices they made to the classes they took. From this, Eckert identified two groups in the school social order: the 'jocks', typically the students who engaged in school life and who were from upper-middle-class homes; and the 'burnouts', typically the students who did not engage with school life and who were from working-class homes. Eckert found that these non-linguistic characteristics correlated with linguistic **variables**, and that students who shared the same social group spoke more similarly than those who did not. In this study, Penelope Eckert used ethnographic methods to closely observe the students engaging in their shared social practices, as well as how those social practices were meaningful within the wider context of the school setting.

etymology

This is an area of **historical linguistics** that is focused on the history of **words** and word **meanings**. Etymologists aim to discover the origins of words and are thus interested in word formation processes (*see*, for example, **acronym, back-formation, blending, borrowing, clipping, compound word, conversion, derivation, grammaticalisation, lexicalisation, loanword, neologism, nonce formation** and **portmanteau**). The lexical source of a word is known as its *etymon*. For example, the word *city* was borrowed into English from French. But the French word *citée* derives ultimately from the Latin word *cīvitās* (an organised community). *Citée* is therefore the etymon of *city*, while *cīvitās* is the etymon of *citée*.

euphemism

This involves the substitution of an inoffensive term for a more troublesome one. There are certain topics for which people are particularly adept at coming up with euphemisms – notably sex, death and bodily functions. Think, for instance, of *rolling in the hay* and *making love* for sex, *to pass away* for *to die*, and *doing a number two* for defecating. While familiar euphemisms such as these often make it easier for us to discuss sensitive or taboo topics, other creative euphemisms can be used in a more deceitful way to cover up unpleasant or disagreeable actions. These are often found in politics: the Nazis infamously used the phrase *enhanced interrogation* to refer to the torture of prisoners, while, more recently, *post-truth* can be seen to refer to what we might more damningly call *lying*. The linguist Kate Burridge notes an interesting example used by

medieval Dutch physicians: would you have guessed that having *figs in the secret passage* refers to piles? Related to euphemism is the concept of ***dysphemism***, which is an expression with potentially offensive connotations. Think, for instance, of *pushing up the daisies* to refer to being dead, and *shithouse* for toilet.

exemplification

This is the process of providing an illustrative list in order to explain a particular phenomenon. Note that, by contrast, **enumeration** is concerned only with listing, not explaining. Moreover, exemplification, unlike enumeration, does not necessitate giving a full list. A phrase such as 'for example' is used to makes it clear that a list of things is not comprehensive, e.g. 'On this linguistics course we will, for example, talk about syntax, phonology and semantics.'

existential presuppositions

These are a type of assumption that we make all the time in using **language**. When we use a **noun phrase** like *the controversial striker* or *their troublesome washing machine*, we presuppose the existence of the thing to which we refer (*see* **reference**). These noun phrases can be seen as bits of language that refer to something in the world around us. Note that existential presuppositions begin with definite **determiners** such as *the, their* and *this*. A noun phrase like *a cheeky chappy* does not give rise to an existential presupposition, as it does not point to a specific **referent**. Existential presuppositions can have a powerful effect. For example, someone could use the noun phrase *the decline in morals* to make it sound more like a thing than a process. This makes the reality of the alleged decline difficult to argue with. That is, we can argue with a statement such as 'Morals are declining' ('No they are not!'), but it's harder to argue with the existence of a thing. Note that the qualities noted in existential presuppositions are also hard to argue with. For instance, by labelling a footballer *the controversial striker*, we assume that they have some sort of controversial quality.

exophoric reference
This is a linguistic **reference** to something that is outside of the immediate **discourse**. *See* **endophoric reference** for a full explanation.

F

face

This is a term introduced by the sociologist Erving Goffman to refer to the image that people project when they are interacting with other people. The potential for speakers to offend their listener follows from the notion that all participants in face-to-face communication are concerned with upholding their social value by protecting their *face*. The idea was later developed into a theory of politeness by the **linguists** Penelope Brown and Stephen Levinson, who distinguished between ***positive face***, which is the desire to be approved of, and ***negative face***, which is the desire to be free and unimpeded by others. A simple example of a threat to positive face is the **speech act** of apology, which damages the positive face of the speaker by their admission of prior wrongdoing. An example of negative face threat is the speech act of requesting, which attempts to restrict the hearer's freedom of action.

feature matrix

A feature matrix is a table that provides a means of documenting the characteristics of something in order to differentiate it from other things in the world. Feature matrices are used in a range of linguistic subfields. In lexical **semantics** (the semantics of **words**), feature matrices can be used to compare the **meanings** of words according to a set of common features, as in the example for the words *woman, man, girl* and *boy* below. The words of interest appear down the first column and the 'features' appear across the top row. By exploring whether each word encodes specific features, i.e. + or − female, we are able to differentiate between the meanings encoded by each word.

	female	male	adult	child
woman	+	−	+	−
man	−	+	+	−
girl	+	−	−	+
boy	−	+	−	+

Looking in closer detail at word meaning via feature matrices is sometimes referred to as ***componential analysis***. Feature matrices are useful for comparing between words that are closely related within a specific **semantic field**. For example, the **verbs** *run*, *walk* and *hobble* all fall within the semantic domain of movement but there are clear distinguishing features between each word – for example, the speed at which each action is carried out.

felicity conditions

The word *felicity* is Latin in origin and refers to a state of happiness or contentment. In **pragmatics**, which is the linguistic study of **meaning** in context (as opposed to **semantics**, which is the study of meaning in **language**, such as individual **word** meaning), felicity conditions are the name given to the circumstances that have to be true in order for a particular **speech act** to achieve its purpose. For example, the speech act 'I now pronounce you husband and wife' is a ***declaration***, which means that it changes the world in some way. Declarations are only deemed felicitous if certain conditions are met. For example, participants in a ***speech event*** (an event in which a speech act is uttered) must understand the language that is being used, the speech act must take place in a context that is appropriate, the speaker must intend for the speech act to be true, and the participants involved must accept the speech act – e.g., if it is a promise, then the promiser must intend to carry out the promise. To return to the marriage example, in order for the speech act to be felicitous, the participants need to be gathered in a place that is an approved premises for marrying people, i.e. a registry office or a church; the person doing the marrying must have the right to do so – e.g. they must be an ordained person; and the persons being married should understand and intend to keep to the agreement they are making with one another (i.e. their marriage vows). If these

figure 93

conditions are met, then the speech act is felicitous. The same speech act wouldn't be felicitous in the context of, for example, children playing a game in which they pretend to get married, even if they utter the same words. This is because the context of the speech act does not meet the conditions listed above, and as a result is not deemed felicitous.

figure

If you're reading this entry in *The Babel Lexicon of Language*, then what you are subconsciously doing is paying attention to the little black marks on the page that appear to be placed over the white background. These black squiggles on the page that we call letters (in this case, the letters of the English alphabet) are **foregrounded** against the white background of the page. In this example, the letters on the page are the figure (the thing that stands out) and the white background of the page is the **ground**. Separating something that is foregrounded in an image or **text** from the things that are backgrounded is a natural human phenomenon, and there are many optical illusions that demonstrate how we perceive the figure and ground in the visual mode – for example, Rubin's vase (see below), an optical illusion from 1915 which demonstrated that some people see two faces in profile first, while other people see a vase first. Rubin's work also showed that a person could not focus on both the vase and the profiles at the same time (i.e. the vase and the profiles could not both be the figure of the image). This finding showed there to be a distinction between figure and ground in human perception.

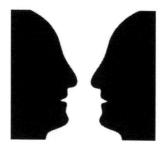

In **cognitive linguistics,** the terms *figure* and *ground* have been explored by Leonard Talmy, who applied the terms to **language** (as opposed to images, like Rubin). Talmy applied figure and ground to **sentences** such as 'the bike is near the house', in which language is used to place an object (in this case 'the bike') in reference to some other (more stable) object in the text (in this case 'the house'). The notions of figure and ground have been adopted in a range of theories and analyses in cognitive linguistics, such as Ronald Langacker's *cognitive grammar* where the terms *trajector* and *landmark* broadly correspond to figure and ground, respectively.

finger spelling

This is a way of representing the letters of the alphabet using the hands. Finger spelling is a part of some **sign languages** and is often used to spell the names of people and places that have no established sign, or in order to clarify a sign. In addition to spelling out the names of people and places like this, finger spelling is sometimes used as part of a sign – for example, in British Sign Language (BSL), the sign for *gold* is the finger-spelt <g> followed by the hands moving away in a shimmering motion. Finger spelling conventions differ between sign languages – for example, the finger spelling used in American Sign Language (ASL) is done on one hand only, whereas finger spelling in BSL uses two hands. The **linguists** Trevor Johnston and Adam Schembri point out that there are also **varieties** of Australian Sign Language (Auslan) that use two hands, and some much more restricted varieties that only use one hand. You can learn the BSL alphabet online at www.british-sign.co.uk/finger spelling-alphabet-charts.

finite

The terms *finite* and **non-finite** refer to **verb forms**, but by
association also become part of the label of the **clauses** in which
those verb forms occur. The main clause in any **sentence** must have
a **verb phrase** that is finite – that is, one that is linked both to a
(grammatical) **subject** and to a time (through **tense**). For regular
verbs, there are two present tense forms (first, second and all plural
persons on the one hand, e.g. *play*; and third person on the other,
e.g. *plays*) and there is one past tense form (*played*). All other verb
phrases in English combine up to four **auxiliary verbs** and the main
verb, as in *might have been being followed*). In these forms, the first
verb will usually be finite. In a verb phrase such as *has been being
followed*, the first auxiliary verb – *has* – is in the present tense and has
a third person singular form, so it is likely to follow *he* or *she* (or a
longer name). All the other forms that follow *has* in the **phrase** are
non-finite. See what happens, though, if we take off this first
auxiliary, leaving us with *is being followed* – the auxiliary that was
previously *been* now has to agree with the subject and take on the
tense, and so becomes *is*.

flap

This refers to the **manner of articulation** used for producing a
particular consonantal sound. *Flap* and **tap** are often used
interchangeably by **linguists** to describe a **consonant** that is
produced when an active **articulator** (such as the **tongue**) is
thrown against another articulator. However, for those linguists
who do differentiate between flaps and taps, the key difference in a
flap is that it involves the retraction of an active articulator that is
accompanied by a forward-striking motion.

floor

This is a term taken from the study of **turn-taking** in interaction.
When a person is speaking, they are described as 'holding the floor'.
There are many strategies for 'holding the floor' or 'taking the floor'
(i.e. when another person starts talking), including pausing,
changing **intonation** or even using particular **idioms**. The analysis
of turn-taking, and, relatedly, the analysis of who is holding the
floor (and how), is a key area of research in the sub-disciplines of

linguistics that are concerned with the study of interaction, for example **Conversation Analysis** and **Discourse Analysis**.

flout

In **pragmatics**, *flouting* refers to when a person knowingly deviates from one of Grice's maxims (**quantity, quality, relation** and **manner**). According to Grice's **Cooperative Principle**, when a speaker flouts a maxim, they deviate in some way from what is expected. As a result of this **deviation**, non-literal **meaning** is produced. For example, imagine a person breaks the maxim of quality (being truthful in what you say) by saying to a person who has just walked into a meeting late: 'One of your best qualities is your time-keeping.' It is likely that the participants in that interaction would be able to work out that what the speaker said is not true (i.e. the person is not a good time-keeper), and, from that, what effect the speaker intended by flouting the maxim of quality (that they are making a point of the person being late to the meeting). Breaking maxims in this way is called a *flout*, and flouting the maxims can generate a wide range of effects other than the sarcastic *implicature* of the time-keeping example. For example, parents of a small child may flout the maxim of manner (being clear in what you say) to talk about whether they should give their child a T-R-E-A-T without the child knowing what they are talking about. Flouting is a common feature of the interactions depicted in comedy shows and in jokes. Take, for example, this old Lancashire joke that relies on the comedic effect of flouting the maxims of manner and quantity:

> A man from Wigan is waiting at a bus stop when a passer-by asks him for directions:
>
> Passer-by: How do you get to the Red Lion pub?
> Man from Wigan: My brother takes me.

foregrounding

This is a term used in the linguistic sub-discipline of **stylistics** to describe linguistic choices that stand out in some way in relation to the rest of a **text**, or against the norms of a **language** more broadly. Aspects of a text can be foregrounded in two ways. The first of these is through **parallelism**, which relates to the establishment of a pattern within a text through repetition of particular structures of linguistic **forms**. An example of parallelism is the famous 'Hath not a Jew eyes' speech given by Shylock in Shakespeare's *The Merchant of Venice*:

> If you prick us, do we not bleed?
> If you tickle us, do we not laugh?
> If you poison us, do we not die?

Shylock's speech is foregrounded because the syntactic structure of the **sentences** in his speech is repeated in a way that one would not expect normally. The second way of foregrounding elements of a text is through **deviation**. Deviation relates to linguistic choices that deviate from a norm in some way. The limerick below provides an example of foregrounding via the deviation from a rhyme scheme and from our expectations of the genre:

> Six scholars from Yorkshire did write
> A book about language one night
> But when the sun rose
> On the scholars' good prose
> They remembered they had a meeting at 9am and
>   left early to avoid congestion on the M62.

When deviation occurs as a result of breaking a norm that has been set up within a text (as opposed to a norm within the language more generally), the deviation is termed *internal deviation* (i.e. the language is deviant in relation to the norms of that specific text only). When deviation is the result of breaking a norm within the language more broadly, this deviation is termed *external deviation* (i.e. the language would be deviant in any text, not just the one being analysed). In addition to foregrounding in literature, foregrounding through parallelism and deviation is a common feature of advertisements. So, next time you're flicking through a magazine or listening to slogans on the TV, think about what the company is doing to get your attention. Language analysis might even save you some money. This isn't just any advice, this is Babel advice ...

forensic linguistics

In general terms, *forensic linguistics* is the name given to the application of linguistic techniques in legal contexts. Forensic linguistics most commonly involves linguistic analysis in circumstances where **language** is being used as evidence in a legal case. It can include, for example, **authorship attribution** (working out who the likely author of an unattributed **text** might be) or *author profiling* (building up a picture of the writer of a text based on the characteristics of their writing). The term is also used to describe the analysis of legal language (for example, the language of legal contracts) or the use of language in legal settings (for instance, how legal professionals question children in courtroom contexts). Forensic linguistic analysis has been used in many high-profile cases, including that of Derek Bentley. Bentley's 1953 conviction for 'murder by joint enterprise' was eventually quashed (though too late for Bentley, who was hanged for his alleged role in the shooting of a police officer). The overturning of Bentley's conviction was due in no small part to the evidence provided by Professor Malcolm Coulthard, to the effect that Bentley's statement after arrest was not the verbatim record that police had claimed it was, but was instead likely to have been at least partly written by police officers. While the term *forensic linguistics* is often used in a general sense to refer to any application of **linguistics** in the legal sphere, forensic linguists themselves tend to reserve the term for the forensic analysis of written language specifically. The analysis of speech is the preserve of **forensic speech science**. Forensic linguistics is an example of **applied linguistics**.

forensic speaker/voice comparison

This is a task – and typically the most common task – carried out in **forensic speech science**. Forensic speaker/voice comparison involves comparing at least two (or more) recordings – one that contains the speech from a criminal recording, and one that contains speech from a suspect – in order to determine whether the two recordings may have come from the same or different speakers. The term *forensic speaker comparison* tends to be used more often than the term *forensic voice comparison*. Both terms are equally correct and refer to the same general task. However, researchers typically have a preference for *voice* or *speaker* based on their belief either that the task of comparison within speech analysis is looking at the voice as an isolated entity (forensic voice comparison), or that a comparison is not necessarily able to separate the voice from the individual/speaker and considers the voice to be a part of the speaker (forensic speaker comparison). More importantly, those in the field of forensic speech science are careful to use the term *comparison* over *identification*. This is due to the complex nature of speech, and the notion that no two **phrases** uttered by an individual will ever be identical. A forensic speech scientist would always be able to find some difference, whether at the auditory or acoustic level, which would mean that you can never even have identity within an individual. For this reason, it is technically impossible to achieve an identification, and *comparison* is a more aptly applied word. Forensic speaker/voice comparison has been featured in many high-profile cases around the world, including: the Yorkshire Ripper Case (UK), the Trayvon Martin and George Zimmerman trial (USA), the murder of the former head of the Civil Service of Mauritius (Mauritius), and the trial of General Radislav Krstic at the International Criminal Tribunal (United Nations).

forensic speech science

This is a relatively new term that only began to be used in the mid-2000s. The term *forensic speech science* is used to describe a branch of **linguistics** (more specifically, a type of **forensic linguistics**) that applies areas of linguistics, **phonetics**, computer science and engineering, statistics and even physics to examining speech for criminal and investigative purposes. *Forensic speech science* is often used interchangeably with *forensic phonetics*; however, the term *forensic speech science* goes slightly further than *forensic phonetics* in its description, to encompass all of the types of research and practical work that are undertaken in relation to speech in the forensic context (not just phonetic analysis). *Forensic speech science* is the preferred catch-all term that allows those in the field to refer to both linguistically based and engineering- / computer science-based methods for evaluating speech in a forensic context. Forensic speech scientists are asked to consult on a variety of tasks in relation to speech evidence. The most widely undertaken task is **forensic speaker/voice comparison**, whereby the expert is asked to consider whether a criminal and a suspect voice sample have come from the same or different people. Forensic speech scientists will also consult on a variety of other tasks, including: voice line-ups, speaker profiling, disputed **utterances**, transcription tasks, trademark disputes, lay witness identification, and language analysis for the determination of origin.

form and function

These are terms that can be used to describe all linguistic forms and relate to how they look/sound (*form*) and what they are doing in use (*function*). This split works for all levels of structure, so that a **noun** such as *dogs* can be described formally – as being made up from a **free morpheme** *dog* and a bound plural **morpheme** *s* – and also functionally, as the **head noun** in the **noun phrase** *those long-haired dogs*. In turn, the noun phrase itself can be described formally as having a **determiner** (*those*), a **modifier** (*long-haired*) and a head noun (*dogs*), while its function may be as either a **subject** (*Those long-haired dogs keep chasing my sheep*) or an **object** (*I will shoot those long-haired dogs*).

formants

Formants are bands of energy in the acoustic frequency spectrum that result from the resonance characteristics of the **vocal tract**. Formants can be used as a means of identifying **vowel** types by their physical properties. This can be done using spectrographic images (see **spectrogram**). The first and second formants (usually labelled F1 and F2) are most frequently used in vowel analysis. F1 relates to the openness of the **oral cavity** when the vowel is pronounced, with open vowels having high F1 frequencies and close vowels having low F1 frequencies. F2 is related to the frontness of the highest part of the **tongue**. Back vowels have low F2 frequencies and front vowels have high F2 frequencies. In combination with F2, the F3 formant (which is less commonly used by analysts) can reflect the roundness of a vowel.

fortition

This is a phonological process whereby **consonants** change over time to become 'stronger'. An example is how in some British urban youth subcultures, *thing* is pronounced with an initial /t/ as opposed to /θ/, i.e. /tɪŋ/ rather than /θɪŋ/. The opposite of fortition is the more common **lenition**, which refers to the 'weakening' of consonants.

fossil word

Fossil words are **words** that are *obsolete*, or almost obsolete, but which are still used in set **phrases** or **idioms**. For example, the common set phrase *to and fro* features the fossil word *fro*, which the *Oxford English Dictionary* lists as obsolete. Other fossil words include *vim* used in *vim and vigour*, and *petard*, used in the idiom *hoisted by [my/ one's] own petard*.

fossilisation

In *second language acquisition*, fossilisation is the term given to the process by which nonstandard linguistic features of a **language** (such as pronunciation or grammatical structure) become a permanent, or *fossilised*, part of a language learner's second language – for example, the retention of pronunciation features of an **L1** constitutes fossilisation. The concept of fossilisation is a problematic one, because it suggests that there exists an ideal version of a language that a learner can and should acquire, which is not accurate. If we base a definition of fossilisation errors on a standard **variety** of a language – say, for example, **Standard English** – then many people who are **native speakers** of English would have entrenched 'inaccuracies' in their language, such as regional pronunciations of **words** or the use of nonstandard **syntax** as a result of speaking in a **dialect**.

frame

In the **semantic** theory known as *frame semantics*, a *frame* is the world knowledge that a person must have in order to fully understand and use a **word**. According to frame semantics, in order to understand the word *swim*, one would have to have knowledge of the concepts related to swimming, such as water, a type of swimming stroke, or the fact that in order to swim there must be a swimmer, etc. Therefore, when we think of the word *swim*, we are also thinking about a set of concepts related to swimming. The theory of frame semantics was developed by Charles J. Fillmore, who was Professor of Linguistics at the University of California–Berkeley. He took the view that words are representations of different categories of experience. Frame semantics is notable because it takes into account cultural differences in the understandings of words, i.e. whether words in different **speech communities** invoke a different set of related concepts.

free morphemes

These are **morphemes** that look like individual **words** and can occur on their own without **affixes**. The morpheme is often said to be the smallest unit of **meaning**. So, although individual sounds (such as /f/, /ɪ/ or /g/) have no intrinsic meaning in a **language**, when they are combined, for example in the word /fɪg/, they produce a morpheme (*fig*) that has **reference** (to a fruit). *Fig* is one such free morpheme, and although it can be combined with the plural **phoneme** /z/ to make /fɪgz/ (i.e. <figs>), it can also stand alone. This is not the same for **bound morphemes**, such as the plural morpheme, which cannot occur on its own as <s> or /z/. *Disinterestedness*, for example, is made up of the free morpheme *interest* and three bound morphemes: the negative <dis>, the past participle ending <ed>, and the nominal ending <ness>. Note that morphemes do not necessarily equate to **syllables**. The word *establish*, for instance, is polysyllabic but consists of just one free morpheme.

free variation

The minimal meaningful unit of sound in a **language** is called a **phoneme**, and phonemes can have variants, which are called **allophones**. While some allophones are in **complementary distribution** – meaning where one allophone appears, another does not – others are in free variation. This means more than one allophone can appear in the same position without affecting the **meaning** of the **word**. For example, the /t/ in the English word *cat* can be produced with a number of different variants, such as a [t] ([kæt]), a **glottal stop** ([kæʔ]), or an **ejective consonant** ([kæt']). In this example, [t], [ʔ] and [t'] are in free variation because the three allophones can be swapped without changing the meaning of the word.

fricative

This is the label for one of the **manners of articulation** in the phonetic description of **consonants**. Consonants are generally produced on an **egressive** (outward) airstream from the **lungs**, and as the air exits the mouth (and/or nose), it is obstructed to a greater or lesser extent by the **articulators** in the mouth coming together in its path. While **plosives** and **nasals** produce a complete obstruction, fricative consonants produce a close but not complete closure, and the result is a kind of 'whistling' sound as the air passes through the small opening left between the articulators. Thus, for example, the sounds /f/ (*fat*) and /v/ (*vat*), which are articulated by raising the lower **lip** towards the upper teeth, produce a sound of escaping air, with the only difference between them being the **voicing** (**vocal fold** vibrations) in /v/.

function word

This is an alternative term to **grammatical word** and describes **words** that express grammatical **meaning** in **sentences**, such as articles like *the* and *an*, or **conjunctions** like *and* and *but*. Function words are vital for constructing **phrases** as they act as a kind of glue to stick together semantically richer terms, or **content words**. Unlike content words, function words are **closed class**, which means that there are a finite number of them and words are rarely added to – or lost from – these **categories**.

fundamental frequency

This term, or F0, is used in **phonetics** to describe the rate at which the **vocal folds** vibrate. Vocal folds that vibrate at a faster rate produce a higher fundamental frequency (e.g., up to 255 cycles per second, or hertz (Hz), for a typical adult female), while vocal folds that vibrate at a slower rate have a lower fundamental frequency (e.g., up to around 150 Hz for a typical adult male). Fundamental frequency should not be confused with **pitch**, though the two are related to one another. *Pitch* is the term used to describe the perceived level of the voice and is often just described as high or low, while fundamental frequency provides the numerical frequency at which the vocal folds are vibrating.

fusional language

Fusional languages are **languages** that encode a wide variety of information in single features. For example, a single **morpheme** might encode not only the **tense** and **aspect** of a **word**, but also whether it denotes the first, second or third person. Most languages feature a degree of both fusional and agglutinating **morphology**. Many of the **Indo-European** language family are fusional, as well as some Semitic languages. An example of a fusional morphology in a language is the Spanish **verb** *hablar* (to talk), in which the final morpheme in the word is changed to denote both the tense and aspect of the verb and whether the verb relates to a singular or plural **pronoun**:

> *hablo* → I speak (first person, singular)
> *hablas* → you speak (second person, singular)
> *habla* → she/he speaks (third person, singular)
> *hablamos* → we speak (first person, plural)
> *hablais* → you speak (second person, plural)
> *hablan* → they speak (third person, plural)

See also **analytic language** and **synthetic language**.

fuzzy

This is a term from **cognitive linguistics** that describes **categories** that are not discrete, but which instead seem to blend into one another. For example, a strawberry clearly belongs to the category of *fruit*, while a carrot clearly belongs to the category of *vegetable*. But what about a tomato? It has seeds, which suggests it is a fruit, but it is conventionally thought of as a vegetable. It would seem, then, that the categories of *fruit* and *vegetable* have fuzzy boundaries. *See also* **prototype**.

garden path sentence

A garden path sentence is one which turns out not to have the syntactic structure or semantic **meaning** that you expected when you started to read it. For example, in the **sentence** 'The old badger the young about money', it is likely that readers will first understand *badger* to be a **noun**, premodified by the **adjective** *old*. However, this makes the rest of the sentence impossible to interpret. The reader is therefore forced to re-parse the sentence, at which point it should become clear that *badger* is actually a **verb** and *old* is a noun.

geminate

A geminate is defined as two identical sounds that are adjacent to one another. The term comes from the Latin **word** *gemini*, meaning 'twins'. **Vowels** and **consonants** can both appear as geminates. Geminate vowels are often denoted as a long vowel when annotated in the **International Phonetic Alphabet** (IPA), while geminate consonants are often transcribed twice. Geminate consonants are prevalent in Italian and appear in words such as *fatto* (fact), *notte* (night) and *tutti* (all).

gender

In formal linguistic terms, gender has nothing to do with sex. It is instead a classification of **nouns**. In **languages** that have gender, nouns fall into one of two or more **categories**. For example, in German, nouns may be masculine, feminine or neuter, whereas Italian uses only masculine and feminine. Nouns with gender must agree with their associated **determiners** and **adjectives**. So, for instance, in the **phrase** *la nuova macchina* (Italian: the new car), the feminine forms of the determiner and the adjective are used because the noun *macchina* is feminine. Compare this to the following phrase in which the noun is masculine: *il nuovo mondo* (Italian: the new world). Note, too, that neither cars nor the world have natural gender – that is, grammatical gender is not necessarily determined by whether the **referent** of the noun is male or female. The term *gender* is also used in **sociolinguistics** but here it has a very different **meaning**. *Gender* in this case refers to a non-linguistic **variable** – that is, a factor that might influence the kind of language that someone uses (in the same way that, say, age or social class might also determine your language use).

generative grammar

This refers to the development of a cognitive approach to **grammar**, initiated by Noam Chomsky, who borrowed the term *generative* from mathematics in order to signify the process that speakers are engaged in when they produce the **sentences** of a **language**. Chomsky's idea was that, rather than producing a static description of the possible constructions in a language, as **structuralism** tended to do, we should be trying to simulate the kinds of processes that a human brain may go through in order to produce a well-formed (i.e. grammatical) sentence in the language concerned. Chomsky's initial model of what a generative grammar might look like was one that 'generated' simple **clauses** by means of *rewrite rules* successively applied in order to produce the acceptable structures in a language. In English, this starts by writing S (= sentence) as *NP + VP* (= **noun phrase** + **verb phrase**), creating the **rule**: S → NP + VP. The next part of the process was to 'expand' each of the parts of the resulting structure in order to produce more complex structures. So, for example, there would be a rule 'rewriting' NP with a **determiner** and a **noun** as well as optional pre- and post-modifiers (in brackets): NP → det + (Aj) + N + (comp). This rule means that there must, at a minimum, be a **head noun**, and there may be a determiner, an **adjective** (usually more than one) and a post-modifying **phrase** or clause, represented here as a **complement**. If these rules look a little bit like primitive computer code, this is no accident. Early generative grammars were being formulated around the same time that computer programming started to infiltrate every aspect of modern life, and the metaphor of the brain being like a computer started to be naturalised around the same time. Chomsky's approach has been hugely influential since the 1970s, but not all approaches to grammatical theory accept this generative view as being the most accurate model of human language production.

Genie

This is the pseudonym given to a woman born in the USA in 1957 who had been badly mistreated as a child and isolated from normal human interaction. As a result, by the time she was discovered by authorities when she was 13 years old, she had failed to acquire **language**. After her admission to the Children's Hospital Los Angeles, hospital staff began teaching Genie English. Genie then became the object of study for **linguists** interested in testing hypotheses about **language acquisition** (such as the **critical period hypothesis**) and whether, as the generative linguist Noam Chomsky had argued, language was innate in all humans. The study showed that Genie was eventually able to acquire some form of language, even though the previously assumed critical period for language acquisition had passed. This provided some evidence to support the linguist Noam Chomsky's view of the innateness of language. Nonetheless, what the study of Genie also showed was the importance of early socialisation to language development, leading to the view that language acquisition is a result of both nature and nurture. *See also* **generative grammar**.

genitive

This is a grammatical **case** that is used to indicate a possessive relationship. The genitive is marked by a morphological **affix** on the **noun**. Here's an example from Hungarian of how this works:

> *macska* (cat)
> *macskám* (my cat)
> *masckád* (your [singular] cat)
> *masckája* (his/her cat)
> *masckánk* (our cat)
> *masckátok* (your [plural] cat)
> *masckájuk* (their cat)

Because **Old English** was also a case **language**, it too marked possession by an **inflection** on the noun. For example, consider the difference between *se eorl* (the earl) and *þæs eorles bōc* (the earl's book). Note too how the form of the **determiner** changes to agree with the noun (compare subjective *se* and genitive *þæs*). The remnants of the Old English genitive can be seen in the apostrophe -*s* used in **Present Day English** to mark possession (e.g. *the earl's book*), though to describe this as a genitive is not strictly accurate as Present Day English is no longer a case language.

gesture

This is a type of expressive use of the hands that is often used in conjunction with speech. Looking at gestures that accompany speech can provide meaningful information about how speakers perceive, say, an utterance's meaning or metaphorical **language**. For example, it is often the case that when we use the expression 'on the one hand X, but on the other hand Y', we accompany the phrase with co-speech gesture that conveys this message literally: i.e. by placing one hand to one side of the body, and the other to the other side of the body, as if we are holding the concepts we are discussing. While this kind of communication is sometimes referred to as ***body language***, **linguists** prefer the term *gesture* because of its more specific reference to actions (note that body language encompasses such behaviours as eye movement, blushing, posture, etc.). Gestures are not expressive on their own but rely on the content of the speech they accompany. However, their communicative import is determined by the speaker's communicative intention. By this definition, the activity that aircraft marshallers engage in when directing planes where to park is not gesture but flag semaphore.

glide

A glide is a semivowel with acoustic properties similar to those of a **vowel**. An example in English is /j/. Glides affect the vowel sounds that precede or follow them. So, for instance, in the **word** /jɛs/ (*yes*), the /ɛ/ will have a different quality from the /ɛ/ in /dɹɛs/ (*dress*) because of the preceding /j/. For this reason, in **acoustic phonetic** studies, vowels that appear next to a semivowel are usually treated separately from those that do not. *See also* **hiatus**.

gloss

A gloss is a brief explanation of a specialist term. This explanation of the **word** *gloss* is therefore a gloss. A collection of glosses is called a *glossary* – and that's what *The Babel Lexicon of Language* is. Glossaries differ from dictionaries in focusing on explaining terminology. While dictionaries do this too, they also provide additional information about pronunciation, **etymology**, usage, and so on. The first glosses were originally inserted between the lines of a manuscript, or in its margins. The first reference to a gloss in English is in a **Middle English** poem from 1340: 'Some clerkes says, als þe glose telles / þat Gog and Magog es noght elles / Bot þe host of ontichrist' (Some clerks say, as the gloss tells / that Gog and Magog are nothing else / but the host of the Antichrist). Nowadays, glossaries are often found in the appendices of academic books, particularly textbooks.

glottal stop

This is the name of a speech sound used a great deal in British English, particularly in urban **accents**, as a replacement for the **phoneme** /t/. The glottal stop occurs at the **glottis**, which is the bony structure inside the **larynx** that holds the **vocal folds**. The term **stop** refers to the complete closure of any **articulators**, and so includes **plosives** (such as /p/ and /b/) and **nasals** (such as /m/ and /n/). In this case, the glottal stop is a plosive sound where the vocal folds are clamped tight shut for a moment, causing the build-up of air from the **lungs** to burst out between the vocal folds as the pressure becomes too great to hold back. The resulting sound is similar to the sound made when we are straining (for example, when moving heavy furniture). It is a sound articulated a long way from the **alveolar** ridge, where /t/ is usually pronounced; nevertheless, it often replaces /t/, particularly at the ends of **words** when they are not followed by another sound, as in *that* or *put*. In urban accents in the UK, the glottal stop is also found in the middle of words such as *water* or *better*, where some US accents may have a **voiced** alveolar /d/ instead. While sociolinguistic prejudice may cause some people to argue that accents that use glottal stops are 'lazy' or 'ill-informed', there is no evidence that a glottal stop is any easier to pronounce (it's like straining, after all!), but plenty of evidence that most English speakers use it, at least at the ends of **utterances** where /t/ occurs.

glottis

The glottis is the space between the **vocal folds**. **Voiceless** sounds are produced when the vocal folds are apart and only a small amount of air passes through the glottis. By contrast, **voiced** sounds are made when the vocal folds are almost touching and there is significant **airflow** through the glottis. The shape of the glottis can also result in a range of other sounds, such as **creak**. *See also* **airstream mechanism** and **voicing**.

Goal

This refers to the entity that is affected by the action in a **clause**. Often, but not always, the same as the grammatical **object**, this is a label associated with **Systemic Functional Linguistics**, which prioritises semantic over syntactic functions.

gradable antonym

A gradable antonym is just one of a number of logically different types of **opposition** between **words** in a **language**. It reflects the tendency in languages to prioritise the end points of a real-world continuum, such as size or temperature, and treat them as opposites, rather than treating all points on the scale equally. Examples such as *hot* and *cold* or *large* and *small* demonstrate that gradable antonyms are often **adjectives** with *gradable meaning*, though they can be found in other **Categories** as well – for instance, the verbs (and nouns) *love* and *hate*. Some **linguists** use the word **antonym** to refer only to the gradable type. *See also* **complementaries, converse** and **directional opposite.**

grammar

This refers to the system of **rules** that governs how **morphemes, words, phrases** and **clauses** may be combined to form acceptable **sentences** in a **language. Morphology** is the branch of grammar that focuses on how **morphemes** combine, while **syntax** refers to the rules that govern sentence structure. Everyone understands the grammar of their first language; this must be the case – otherwise, we would not be able to form acceptable sentences. When people say they don't know any grammar, then, what they usually mean is they don't have a **metalanguage** for talking about grammatical structure.

grammatical word

This is an alternative term for **function word**. Examples of grammatical **words** include **conjunctions, determiners, prepositions** and **pronouns**, of which there are a finite number in **languages.** *See also* **closed class.**

grammaticalisation

This is a process of **language** change during which **lexical words** gradually start to function more like **grammatical words**, to the extent that, in some cases, they may even become **morphemes** (i.e. part of a **word**, rather than a whole word). This is a long process that involves a number of stages. An example of grammaticalisation in Romance languages is the morpheme *-ment(e)*, which originated as the lexical item *mente* in Latin (meaning 'with a state in mind') and gradually became attached to **adjectives** in French, Spanish and Italian, to produce **adverbs** indicating a quality, as in *lentamente* (Italian for *slowly*) or *absolutamente* (Spanish for *absolutely*). In English, *shall* is undergoing grammaticalisation. Indications of this are: (i) that it is now commonly reduced to *'ll* (e.g. 'I'll do it' rather than 'I shall do it'); and (ii) that its **meaning** is being lost (that is, it is undergoing *semantic bleaching*) – i.e. it is now often thought to

mean the same as *will*. The opposite of grammaticalisation is
lexicalisation.

grapheme

This refers to the written equivalent of a **phoneme** (a speech sound).
We could call them *letters* or *characters*, but this term makes the link
between sound and written form clearer. Most definitions of
grapheme state that it is a written symbol that links to a phoneme.
However, many **languages** have sounds that require more than one
symbol to represent them, and there are also 'silent' letters in many
languages that may show grammatical or lexical family
resemblances, but which have no phonemic counterpart.
Nonetheless, *grapheme* is used to refer to all such linguistic marks on
paper or screen. Note, incidentally, that, just like phonemes, which
have slightly different realisations depending on the context,
graphemes also all look slightly different when produced by
different people or machines. Thus, we are able to recognise each of
the following shapes as a letter 'a' even though they differ
substantially:

a   a   a   a   **a**

Great Vowel Shift

The Great Vowel Shift (GVS) occurred between approximately 1400
and 1750. It refers to the gradual modification in the pronunciation
of the seven long **vowels** in Middle English. These were /iː/, /eː/, /ɛː/,
/aː/, /ɔː/, /oː/ and /uː/. 'Long' in this case refers to the duration of the
vowel sound. As an example of what happened during this period,
consider the **word** *name*. In the **Middle English** period, this would
have been pronounced /naːmə/. By the Early Modern period,
however, the pronunciation had shifted to /nɛːm/. That is, the /aː/
vowel had been raised to /ɛː/. This means that, in the pronunciation
of the /aː/ vowel, the **tongue** was closer to the **hard palate** in the
Early Modern English (EModE) period than it was in the Middle
English period. A further raising of the vowel eventually resulted in
the common pronunciation containing a **diphthong**: /neɪm/. But
sound changes don't always happen in isolation, and a change to
one vowel can have knock-on effects on other vowels. Because the

/aː/ vowel raised to /ɛː/, the pronunciation of any words containing an /ɛː/ vowel also had to change. As a consequence, the pronunciation of /ɛː/ was raised to /eː/. Hence, the word *meat*, which was pronounced /mɛːt/ in the Middle English period, changed to /meːt/ in the EModE period, before the vowel was raised again to result in the modern-day pronunciation /miːt/. **linguists** refer to the kind of change that we observe in the GVS as a ***chain shift***. This assumes that **phonemes** are like links in a chain: as one moves, so do the others. The question is whether one phoneme is dragging the others in its wake (a drag chain), or whether phonemes are pushed into an already occupied position in the vowel space (see **International Phonetic Alphabet**), thereby pushing other phonemes into higher positions (a push chain). The Great Vowel Shift begins to explain why English spelling often seems to bear little resemblance to pronunciation. The **standardisation** of English spelling had started to happen from around the late 1400s. But the GVS went on for much longer than this, meaning that in many cases the now standardised spellings no longer appeared to match pronunciation. Consider the word *name*, discussed above. A spelling that more accurately reflects its modern pronunciation would be *neim*. The GVS began in the south-east and gradually spread across the country, but it did not take hold to the same degree everywhere. For example, in Scotland today you will still hear *house* pronounced as /huːs/, as the GVS did not affect areas in the far north of the country; essentially, the /uː/ vowel has not been raised.

Grimm's Law

This is named after Jacob Grimm (1785–1863), better known to non-linguists as one half of the Brothers Grimm, the duo famed for their fairy tale collection. Grimm, though, was first and foremost a philologist (what we would nowadays call a historical linguist). Grimm's Law describes how Germanic (the ancestor of such **languages** as English, Swedish, German and Danish) developed from **Proto-Indo-European** (PIE). PIE is a **reconstruction** of the language from which modern **Indo-European** languages developed. Proto-Germanic began as a dialect of PIE but, at some point, its **consonants** started to be pronounced differently from those of PIE. For example, PIE /p/ started to be pronounced as /f/. That is, the consonant shifted from being a **voiceless bilabial plosive** to a voiceless labiodental **fricative**. Similarly, **voiced** /b/ in PIE shifted to voiceless /p/ in Proto-Germanic. Grimm discovered that these changes were not arbitrary but systematic, and Grimm's Law describes the stages of these sound shifts. Grimm's Law describes why, for example, the word *foot* begins with a /p/ in Latin and Greek (*pes* and πόδι, pronounced /poδi/) but with a /f/ in English and German (*foot* and *Fuß*). The reason is that Latin and Greek are developments of Italic and Hellenic respectively, offshoot languages of PIE which retained PIE consonants, while English and German are developments of Proto-Germanic, which did not. *See also* **Verner's Law**.

ground

This refers to the background against which something may be foregrounded – either visually or in the written mode. Thus, the ship in the foreground of a painting is the **figure**, whereas the sea is the *ground*. Similarly, a **text** written in **Standard English** may be the ground for a foregrounded figure when there is suddenly a **phrase** or **sentence** in a nonstandard **dialect**. **Stylistics** has used this psychological notion of **foregrounding** to explain how readers pay more attention to those features of **language** that stand out against their context.

H

hard palate

This is often referred to as the roof of the mouth. The hard palate is the bony structure in the **oral cavity** that is found behind the **alveolar** ridge and in front of the soft palate (or **velum**). If you run your **tongue** along the roof of your mouth from your alveolar ridge and as far back as it will go, you should be able to feel the roof of your mouth go from hard (i.e. the hard palate) to soft (i.e. the velum).

head noun

The head noun is the irreducible core of a **noun phrase**. So, although there are seven **words** in the **phrase** *that incredibly expensive pizza restaurant in Soho*, and three of them (*pizza, restaurant, Soho*) are **nouns**, only one of them – *restaurant* – is the head noun. Note that the shortest possible version of this phrase that would remain grammatical is *that restaurant*. Apart from the **determiner** (*that*), the only word that remains is the head noun.

head word

This refers to the most essential part of a grammatical **phrase**, and determines the **category** of the phrase. For example, *the merry linguists* is a **noun phrase**, with the **noun** *linguists* as the head of the phrase. The head of a phrase is often the one part of a phrase that is essential in order for it to be grammatical. For instance, the **sentence** 'The merry linguists love grammar' would still make sense – and be grammatical – if the noun phrase *The merry linguists* was reduced to just its head, *linguists* ('Linguists love grammar').

heritage language

This is a term used to describe **languages** that are not the dominant language(s) in a given region / area / social context. For example, in the United States, English is the dominant and national language and is used for education, in government, and in the media. As a result, any language spoken in local communities, other than English, could be considered a heritage language. A heritage language is typically a second (or third) language learned by an individual at home, but it may not always be fully developed. The development of the heritage language is largely dependent on the input from the surrounding environment. Scholars place speakers' fluency in a heritage language on a continuum, where speakers range from completely fluent in the language, to individuals who may not speak or understand the language at all, but identify with the cultural associations of the language after growing up in that culture. In foreign language teaching, *heritage language* is generally used slightly more specifically, to indicate that an individual has grown up where a non-majority language was spoken and they have some level of proficiency in it. The more general definition of *heritage language* does not assume that an individual necessarily has a level of proficiency in their heritage language.

hesitation

Hesitation markers are commonly analysed in both **Conversation Analysis** and **phonetics**. Hesitations can be filled when someone produces an audible form of a hesitation (e.g. *um* or *uh*), or unfilled, which is marked by silence. Hesitations are believed to serve many purposes, such as **floor** holding, **word** searching, and **utterance/ sentence** planning. In phonetics, hesitation markers such as *um* and *uh* are found to be very common in spontaneous speech, and individuals unconsciously tend to exhibit their own hesitation patterns (in terms of both hesitation choice – *um*, *uh*, *er* – and hesitation quality).

heterodiegetic narrative

This refers to a narrative whose narrator is not a part of the story they are telling. The concept of ***diegesis*** comes from the work of Gerard Genette, who distinguished between those narratives where the narrator is present in the story being related (*homodiegetic*) and those where the narrator is outside the story (*heterodiegetic*). Although this often corresponds to the distinction between first person diegesis (*homodiegetic*) and third person diegesis (*heterodiegetic*), there are in fact many ways in which the two sets of **categories** are not equivalent. Thus, a narrator may well refer to him/herself in the first person while still being absent from the events of the story. Likewise, a third person narrative (or even, sometimes, a second person narrative) may actually present the thoughts, feelings and viewpoint of a character internal to the story. *See also* **homodiegetic narrative**.

heteroglossia

This is the concept of 'multiple voices'. The literary theorist Mikhail Bakhtin claims that multiple voices are present in any **text** (written or spoken). The idea is that no text is completely the product of the speaker or writer, since their own **words** are based on their whole experience of **language** up to that point in time. Many other 'authors' are, therefore, responsible for anything that we say or write through the intertextual **references** that we (albeit unwittingly) make.

heteronym

A heteronym is a type of **homograph**. Like homographs, heteronyms are **words** that are spelt the same but have different **meanings**. The difference is that heteronyms are always pronounced differently. Examples include *wind* (**verb**: 'to twist something round' / **noun**: 'moving air currents') and *bow* (verb: 'to bend the upper body forwards as a mark of respect' / noun: 'a weapon for shooting arrows'.

hiatus

This refers to the phenomenon whereby two adjacent **vowels**, instead of being combined into a **diphthong**, retain their syllabic status and are given their full values. This occurs, for example, in the English **words** *re-elect* and *re-assemble*, in which the **prefix** is not run into the base **morpheme**, but instead retains its separate identity. The words have three and four **syllables**, respectively. English avoids the difficulty of pronouncing vowels consecutively without turning them into a diphthong by using a **glide** (examples 1–3) or linking /ɹ/ (example 4) to keep the vowels separated:

1. Do ask → [duː^{w}ɑːsk]
2. Three acres → [θɹiː^{j}eɪkəz]

3. How old → [haʊʷəʊld]
4. Far and wide → [faːɹənwaɪd]

The glide is indicated by a superscript **International Phonetic Alphabet** symbol. What you might notice is that the /w/ glide is used following close back vowels, while the /j/ glide follows close front vowels. Linking /r/ shows up anywhere there's a historical /r/ that's shown in the spelling (for example, *fear of* /fɪəɹəv/, *pair of* /pɛəɹəv/, *sure of* /ʃʊəɹəv/, etc.). Notice that rhotic **accents** pronounce the /r/ as a matter of course (hence, in such accents it is not a linking /r/), while non-rhotic accents only pronounce it when it is followed by a vowel. *See also* **connected speech**.

hierarchical structure

Some models of **grammar** see the units of **language** as being arranged hierarchically, from the smallest to the largest. In this view of language, small units can be combined to form ever larger units. So, the smallest unit of language that can change **meaning** is the **phoneme**, which combines into the next smallest unit which carries meaning: the **morpheme**. When combined together, morphemes form **words**. When words are combined, they form **phrases**. And when phrases are combined, they form **clauses**. But from this point on, the definition of hierarchy becomes slightly stretched. We can combine clauses to form **sentences** (e.g. 'Dan played drums while Lesley played trumpet'), but a clause on its own constitutes a sentence (e.g. 'Hazel and Dan argued for ages'). Above the level of the sentence, the situation becomes increasingly unclear. Some **linguists** have suggested that **discourse** constitutes the next level up. That is, discourse is formed from the combining of sentences. However, this depends on how we define *discourse*, which is a notoriously slippery term. Moreover, some of the units described above are units of written language, rather than speech. For example, while clauses can be clearly defined in writing, they operate slightly differently in spoken language (*see* **C-unit** and **spoken grammar**), suggesting that the concept of hierarchical structure may not adequately describe both writing and speech. Another problem is what to do with **semantics** in this model, as it seems to sit at all levels of grammar. Some grammars do not subscribe to the notion of hierarchical structure in the way described here, preferring to see language as made up of *units of meaning* or *constructions*. *See* **construction grammar** and **pattern grammar** for examples of such models of language.

historical linguistics

This refers to the study of how **languages** change over time. Historical **linguists** are interested both in identifying change and in explaining why it happens and how it spreads. The **Great Vowel Shift** is an example of a linguistic change. Changes can be caused by language-internal factors or by language-external influences. An example of a language-internal change is when a modification to the pronunciation of one **phoneme** has a knock-on effect on the pronunciation of other phonemes (*see* the entry on the Great Vowel Shift for an example of this). An example of a language-external factor influencing language change is the German spelling reform of 1996, when the governments of Austria, Germany, Liechtenstein and Switzerland signed an international agreement to enact this reform. Linguistic change can occur at all levels of language: **phonology**, **grammar**, **lexis** and **meaning**. To study linguistic change, historical linguists rely on three types of evidence: primary data, secondary data and linguistic **reconstruction**. Primary data consists of samples of actual language from the period we are interested in. For example, historical linguists interested in morphological change in **Middle English** would study **texts** written in that period, such as Chaucer's *Troilus and Criseyde* (written in the 1380s) or the twelfth-century *Ormulum*. Secondary data consists of contemporary commentaries on language use. For instance, a historical linguist studying syntactic change in **Early Modern English** might, in addition to consulting primary data, also look at dictionaries, grammar books and style guides of the period, to see what (if any) comments their authors make about Early Modern **syntax**. Finally, linguistic reconstruction is used in the absence of primary or secondary data and refers to the practice of estimating what a language must have been like at a particular point in time, based on indirect evidence. Perhaps the most famous example of linguistic reconstruction is how the Rosetta Stone was used to decipher Egyptian hieroglyphs. Discovered in 1799, the

Rosetta Stone was inscribed in 196 BCE with three versions of a royal decree of Ptolemy V. These three texts were written in hieroglyphs, demotic Egyptian and Greek. The ability to read hieroglyphs, the writing system of ancient Egypt, had been lost in the medieval period. However, once it had been established that the demotic and Greek inscriptions on the stone were the same, thereby suggesting that the third text was likely to be identical in content, linguistic reconstruction enabled linguists to interpret the hieroglyphs. The value of historical linguistics is that it helps us to explain why languages are as they are today and supports arguments against prescriptivist views by showing that linguistic change is normal and inevitable. It also helps us to read and understand older texts, thereby enabling us to understand the cultures of past societies. *See also* **actuation** and **propagation**.

holophrastic stage

This is the one-word stage that occurs in child **language acquisition**. The holophrastic stage becomes more language-specific following the babbling stage, and comes just before the two-word stage. **Language** development in children follows a generally predictable pattern – however, there is often a great deal of variation in the age at which different children reach these certain stages or milestones. The holophrastic phase is said to occur around 9 to 18 months of age when children will typically be producing single **open-class words** (i.e. **lexical words**) or word stems (i.e. **base forms**). It is common during the holophrastic stage for children to overgeneralise their word use. Many children will often use the word *dog* or *cat* to refer to any animal that has fur and four limbs – don't be surprised if your little one uses *dog* to refer to the lion or the bear the next time you are at the zoo. In addition to simple labelling overgeneralisations, children that are further into the holophrastic stage will often use one word to communicate more complex messages. For example, the word *food* may variously be used to mean: 'I want food', 'Where is the food?', 'Look dad, food' or 'I have food.'

homodiegetic narrative

This is a type of storytelling in which the narrator is a character within the story. In Herman Melville's *Moby Dick*, Ishmael is a homodiegetic narrator, recounting the story of a voyage in which he took part. Famously, he introduces himself to the reader in the very first **sentence**: 'Call me Ishmael.' In a homodiegetic narrative, the point of view that the reader has access to tends to be restricted to that of the narrator, whose perspective is limited to their own perceptions of events – although, like Ishmael, the narrator may, of course, be recounting what happened with the benefit of hindsight. Homodiegetic narratives contrast with **heterodiegetic narratives**, in which the narrator reports on events of which they are not a part and often has a more 'omniscient' view of events, with access to various characters' points of view.

homograph

Homographs are **words** that are spelt the same but have different **meanings**. Their pronunciations may be the same or different. In English, these include *lie* (**verb**: 'to make an untrue assertion' / **noun**: 'an untruth'), *content* ('happy' / 'that which is contained within something else'), *refuse* ('say no' / 'garbage') and *wind* ('to turn' / 'moving air currents'). Notice that, in the case of those examples whose pronunciations differ, often it is the **stress** pattern that changes. If both pronunciation and spelling were the same, they would be **homonyms**. *See also* **heteronym**.

homonym

Homonyms are **words** that sound the same when pronounced, and have the same spelling but different **meanings**. These meanings can only be disambiguated in context. Homonyms include *bat* ('small flying animal' / 'sports equipment'), *scale* ('measure'/'climb') and *fair* ('equitable' / 'outdoor entertainment'). *See also* **heteronym** and **homograph**.

homophones

Like **homonyms**, homophones sound the same when pronounced and have different **meanings**. Their spellings may be the same or different. Examples include *to/two/too* and *flower/flour*.

honorifics

These are linguistic elements that encode an addressee's status and convey esteem when addressing or referring to someone. In English, these are **words** such as *sir* or *madam*. In some **languages**, the system of honorifics is considerably more complex. In historical Chinese, for example, the system of honorifics involved not only complimenting your addressee, but also denigrating yourself, and your choice of honorifics was governed by your own social status.

hypercorrection

This refers to one effect of the tendency for speakers to aspire to linguistic habits that they think are more prestigious. Sometimes, this can result in a **form** that is not really attested as a genuine form for the higher social group but has been created as the result of an over-generalisation of a **rule**. For example, a speaker of English who suspects that ***h-dropping*** is something that only lower-class speakers do may try to put in all the /h/ **phonemes** at the beginnings of **words** such as *house* and *however*, when in a formal situation in which it would be advantageous to be seen as belonging to a higher social class. In addition, this speaker may start adding /h/ to the beginning of words that start with a **vowel**, as the supposed rule of adding /h/ to words they normally pronounce starting with a vowel (like *'ouse* and *'owever*) is spread too widely. This is the mistake that the character Eliza makes in the play *Pygmalion* (and its musical version, *My Fair Lady*), where she starts to add /h/ to only the wrong words, thus showing her 'umble origins: 'In 'Artford, 'Ereford, and 'Ampshire, 'urricanes 'ardly hever 'appen.'

hypernym

A hypernym is a **superordinate** term. For example, *building* is a hypernym for *house, factory* and *garage; cat* is a hypernym for *Maine Coon, Russian Blue* and *British Longhair; footwear* is a hypernym for *boot, sandal* and *trainer;* and *walk* is a hypernym for *dawdle, stroll* and *saunter. See also* **hyponym**.

hyponym

Hyponyms are **words** that share the core semantic components of a more general word (a **superordinate**) but are more specific in **reference**. So, the word *boxer* is a hyponym of *dog*. So, too, are *Labrador* and *terrier. Daisy* and *daffodil* are hyponyms of *flower*. Note that you can test for this relationship by seeing whether you can fit the words into the frame 'X is a kind of Y.' Thus, you could say that

'ash is a kind of tree' and that 'a dog is a kind of animal'. This relationship is hierarchical and has more than one layer, so that the word *dog* is both the superordinate of *retriever* in English and a hyponym of *animal*. *See also* **hypernym**.

hypotaxis

This is an older term for what is now more commonly known as *subordination* (*see* **subordinate clause**). Hypotactic (i.e. subordinate) **clauses** are dependent on a main clause, i.e. they cannot stand on their own. Spot the hypotactic clause: 'Although some linguists prefer the term *subordination, hypotaxis* is still used.'

I

I-language

This is a term introduced by Noam Chomsky. It is often used as a replacement for **competence**. This is partly because, since its introduction, the term *competence* has been extended to encompass such broader concepts as **communicative competence** and **pragmatic competence** (both of which essentially refer to a speaker's knowledge about the social appropriateness of their use of **language**). The *I* in the term indicates that I-language is internal (that is, *I-language* refers to your internalised knowledge of your own language and how it works). The term *I-language* contrasts with what Chomsky calls **E-language**. While *I-language* essentially refers to the same concept as *competence*, the related term *E-language* is not quite the same as its precursor, **performance** (*see* **E-language** for a more detailed explanation of why). Chomsky's view is that the proper object of study for **linguistics** is I-language (this view is not shared by all **linguists**). His reasoning for this is that we are born with **Universal Grammar**, which provides our I-language – and I-language generates E-language.

idiolect

This is the term that is sometimes used to refer to the individualised **dialect** (and **accent**) that a speaker uses. Of course, we all change features of our accent and dialect on a daily basis according to situation – for example, when we try to use a more prestigious accent in formal situations (such as adopting a 'telephone voice') or when we try to be accepted by younger members of society by using what we might imagine to be modern slang expressions (e.g. 'Yo dude!'). Like dialects, then, idiolects are variable even within a particular speaker, though they have some stability across time. Say you were born in the USA, live in Canada and have one British and one

Canadian parent: this background, together with the experiences you have in life (education, work, travel, etc.) will produce a unique combination of accent features as well as grammatical structures and lexical resources that make up your own special idiolect.

idiom

This refers to a lexical unit (usually a **phrase** or **clause**) where the **meaning** cannot easily be figured out from its constituent parts. A famous English example is 'kick the bucket', which **native speakers** will recognise as meaning 'to die'. Second language and other speakers may be unlikely to recognise this meaning, even if they had a confident grasp of the individual **words** *kick*, *the* and *bucket*. Note that no speaker can be sure why this idiom has this meaning – its origins, like those of many idioms, are contested. The figurative nature of idioms means that they are often used to refer to things that are taboo. *Bite the dust* and *six feet under* are other idioms for death. Others, such as 'to park the bus' (Swedish) refer to sexual activity – although note that this particular idiom has proved itself adaptable, with Portugese football manager Jose Mourinho bringing it into English to refer to teams who place the emphasis on defending their own goal, rather than attacking the opposition's.

idiom principle

The idiom principle was proposed by the **corpus linguist** John Sinclair (1933–2007) and underpins the concept of **pattern grammar**. According to the idiom principle, we do not form **sentences/utterances** by filling grammatical slots with single **words**. Instead, we rely on our knowledge of how words pattern together in chunks. That is, rather than seeing **language** as consisting of a **lexicon** and a set of grammatical **rules** for combining the words within that lexicon, the idiom principle suggests instead that language is structured around pre-existing patterns. Sinclair illustrates what he means by referring to how we use the expression *naked eye*. If we look in a corpus, what we find is that this expression always follows the same pattern, which can be summarised as follows: some reference to visibility, followed by a **preposition**, followed by *the naked eye*. Examples from the **British National Corpus** include 'abundantly clear to the naked eye', 'very obvious with the naked eye' and 'it would barely be discernible to the naked eye'. This, then, is the structure that we draw on when we use the phrase *naked eye*. Consequently, it would be very unlikely for us to come across usages such as 'It was extremely warm to the naked eye', unless the speaker was trying to be deliberately creative. Sinclair's view was that we rely primarily on the idiom principle when formulating utterances and sentences. It is only when we do not have a pre-existing pattern as an option that we use what he calls the **open choice principle** (that is, the practice of choosing single words from the lexicon and combining these according to syntactic rules). The idiom principle also plays a role in how we interpret language. For instance, consider the expression *on top of it*. This has two idiomatic meanings. The first is 'to understand an issue and be able to deal with it' (as in this example from the BNC: 'now that we know what the problem is [...] we're on top of it'). The second is 'in addition to' (as in 'On top of it all, the remorseless heat was becoming too much for Hugh'). If we see *on top of it* in contexts such as these, we are most likely to interpret the **phrase** using the idiom principle – that is, we see it as a complete pattern and understand its idiomatic meaning. Alternatively, *on top of it* can be used in a literal sense, as in 'I went over to the bed, climbed on top of it, put my head on the pillow and fell asleep.' Interpreting language, then, means working out whether a phrase is best understood using the idiom principle or the open choice principle. Sometimes, it is only through considering the context that we can work out whether the idiom principle interpretation or open choice interpretation is the most appropriate, as in this example: 'The boiler was like an upright wooden barrel banded with copper. On top of it there was a copper funnel.'

illocutionary force

This refers to the intention behind a particular **utterance**. This concept arose from the work of J. L. Austin and John Searle, who introduced **Speech Act Theory** and changed our fundamental view of **language** from being a means of information transfer and labelling to being a means of carrying out action. So, we threaten, promise, deny, refuse, persuade, and perform many other actions, through the means of language. The illocutionary force of our utterances refers to the speech act we are performing. This does not always match the apparent surface **meaning** of the utterance, so that 'I wouldn't put your glass on the edge of the table' is likely to be a warning about danger more often than it is a statement about the speaker's behaviour, although this is what the superficial linguistic meaning seems to be. Likewise, a notice reading 'Thank you for not smoking' is usually a request or even a command, rather than an expression of gratitude. *See also* **locution** and **perlocutionary effect**.

imperative

This is a grammatical **mood**. The imperative is used to form a command or an indirect request, such as 'Stop writing now' or 'Let's go.' In English, imperatives are notable for their deletion of the **subject pronoun**, as in 'Leave this place of worship!' (compare *'You leave this place of worship!'). Imperatives can often consist of a single **word**, i.e. one **verb** on its own, as in *Go!*, *Stop!* or *Attack!*

implicature

This refers to **meaning** that is conveyed without being explicitly stated. The term was coined by the language philosopher H. Paul Grice, who wanted a term that was both wider and more precise than *implication*. In a famous example of his, a reference letter for a job applicant that says that s/he is always punctual – but says nothing else – carries the implicature that there is nothing else that can be said about the applicant (and that therefore s/he is actually not much good) because in this situation a comprehensive, and largely positive, assessment is expected. Implicature works in this way, as a result of the context supplying extra meaning to the **words** used, and often, as in this example, by breaking expectations. *See also* **Cooperative Principle**, **flout** and **inference**.

implosive consonants

These are common in some of the world's **languages**, including Vietnamese, Khmer, Swahili, Zulu, Xhosa and Hausa. They are similar to **plosive consonants**, where there is a complete closure somewhere in the mouth or throat, and where, for pulmonic **egressive** plosives, the pressure of air builds up as it leaves the **lungs**, until it forces the closure apart, resulting in a small explosive sound and the release of the air as this happens. Implosives, as the name implies, involve the opposite direction of travel of the air, so that the closure is forced apart by air entering, rather than leaving, the **vocal tract**. It is not easy to achieve the same kind of pressure build-up outside the mouth except by making the pressure inside the mouth lower, so that the air outside is naturally under higher pressure than the air inside the mouth, causing it to force its way in, to balance the pressure. The way that speakers make this happen is to suddenly plunge their **larynx** downward, causing the air between the **glottis** and the closure in the mouth to become rarefied (i.e. lower in pressure). You may like to try to articulate these sounds by putting your **lips** and **tongue** in the right place to say [b], [d] or [g]: instead of breathing out as you say the sound, pull your larynx down sharply as you do when you swallow. It takes a bit of practice to get it right and it only makes a sound if you also voice (vibrate your **vocal folds**) at the same time! The symbols for the implosive versions of these **voiced** sounds are [ɓ], [ɗ] and [ɠ].

indefinite article

In some **languages**, including English, there are two ways of introducing a **noun** with a **referent**, such as *cup* or *sugar*. These are definite and indefinite articles. The indefinite article, which is *a* or *an* in English, is used only with **countable nouns** (i.e. we can say *a cup* but not *a rice*) and introduces only a single referent (i.e. we don't say *a cups*). The **meaning** of the resulting **noun phrase** (e.g. *a cup*) is either that there is no specific item being referred to (e.g. 'Can you get me a cup?') or that it is irrelevant which of many items is the one being referenced ('She picked up a cup'). In order to get the same meaning for plural countable nouns in English, we have to use the **quantifier** *some*, but in other languages, such as Spanish, the indefinite article can have plural versions (e.g. *una taza* becomes *unas tazas*).

Indo-European

Currently, the Indo-European language family is made up of close to 450 related, living **languages**, and there are over 3 billion speakers who claim an Indo-European language as their first language. The Indo-European language family can be further divided into many

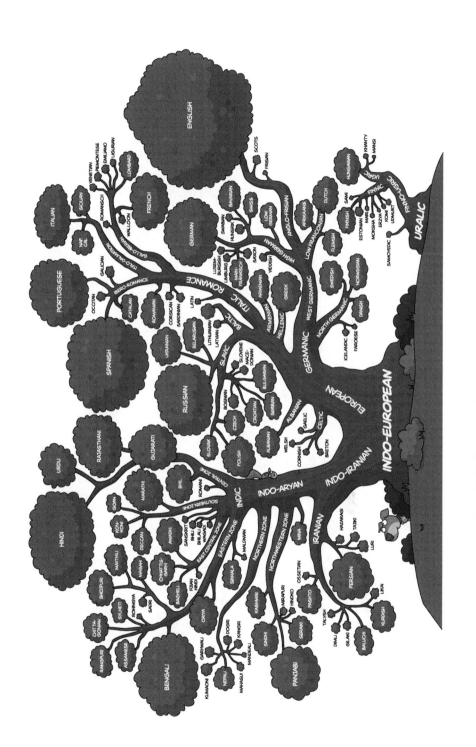

sub-groups like those of Germanic, Indo-Iranian, Celtic and Italic, grouping similar languages into even more related sub-families. However, all Indo-European languages descended from a single prehistoric language, reconstructed as **Proto-Indo-European**, which was believed to have been spoken in the Neolithic era. Indo-European languages include many of the languages found across modern-day Europe and parts of Asia. You will also find Indo-European languages spread even farther afield – such as in North America, South America, Southern Africa and Australia. It is believed that Indo-European languages began around the Black Sea and then slowly spread out to the rest of Europe and Central Asia, all the way to what is now Northern India. The most widely used Indo-European languages include: English, Spanish, Hindi, Punjabi, Russian, French and German. Be careful, though. Not all modern European languages belong to the Indo-European language family. There are a few language **isolates** in existence that do not (e.g. Hungarian, Finnish and Turkish).

inference

This refers to the **meaning** that a reader or hearer derives from a piece of **language**. In particular, it is used to refer to the conclusions that we draw from a piece of language where someone has made an **implicature**. Imagine that the film is just getting started at the cinema, and your friend turns to you and says 'I'm hungry.' You may make the inference that, rather than just a statement of fact, this is a request – your friend means to imply that they would like you to share your popcorn with them. Note the difference between **imply** (what the speaker or writer does) and **infer** (what the hearer or reader does) – these two are often confused. Such is the non-literal nature of implicature that we don't always understand the intended **reference**. You could just as well infer that your friend is asking you for money to buy their own popcorn or is not all that interested in the film. Sometimes we choose not to make the intended inference. A nice example comes in the TV comedy series *Black Books*. A customer makes a statement to the bookshop owner and enthusiastic smoker Bernard Black, observing that 'I'm probably getting a lot of second-hand smoke off you.' The customer's implied request – 'Please stop smoking' – is ignored by Bernard, who chooses to make the inference that the customer is acknowledging a debt to him: 'Don't worry about it. You can get me a drink some time.' *See also* **Cooperative Principle**.

infinitive

This refers to a particular **verb form**. A bare infinitive is the basic form that we would find in a dictionary – e.g. *dance, work, climb* – while in English the addition of *to* before the verb produces the *to*-infinitive. *To*-infinitives are **non-finite**, and can serve different functions from finite forms. For example, a *to*-infinitive **phrase** fulfils the role of **subject** in the **sentence** 'To dance to techno is his preferred way of spending the evening.' *See also* **split infinitive**.

infix

An *infix* is a type of **affix** that has been inserted into a **word**, rather than being added at one end or the other. For example, in Tagalog, -*um*- is an infix that is used to indicate that an event has been completed, marking the difference between *lakad* 'walk' and *lumakad* 'walked'. Infixes do not generally occur in English, although you might hear (nonstandard) sweary examples such as *evibloodydently* or *absofuckinglutely*. They can also be used humorously to indicate that someone lacks intelligence or understanding of something – as when Homer, the cartoon character from *The Simpsons*, attempts to play his daughter Lisa's saxophone by intoning the word *saxamaphone* into the instrument.

inflection

This is the process whereby a **morpheme** is added to a **word** in order to indicate a grammatical change. For instance, we can add different inflectional morphemes to a **verb** such as *peruse* to indicate **tense** – *perused, perusing, peruses* – or add the plural marker *s* to a **noun** to indicate that there is more than one of something, e.g. *tables, cupboards, carpets*. The change from one tense to another, or from singular to plural, is grammatical, but does not affect **word class** – *perused* is still a verb, *carpets* is still a noun. **Derivation**, on the other hand, causes a change in **meaning**, but can also cause a change of word class.

ingressive

Ingressive sounds are those sounds produced with an **airflow** that comes in through the mouth or nose (*see* **egressive** for airflow that moves in the opposite direction). There are three different types of ingressive sounds: velaric/lingual, glottalic and pulmonic. All of these terms can be used to modify the **word** *ingressive* to describe where the initiation of the airstream occurs. *See also* **implosive consonants**.

intensifiers

These are **words** that stress the degree of something. When attached to an **adjective**, words like *very* and *really* intensify the degree to which it is the case – 'Grammar is very interesting', 'Linguistics is really eye-opening.' Note that these intensifiers have little **meaning** on their own and are not essential to the **propositions. adverbs** of degree are also intensifiers – e.g. 'his remarkably sullen features', 'her particularly strange sense of humour'.

interdental

This describes an articulation where the **tongue** is placed between the top and bottom **teeth** to produce a sound. It is common for **dental** sounds [θ ð], especially in American English, to be produced interdentally. To a lay person, the slight fronting of the tongue for these articulations may not sound particularly different, but visually one may notice a habitual interdental speaker's tongue poking out of their teeth (or even mouth) at times when they speak.

interjection

Interjections are fairly peripheral, and somewhat primitive, aspects of our **vocabulary**. Some **grammars** count interjections as a **part of speech** (or **word class**). They include expressions of feeling (*ouch!*, *ugh!*), greetings (*hi*, *hello*) and signals such as *okay*, *no* and *goodbye*. *See also* **discourse markers**.

interlanguage

This is the term used to refer to the **language** system that a second language learner has available to them at any point in the learning process. In successful language learning, the nature of the interlanguage the speaker has available will become more and more like the target language and reflect less of the speaker's first language(s). This concept arose among researchers in second language learning from the 1960s onwards, as the Chomskyan revolution in thinking turned away from a behaviourist explanation of how human beings learn languages and towards a more cognitive approach to such questions. Thus, the supposed errors of language learners were no longer seen as defective, but as a step on the way towards a first language type command of the target language. The kinds of errors that indicate progress in language learning, for both first and second language learners, include the over-generalisation of grammatical **rules**, such as the addition of the past **morpheme** in English, which results in **forms** like *goed* (for *went*) and *swimmed* (for *swam*).

interlocutor

This is a term commonly used in **Discourse Analysis**, **sociolinguistics**, **phonetics** and many other sub-disciplines of **linguistics** that are interested in interaction. *Interlocutor* is typically used to refer to the person someone is speaking to. A conversation will minimally have two interlocutors, and they are each other's conversation partner, hearer or addressee. In phonetics, it is common to talk about the person whose speech is being analysed as the **participant**, reserving *interlocutor* to refer to the addressee, whose own speech might not necessarily be under analysis.

International Phonetic Alphabet

The International Phonetic Alphabet, or *IPA* for short (not to be confused with Indian Pale Ale!), was developed in 1888 in order to represent the sounds in all the world's **languages**. The alphabet is comprised of both ordinary letters and symbols that were invented specifically for the IPA. The alphabet was created such that each symbol is intended to represent one value, or general sound, across all languages. The idea is that anyone who knows the IPA would be able to pick up something written in the alphabet, in any language, and be able to pronounce it. The International Phonetic Alphabet is not a fixed alphabet insofar as the International Phonetic

Association provides updates to the alphabet when new sounds are discovered in languages that have not been previously documented. The year 2005 saw the latest update to the IPA that included an entirely new symbol, introducing the **voiced** labiodental **flap** [v]; a sound found primarily in languages in Central Africa.

interrogative

Interrogative **sentences** pose a question. In English, these tend to be produced through subject–auxiliary inversion: an **auxiliary verb** such as *do* is placed at the front of the sentence, to produce an interrogative such as 'Do you like rock music?' These interrogatives are commonly referred to as **yes/no questions**, whereas **wh-questions** use a wh-word to indicate the type of answer that the interrogative seeks – '*Who* do you love?', '*Where* do you go to, my lovely?', '*What* is love?' *See also* **question forms**.

intertextuality

This is the relationship between **texts** that are somehow associated with each other. This association can be through quoting or referencing. For example, the Oasis song 'Morning Glory' features the line 'Tomorrow never knows what it doesn't know too soon', referring back to a song by The Beatles ('Tomorrow Never Knows'). Intertextuality can also be seen over longer stretches of text. A parody song like 'Ouch!' by the Beatles pastiche, The Rutles, is based on an entire text (in this instance, The Beatles' 'Help!'), while Charlotte Brontë fans will notice how characters and plot elements in Jean Rhys's *Wide Sargasso Sea* correspond to those from Brontë's *Jane Eyre*. Whereas the song by The Rutles is a simple parody of another, Rhys uses intertextuality in a more complex way, inviting readers to look at *Jane Eyre*'s characters and themes in a different light.

intonation

This refers to linguistic (meaningful) variation in **pitch** over a whole **utterance**, and is not to be confused with the terms **inflection** or **tone**. Intonation is perceived and identified through different **fundamental frequency** contours over an utterance. Intonation is not intended to differentiate between **word meanings** like tones can (*see* **tone language**), but it may affect meaning more generally.

The contours created by intonation in fundamental frequency patterns are described in terms of their shapes. In English, we may describe intonation patterns as being a fall, fall-rise, rise, rise-fall or level. For example, **wh-questions** in English tend to use a rising intonation on the word that is the focus of the question (e.g. 'What did you think of the ↗ book?').

isogloss

In regional dialectology, an isogloss is a boundary between **accents** or **dialects**. Thus, in England, there is a boundary between the north, where the **vowel** in *bus* is largely pronounced as /ʊ/, and the south, where it is mainly pronounced as /ʌ/. Of course, there are other subtler differences in the pronunciation of this vowel, and there are other differences between the northern and southern accents of British English, but the isogloss between /ʊ/ and /ʌ/ identifies one of the major boundaries between different accents in the UK. Where there is a bunching together of different isoglosses, this can be seen as the boundary between accents or dialects as a whole.

isolate

An isolate is a **language** that researchers have not been able to place in a particular language family tree. A well-known example is Basque, spoken in Northern Spain and Southwestern France. While other European languages are **Indo-European**, Uralic or Turkic, no relationship has been found between Basque and other languages or shared ancestral languages. Basque, Korean and the Kashmir language of Burushaski are living languages that are often categorised as isolates, although some **linguists** do posit relationships to other languages. Other isolates, such as Pictish (from Scotland) and Etruscan (from Northern Italy), are extinct languages. Note that isolates are natural languages; we would not expect constructed languages such as Esperanto, Klingon or Dothraki to fit into established language family trees.

J

jargon

John le Carré's fictional spymaster George Smiley, the antihero of *Tinker Tailor Soldier Spy*, inhabits a murky world populated by *scalp hunters*, *pavement artists* and *lamplighters*. These terms are part of the jargon of the secret service that Smiley is employed by. They refer to agents responsible for dirty work such as burglary and assassination, surveillance operatives assigned to follow suspects, and couriers, respectively. Le Carré does not explain these terms explicitly in the novel. This has a strange, alienating effect, helping make Smiley's world seem impenetrable to us. It also helps to heighten the sense of realism that Le Carré is able to create, since all workplaces use jargon that is often difficult for outsiders to make sense of. Jargon may thus be thought of as part of the **sociolect** of a particular industry or social group. It works both as shorthand terminology for complex phenomena and as a means of marking group identity. It can also be euphemistic, as in the case of *subprime lending*, a banking term for the practice of offering loans to people who are unlikely to be able to pay them back, or the British and American military term *collateral damage*, which refers to the unintended death or destruction arising from a military attack. In cases such as these, jargon is used to make morally dubious concepts appear more palatable to outsiders – and even, perhaps, to those using the terms. The effects of using jargon can also be humorous: stories of builders' apprentices being sent to ask for a *left-handed screwdriver* or a *long stand* are pranks that derive from the unwitting apprentice's lack of knowledge of the jargon of the trade.

jargon aphasia

This describes a type of language deficit (or **aphasia**) that results from damage to the brain. Jargon aphasia is a type of fluent aphasia where speakers produce strings of **phonemes** that sound, intonationally, like the **language** that they are trying to speak, but which do not combine to produce real **words** in that language. *See also* **Broca's aphasia** and **Wernicke's aphasia**.

jawbone

If you've ever watched a ventriloquist, you'll have noticed that they manage to keep not only their **lips** but also their jaw still while talking. They don't need to move their jaw because the jawbone, or mandible, is not essential to speech production. You can see for yourself by holding a pencil between your **teeth** while talking; you should find that you are still able to talk fairly clearly. That said, when you talk normally, the jawbone does act as an **articulator**, particularly in relation to certain labial (**lip**) and lingual (**tongue**) movements. Say the words *ham* and *harm*, for example. If, in your **accent**, you make a distinction between the **vowel** quality in these two **words**, your jawbone will lower your tongue to produce the long /ɑː/ **phoneme** in *harm*. (If your accent only distinguishes between the two words in terms of vowel duration, this movement won't occur.) You will also feel some jaw movement when you produce **stop consonants** such as /p/.

jitter

This is a term used to describe **voice quality**, specifically in reference to the movement of the **vocal folds**. Jitter describes and measures the instability – or irregularity – of **fundamental frequency**.

joint attentional frame

Part of the process by which children acquire **language** involves the acquisition of what are called intention-reading abilities. It isn't enough for children to be able to identify linguistic units such as **phonemes** and **lexemes**. To be able to use them properly, they need to understand the relationship between linguistic **form** and **meaning**. Children develop an intention-reading ability at around the age of 1, and this helps them to do this. Intention-reading means comprehending that communication is intentional, and that the actions of the adults around them are deliberate. For instance, gaze direction is integral to communication, and understanding this is part of intention-reading – that is, from the age of 1, a child will comprehend that there is likely to be a connection between what an adult is saying and the object(s) that he or she is looking at (e.g. 'Would you like a banana?'). Successful intention-reading necessitates establishing a joint attentional frame. According to the psychologist Michael Tomasello, joint attentional frames are the common ground within which communication takes place. Imagine a child playing with a toy and intermittently drinking from a beaker of water. If an adult kneels down and joins in with the child's playing, then the adult, the child and the toy form the joint attentional frame. Anything the adult says is likely to be understood (or 'read') by the child as relating to this frame. If, on the other hand, the adult kneels down and picks up the beaker, then the child, the adult and the beaker become the joint attentional frame, and the child is likely to understand that anything the adult says will relate to the activity of drinking, even though the toy may still be in sight.

journalese

This refers to the common elements of journalistic style that transcend the house styles of individual newspapers and magazines. For example, in English, newspaper headlines tend to use the **infinitive** to refer to future events, rather than the present progressive or a **modal verb** such as *will* or *shall* ('Stephen Fry to wed' rather than 'Stephen Fry is getting married'). Strings of premodifiers (see **premodification**) in **noun phrases** are also noticeable (*Unemployed father-of-five Lee*) and it is common to place reporting **clauses** after, rather than before, the reported clause ('UK must wake up to CCTV risks, says surveillance chief'). Even elements of propositional content might be thought of as journalese. For example, it is common for court reports to routinely describe what the accused was wearing ('The accused appeared at Southwark Crown Court wearing a dark grey jacket, black trousers, white shirt and red tie'). On the whole, though, there are relatively few linguistic markers that are exclusive to journalistic style, and *journalese* tends to be used as a term primarily to disparage journalistic writing.

K

Kanzi

Kanzi is a bonobo (relative of the chimpanzee) who has learned to communicate in **sign language** in Iowa with American psychologist Sue Savage Rumbaugh, to the point where he knows as many as 348 symbols referring to objects and actions, and even some qualities (*good*, *bad*, etc.). He can understand spoken **words** and point to the right *lexigram* (symbol). Although it is thought that apes do not have the requisite physical characteristics to develop human-like spoken language, one story about Kanzi suggests that, while in a room adjacent to one containing his sister, Panbanisha, he made a number of vocalisations when he was shown some yoghurt and she pointed to the lexigram for *yoghurt*. Kanzi is thought to have developed the ability to combine symbols in a form of *proto-grammar*, for example in combining the signs for marshmallows and fire so that he could toast the marshmallows by starting a fire with matches. Much of the evidence of Kanzi's 'language' is anecdotal but indicates that these near relatives of human beings may have the capacity for a more complex system of communication closer to our own languages.

kennings

Kennings have their origins in Old Norse literature. They are **words** or **phrases** that refer to something or someone via a metaphorical expression. The **Old English** name *Beowulf*, for example, comes from the kenning *beo wulf* (bee wolf), meaning 'bear', which alludes to the fondness of bears for honey. Other examples are the use of *whale road* to refer to the sea, and *oar-steed* to refer to a ship.

keyness

This is a statistical measure used in **corpus linguistics**. It allows us to see whether, for example, a particular word-form is more typical of one **corpus** than another. For instance, imagine that in a corpus of 100,000 **words** the word *animal* occurs 10 times. If we then look in a corpus of 1 million words, assuming that the corpus consists of roughly the same kinds of **texts** as our 100,000-word corpus, we would expect to see the word *animal* turning up about 10 times more often (since the corpus is 10 times bigger than our first one). That is, we would expect to see *animal* occurring 100 times in the million-word corpus. If *animal* turns up a lot more than expected, say, 150 times in a million words, then something else might be going on. That is, it appears that *animal* is being used much more frequently that we would expect it to be, based on our observation of frequency in the 100,000-word corpus. In such a case, we would say that *animal* is a **keyword** in the larger corpus – that is, it is a word that occurs significantly more frequently in one corpus than we would expect it to do, based on our observation of how frequently it appears in another corpus. Keyness is measured using statistical tests such as chi-square or log-likelihood. The outcomes of such tests enable us to report the level of confidence we have that a word is key. For example, the test outcome might enable us to say that the probability of the word being key is 95% (or, to put it another way, $p = 0.05$; that is, the *probability* of the result being down to the chance selection of texts when building our corpus is just 5%). The closer our p-value is to zero, the more confident we can be that we have a statistically significant result and not just a chance occurrence. Words that are overused in one corpus compared to another are said to be *positively key*. Those that are underused are *negatively key*. As well as using keyness at the word level, it can also be used to test whether a particular *semantic domain* or **part of speech** is over- or under-used in one corpus compared with another. Keyness can reveal a number of things about a corpus. Keywords or key semantic domains, for instance, might indicate the general topic of the constituent texts of a corpus. This can be useful as a means of gaining an overview of the *aboutness* of a corpus (imagine you have a corpus of government emails, for instance, and you want to find out whether there are any particular topics that officials talk about more than others). Keyness can also indicate *skew* in a corpus – that is, if a particular word is key in our corpus, it might be because we were not sufficiently careful when building our corpus to ensure that it was a balanced and representative sample of whatever form of **language** we were selecting from. Further detailed analysis is required to establish whether the statistical keyness has any contextual importance, or whether it's just an accident of the corpus-building.

Khoisan

This is a term used for a group of African **languages** spoken in Namibia, Botswana and central Tanzania. The term *Khoisan languages* was originally devised by Joseph Greenberg to describe a group of African languages originally believed to be related to each other. However, that is now understood not to be true, and the term is used to describe three distinct language families (Khoe, Kx'a, Tuu) and two language **isolates** (Hadza, Sandawe). There are many languages within the Khoisan group that are endangered, and several that are now moribund or extinct. The most widely spoken language in this group is Koekhoe, spoken in Namibia, with around 200,000 speakers. Like Bantu languages, Khoisan languages are famous for the use of *clicks*. The language of Jul'hoan contains 48 click **consonant phoneme** combinations – that's more than **Xhosa**, which is famous for its clicks.

kinesics

This refers to the study of body language – *gestures* and other movements – that are not linguistic but are used to communicate. A shrug of the shoulders, for example, means 'I don't know' in many cultures, while holding up the palm of a hand to face someone often means *No!* The study of kinesics has struggled to unambiguously define the **meanings** of individual gestures or facial expressions, which should be no surprise given the difficulty of defining even more apparently straightforward meanings in **language**, such as **word** meanings. Kinesic research has focused initially on isolating individual forms of gesture or expression, on analogy with the progress of early linguistic research that began with the word and then moved in two directions, to the lower unit (**phoneme** and **morpheme**) and the higher units (**phrase**, **clause** and **sentence**).

Sequences and complex structures made up of identifiable units of gesture or expression (**kines**) are investigated to discover how they work together, and the variations of a kine (**allokines**) have been found to be as diverse as the raising of an eyebrow, a nod or tap of the hand or foot, or a blink. These kines and their variants may also be seen accompanying, or replacing, intonational **stress** as found in **tone languages**.

kinship terms

Kinship terms in human **languages** have been much studied by linguistic anthropologists as providing an insight into differences of societal organisation. Some kinship systems use a classificatory approach whereby some collateral kin (relatives not in direct lineage with the person we happen to be interested in) are in the same category as lineal kin (i.e. those who *are* in a direct line of descent). The Iroquois, for example, refer to the father and brother by the same term, and the mother and sister likewise. In a descriptive system, however, there is a separation between lineal and collateral kin (e.g. *mother* and *mother's sister*). These descriptive systems are more common where the nuclear family is the main economic and social unit, but there is no absolute division, and many systems combine elements of both. The typical English language systems in the developed Western world, for example, distinguish lineal members of the target person's generation (*siblings*) from collateral members (*cousins*) but group the men and women of the previous generation together (with the exception of *father* and *mother*) as *uncle/aunt*, whether they are lineal or collateral. Even then, English finds a way to make the distinction where it is needed by using **phrases** such as *by marriage* or *blood relation*, or compounds including *in-law* (e.g. *mother-in-law*).

koine

This refers to a mix of two or more mutually intelligible **varieties** of a **language** (as opposed to two or more languages that are not mutually intelligible, i.e. a **pidgin**) that involves some linguistic simplification of the varieties involved. *Koine* derives from the Greek word for 'common'.

L

L1

This is a shorthand term for referring to a speaker's first **language** (sometimes referred to as their native language). For example, if you were brought up speaking French, then French is your L1. By extension, L2 refers to your second language, if you have one; L3, to your third language, and so on.

labial

Labial **consonants** are speech sounds that are produced using one or both of the **lips** as an **articulator**. For example, the /b/ of *brother* is a **bilabial plosive** – i.e. a consonant sound that is produced by stopping the **airflow** from the **vocal tract** by putting both lips together. The air flowing into the mouth causes a build-up of pressure, and when the speaker moves their lips apart, an explosion of air is created. This is what gives rise to the term *plosive*. The /p/ of *party* is another bilabial consonant, the difference between this **phoneme** and /b/ being that the latter is **voiced** – i.e. the airflow causes the **vocal folds** to vibrate. An example of a consonant that only requires one of the lips as an articulator is a labiodental **fricative** such as /f/ or /v/. To produce these sounds, the lower lip is pressed against the upper **teeth**. Try it for yourself and see how many different labial consonants you can produce.

landmark

This is a term from **cognitive linguistics** and is often used in conjunction with the term **trajector**. *See also* **figure** and **ground**.

language

Language is the object of study of **linguistics**. A language is a semiotic system of verbal and non-verbal communication combined. (***Semiotics*** is the study of signs. A sign is anything that communicates a meaning – it may be a **word**, a **gesture**, a picture on a bathroom door, a road sign, and so on.) **Linguists** primarily study ***natural languages*** – that is, languages that have evolved without being consciously planned. Natural languages include **sign languages**. Nonetheless, ***constructed languages*** (***conlangs***) – such as the fictional languages Parseltongue, Dothraki and Klingon, the **universal language** Esperanto, and programming languages such as C++ and JavaScript – can be interesting objects of study for what they reveal about the nature of language as a system. Linguists have attempted to distinguish between the system of language (that is, its underlying **rules** and conventions) and its outward expression (see, for example, the distinction between **langue** and **parole**, **competence** and **performance**, and **I-language** and **E-language**). Language can be expressed verbally (through speech), manually (through signing) or visually (through writing). When linguists use the term *language*, they usually mean human language. The linguist and anthropologist Charles Hockett (1916–2000) introduced the concept of **design features** as a way of explaining how human language differs from the communicative systems used by other animals (**birdsong**, for example).

language acquisition

This is the process by which human beings learn to speak, write and understand **language**. This term includes first language, second or other language, and foreign language acquisition. These processes share some basic characteristics, though the age at which you learn a language and the context in which you do so can affect the type of process you undergo and the rate of learning. Note that there is still an ongoing debate about the balance between nature and nurture in language learning (*see* **Genie**).

langue

This is a term that was introduced by the Swiss **linguist** Ferdinand de Saussure (1857–1913), who is often considered to be the founder of modern **linguistics**. *Langue* is the French **word** for **language**, and in its specialist **sense** means the system of **rules** and conventions that underpin a language. Saussure contrasted *langue* with **parole**, the external realisation of *langue*. The concept of *langue* is very similar to Noam Chomsky's concept of **competence**, except that Saussure's term refers to the underlying systems of language generally while Chomsky's *competence* refers to the underlying knowledge of language that speakers have. Saussure drew an analogy between the concepts of *langue* and *parole* and chess, writing that *langue* can be compared with the rules of chess, while *parole* can be compared with the moves a player makes during a game. *See also* **I-language**.

larynx

This is a specialist term for the everyday **word** *voice box*. This non-specialist term derives from the fact that the larynx is identified as a bony structure in the neck which contains the **vocal folds**. The principal function of the larynx is for cutting off **airflow** in particular situations (e.g. swimming underwater, lifting heavy objects (where cutting off airflow helps to brace the ribcage), defecating, giving birth, etc.). The larynx also plays a role in the production of speech sounds. For example, the larynx responds passively when airflow is increased, resulting in a rise in the frequency of F0 (*see* **fundamental frequency**). It also serves to control the **pitch** of those speech sounds which have it.

lateral

The term *lateral* describes a **manner of articulation**. A lateral **consonant** is one which is produced by air flowing out from the sides of the **tongue**, while the **blade** of the tongue blocks the middle of the **oral cavity**. English has one lateral consonant, which, appropriately enough, is the sound you get at the beginning and the end of the **word** *lateral*. Most **varieties** of English have two **allophones** of /l/, known as *clear l* and *dark l*. Clear /l/ is what you get at the beginning of the word *lift*. Dark l, or [ɫ], is pronounced at the back of the mouth (by the **velum**) but in some **accents** it is closer to a **bilabial semivowel**: /w/. Imagine a Cockney pronunciation of *girl* or *talk*, for example.

lect

This is a **synonym** of **variety**. The term is backformed (*see* **back-formation**) from **dialect** and serves as a neutral **base form** to describe any variety of a **language**. Related terms include **acrolect, basilect, dialect, idiolect, mesolect** and **sociolect**.

lemma

This term is used widely in **corpus linguistics** to refer to all the related **forms** of a **word** (e.g. *rise, rises, rising, risen, rose*) as a single item. In lexicography, it is more usually used to refer to the citation form of the word (in our example, *rise*), which is meant to 'stand for' all forms of the word in the dictionary entry. *See also* **lexeme**.

lenition

This is a phonological process whereby **consonants** change over time to become weaker. For example, in the **Old English** period, the medial consonant in the word for *father* (/fæder/) was /d/ (i.e. /fædə/). By the **Early Modern English** period, lenition had weakened the /d/ to /ð/, hence the **Present Day English** pronunciation /faːðə/. The opposite of lenition is **fortition**.

levels of language

Because **language** is such a complex phenomenon to study, to keep things manageable, **linguists** often choose to focus on just one aspect of it at once. To this end, it is common to hear linguists talk about *levels of language* or *language levels*. This is a metaphor that imagines language to be made up of various strands. Thus, we can talk about the phonological level of language, for example, or the syntactic level or the semantic level. The levels of language can be summarised as follows:

Language level	Focus
Phonetics and phonology	Sound
Syntax	Sentence/utterance structure
Morphology	Word structure
Semantics	Word meaning and sentence meaning
Pragmatics	Meaning as affected by context

The notion of language levels should not be confused with the concept of **hierarchical structure**, which instead describes how units of language can be combined to form increasingly large structures. The concept of language levels is simply a convenient metaphor for thinking about the composition of language.

lexeme

This term is often used as a **synonym** for *word*. However, it has a more particular **meaning**. A lexeme is a unit of meaning that can be realised in a number of **forms**. So, for instance, the **verbs** *sing*, *sings* and *singing* are all inflected forms of the same lexeme, *sing* (*see also* **lemma**, **inflection** and **derivation**). *Singer*, on the other hand, would be considered a different lexeme as this is a **noun** rather than a verb. Lexemes can also be multi-word units, where the meaning of the item is more than the sum of its parts. This is the case for English **phrasal verbs**, such as *look after* or *get over*, which second language learners of English have to learn as a unit, since the lexical meanings 'care for' and 'recover from' cannot be found by simply adding together the meanings of *look* + *after* or *get* + *over*.

lexical bundles

These are also known as ***formulaic sequences***, ***multi-word expressions***, ***recurrent word combinations*** or **n-grams**. These are combinations of (usually three or more) **words** which occur frequently in a given dataset (**corpus**) and which, unlike **idioms**, are semantically transparent. They tend to differ according to **register**. For instance, *one of the most* or *as a result* are lexical bundles found in much academic writing, while *are you going to* is more common in casual speech. These sequences are not always neat grammatical entities and they are only clearly identifiable through **corpus linguistic** methods, so our awareness of these chunks of **language** has increased with the development of powerful computers and more effective software for searching large datasets.

lexical field

This refers to a group of **words** within a **language** that describe a particular **semantic field**, e.g. sport, science or cookery. (Some writers use *lexical field* and *semantic field* interchangeably, though.) *Lexical field* specifically refers to the way in which the area of **meaning** is labelled in a particular language. Thus, English may have a different number of words for a particular field from Spanish or Japanese, or they may simply divide up the field in a different way, so that direct translation is not possible word-to-word. Lexical fields can be more or less specific, so that each general lexical field (e.g. sport) contains a number of more specific ones (e.g. cricket, athletics), and so on down the levels (e.g. running, jumping, throwing). *See also* **superordinate**, **hypernym**, **hyponym**.

lexical gap

This refers to an area of **meaning** (**semantic field**) which has no label in some **languages**, though it may be named by a **word** or **phrase** in other languages. Examples include expressions such as *dedo* in Spanish, which means both *finger* and *toe* in English, so that each language lacks the concept/word pairing (i.e. the ***sign***) of the other. Some lexical gaps have **referents** that are limited geographically or socially and have only been named in the language of their place of

origin. With the rise of global travel and communication, these referents will often need to be labelled in additional languages, leading to an increase in **loanwords** (e.g. *bungalow* in English from Gujarati) which may take on the **phonology**, spelling, or even the **morphology** of the local language. A more technical meaning of *lexical gap* refers to those concepts that existing *lexis* makes predictable, but which happen not to exist. These are known as accidental lexical gaps. An example would be the animal world labels in English where we have words for male and female cows, horses and dogs, for example, but not for male and female mice or spiders. So, we could theorise the possibility of such words, even where they don't exist, and we can, of course, use phrasal circumlocution to explain such concepts in any language.

lexical items

These are the components in the *lexis* (i.e. the **vocabulary**) of a **language** or language **variety**. Although we might be tempted to refer to these as **words**, in fact a lexical item in a language may be compound (e.g. *ice-cream*) or phrasal (e.g. *lunch break*) or even clausal (e.g. 'We'll see'). We also differentiate between lexical items, which are individual occurrences, and **lexemes** or **lemmas**.

lexical richness

Also known as *vocabulary density*, lexical richness in **utterances** or **texts** refers to the ratio of *types* (i.e. distinct words) to *tokens* (total number of words); the higher the ratio, the greater the lexical richness. *See* **type–token ratio** for details of how this is calculated.

lexical word

Lexical words are those that are to be found in the **lexicon** of a particular **language** or area of interest. Lexical words are not just those that we would expect to find in a dictionary (*religion, mellow, shout*), but also smaller and bigger units. Although **bound morphemes** are not recognised as **words** in their own right, <dis>, <s> and others nonetheless have distinct and consistent **meanings** (**negation** and pluralisation). Multi-word units such as **phrasal verbs** and **idioms** are also recognised as lexical words, as their meaning is lost when they are broken up into their constituent words – the meaning of *throw up* cannot be arrived at by simply adding together the meanings of the **verb** *throw* and the **preposition** *up*, just as a newcomer to English would struggle to comprehend the intended meaning of the idiom *sick as a parrot*.

lexicalisation

This is a process of **language** change, during which a grammatical construction such as a **phrase** is gradually converted into a single **word** or **morpheme**. For example, the word *goodbye* is a lexicalisation of the phrase *God be with ye* (the intermediate phase of the lexicalisation can be seen in older hyphenated spellings, i.e. *good-bye*). Similarly, *husband* is a lexicalisation of **Old English** *hus* (house) and *bonda* (master). The compounding of the two words in Old English (i.e. *husbonda*) is indicative of lexicalisation being underway even then. By around 1450, the spelling *husband* was becoming more common, and the change of **vowel** perhaps suggests that the **stress** on the second morpheme had at this stage been reduced.

lexicon

A lexicon is the **vocabulary** of a particular **language** or area of interest, such as business, **linguistics**, or love in 1980s pop music. An individual can also be thought of as having their own, personal lexicon. A lexicon consists of all the words of a particular language, while the **grammar** of a language gives its speakers and writers a means of combining these words into **phrases** and **sentences** and **utterances**. A lexicon consists of all the **lexical words** in a language, plus **bound morphemes** such as <dis>, which can be recognised as having particular meanings (such as **negation** of a connected morpheme), and other meaningful units such as **idioms** – *raining cats and dogs*, *over the moon* – that lose their meaning when broken down into their constituent **words**.

lingua franca

This term originally described a specific **pidgin language** whose **vocabulary** was drawn from southern *Romance languages* and that was used for the purposes of trade around the Eastern Mediterranean region, sometime around the 1600s. (N.B. Romance languages are languages such as Spanish, Italian and Portuguese that can trace their origins to Latin; the term *Romance* comes from the word *Roman*.) A pidgin is a basic language that is developed by two or more groups who do not share a common language, initially for enabling the bare essentials of communication. *Lingua* is from the Italian **word** for *tongue*, while *franca* derives from Greek and referred originally to Franks, i.e. people who came from Germanic nations. *Lingua franca* as a term has broadened in **meaning** over time so that it no longer refers to one specific pidgin. Nor is it a **synonym** for pidgins generally. Its most common contemporary meaning is to refer to any language used as a common means of communication by two or more groups of speakers who do not share a native language. For example, English might be said to be the *lingua franca* of the internet.

linguist

This term often confuses people who are not linguists themselves. There is often an assumption that a linguist is someone who speaks lots of **languages**. It is true that the term can be used in this way. The European Union, for instance, uses *linguist* as a catch-all job title to refer to translators and interpreters. However, this is a specific use of the term. The other meaning of *linguist* (and the one that is more common in academia) is broader, and describes anyone who studies language using the disciplinary techniques of **linguistics**. For example, linguists are interested in how sounds are produced and pattern together, how grammatically acceptable **sentences** are formed, how **meaning** is generated in language, how meaning is influenced by context, what influence society has on language use, and how language varies according to author, text-type or historical period. So, phoneticians, syntacticians, semanticists, pragmaticians, sociolinguists, stylisticians and so on are all linguists. This does not necessarily mean they speak lots of languages (they may study these things in one or many languages without being expert speakers of them) – though some linguists do, of course.

linguistic determinism

This is the idea that your **language** determines the way that you see the world: your language potentially limits the way you perceive your environment. A much-quoted example of this in practice concerns the terms that different languages have for colours. If, for instance, your language does not have a word to refer to the colour that in English is called *indigo*, does that mean that you do not perceive the difference between this colour and, say, purple? The related notion of **linguistic relativity**, attributed to Benjamin Whorf and Edward Sapir, is commonly expressed as the **Sapir–Whorf hypothesis**, of which there is a strong version and a weak version. The strong version says that language determines thought, while the weak version says that language has the capacity to influence thought. Some **linguists** (for example, Steven Pinker) are firmly of the view that thought precedes language. Of those who *do* subscribe to the Sapir–Whorf hypothesis, most now accept only the weak version, rejecting the deterministic view.

linguistics

This is the academic discipline focused on the study of **language**. (Note that studying language is different from learning languages; *see* **linguist**.) The term is often misunderstood and is sometimes seen by administrators in UK schools and universities as synonymous with the name of the school subject *English language*. This is not the case. The best way to properly understand the term *linguistics* is to consider it in relation to other disciplines. For example, biology is the discipline that studies the life of living organisms. Chemistry is the discipline that studies the structure and composition of matter. Physics is the discipline that studies the movement of matter through space and time. Linguistics is the discipline that studies the structure and use of language. That is, the structure and use of language is the *object of study* of linguistics. If you are studying the English language (that is, if you are studying its structure and use rather than simply learning it as a foreign language), then you are doing linguistics; your object of study just happens to be the English language in particular.

lips

This is not a technical term, but the lips are a very important part of the articulatory apparatus we use to speak. They are particularly significant in **labial** and **bilabial consonants**, as well as producing the distinctive sound of 'lip-rounding' in some **vowels**, such as /uː/ (e.g. in *blue* or *you*).

loanwords

These are **words** borrowed into one **language** from the **vocabulary** of another. Examples include Japanese *arubaito* (part-time work) borrowed from German *Arbeit* (work), Italian *sciampagna* (champagne) borrowed from French *champagne*, and German *Kindergarten* borrowed into English. Sometimes, words are borrowed even when the language in question has an appropriate one already. For example, Hungarian *computer* is borrowed from English despite the prior existence of the Hungarian word *szamitogep*. Cases like this often reflect the perceived high status of the donor language. But it is not simply words that can be borrowed. English has borrowed **inflections** (e.g. French plural -*aux*, as in *gateaux*), **prefixes** (e.g. German *uber-*), **suffixes** (e.g. French -*ette*, as in *cigarette*), **phrases** (e.g. Latin *summa cum laude*, particularly in American English), **acronyms** (e.g. French *RSVP*) and even whole **sentences** (e.g. French *C'est la vie!*). Some loans are borrowed without change, as in the above examples, and some are adapted (e.g. *music* from French *musique*). One issue with the term *loan* in relation to **lexical items** is that there is little sense in which these are loans: no-one ever heard of a language eventually giving back its vocabulary. This has led some **linguists** to suggest that *copy* is a more accurate term than *loan*. *See also* **borrowing**.

locative

This is a grammatical **case** used in certain inflectional **languages** to indicate that the **noun** (or **pronoun** or **adjective**) is being referred to as a location – for example, where an action is occurring. There are locative **affixes** in many language groups, but for some of them, the locative has merged with other cases, so that there remain only vestiges of the locative case. In Latin, for example, there are locative versions of city names, such as *Corinthi* (in Corinth) and *Romae* (in Rome). In languages with no morphological cases, the equivalent is the use of **prepositions** with nouns (e.g. 'at the station').

locution

This is the term used in **Speech Act Theory** (originating with the philosopher J. L. Austin and developed by John Searle) to refer to the performance of an **utterance**. The term is used to distinguish it from the purpose for which the utterance is used (**illocutionary force**) and any consequences it may have (**perlocutionary effect**). The locution, therefore, is the core linguistic feature of the utterance, including structure and **meaning**, but not its contextual aspects.

logical presupposition

This refers to a particular kind of **presupposition**. The other kind of presupposition is an **existential presupposition**. Presuppositions are often labelled pragmatic, because they produce an implicit understanding. However, they are nevertheless fundamentally textual in nature (unlike **implicature**) as they are triggered by textual features and cannot be negated. Logical presuppositions can be triggered in a number of ways, including:

- *Change of state verbs* For example, 'Erica stopped taking the dog for a walk' presupposes that Erica had been in the habit of taking the dog out. Even if you negate the **sentence** grammatically ('Erica didn't stop taking the dog for a walk'), the presupposition remains in place.
- *Factive verbs* For example, 'Matt realised he'd lost his keys' presupposes that Matt had indeed lost his keys, because the **verb** *realise* is part of a group of verbs (also including *know*, *regret*) whose **complements** are necessarily true if the sentence is true. If you negate the sentence ('Matt didn't realise he'd lost his keys'), the presupposition is still valid.
- *Iterative words* For example, 'I'm not going to that restaurant again' presupposes that the speaker has been to the restaurant mentioned before. The trigger in this case is the **word** *again*. Other iterative words include all those starting with the iterative **morpheme** <re> (*recalculate*, *rearm*, etc.) and many **adverbs** (e.g. *yet*) and **adjectives** (e.g. *another*), but there is no definitive list of items which produce presuppositions in this way.
- *Cleft sentences* These sentences, such as 'It was Dan that wrote this book', divide the **proposition** into two. The first part ('It was Dan') places an emphasis on the **Actor** by putting it into the top level of **syntax**. The second part ('that wrote this book') places the additional information into a **subordinate clause**, which causes it to be presupposed as true. Thus, negating the sentence

('It wasn't Dan that wrote this book') denies the top-level assertion (it was Dan) but not the second level (a book was written by
someone).

- **Comparative structures** Some comparative structures, particularly those using 'as . . . as . . . ', produce logical presuppositions
too. For example, 'Matt runs as fast as Hazel' presupposes that
Hazel is also fast, as does its negative version, 'Matt doesn't run as
fast as Hazel.'

lungs

While the lungs are primarily involved in respiration, they play
a very important role in speech. Speech begins with the lungs, as we
generally speak while breathing out (although it is also possible to
speak while breathing in). Speech requires some form of airstream,
and the lungs provide this for the production of most speech
sounds. In this respect, the lungs may be the single most important
part of the anatomy for producing speech.

M

manner

This is one of the maxims of Grice's **Cooperative Principle**. The maxim says that speakers should be as clear as possible, summarising the expectation that the person we are speaking to will aim to say things in a way that is clear and unambiguous. If someone flouts the maxim by saying something in a way that is unclear or ambiguous, then we will assume that they are trying to communicate an implied **meaning**, as in Matt's turn here:

LESLEY   Am I the greatest singer in the world?

MATT   You're the greatest singer in the Linguistics department.

Note that Matt's response here does not provide a clear, unambiguous response to Lesley's question, which would usually require a 'Yes' or 'No' answer. Nonetheless, Lesley understood Matt's implied message: while Lesley's vocal abilities may be superior to those of her colleagues, they are not world-beating.

manner of articulation

In **articulatory phonetics**, *manner of articulation* refers to the way in which the **airflow** is obstructed as it moves through the **vocal tract**. The **International Phonetic Alphabet** divides pulmonic **consonants** (i.e. those where the airflow originates in the lungs) into eight different manners of articulation: **plosive**, **nasal**, **trill**, **tap/flap**, **fricative**, **lateral** fricative, **approximant**, and lateral approximant.

markedness

In **linguistics**, this distinguishes between a unit of **language** that is treated as referencing a norm and another that is seen as unusual or nonstandard. For example, *tall* is semantically unmarked in comparison to *short* – it refers not just to having great height, but also to having height at all. So, even if you're short, you still have to be described as *four feet tall*. In some cases, markedness is a morphological matter – *polite* is **unmarked**, whereas *impolite* is marked, in that it deviates from the 'unmarked' **form** by having an extra **morpheme**. Other examples can reveal implicit bias in our understanding and use of language. We can see this with the **word** *nurse*. While the dictionary definition of *nurse* does not specify gender, it may well be the case that the majority of **L1** English speakers will picture someone who cares for those who are unwell and is also female. This is evident from the fact that speakers of English will sometimes use the marked **phrase** *male nurse* to refer to someone who cares for unwell people and who is male. The fact that we must literally mark *nurse* with the **adjective** *male* shows that the unmarked *nurse* is generally assumed to be used for women only. Consider also this title from an internet news article: 'The 30 Most Impressive Female Engineers Alive Today'. By modifying *engineer* with *female*, the writer (i) presupposes that the unmarked form *engineer* refers to male engineers only, and (ii) implies that the female engineers referred to are not among the 30 most impressive engineers in the world generally. We can see similar bias in morphological marking. Consider, for example, *actor* and *actress*, *host* and *hostess*, and *Count* and *Countess*. In each case, it is the form that refers to women that takes the **suffix**. The **base form** in each case refers by default to men. Markedness and its implicit sexism also extends to titles. Note, for instance, that while *Mr* simply refers to an adult male, the equivalent titles for women, *Mrs* and *Miss*, also convey marital status. Attempts to counter marked forms are often made difficult by the fact that sexism is so deeply ingrained in language use. Ms as an alternative to *Mrs* or *Miss*, for example, inevitably indicates a conscious choice to avoid the connotations of *Mrs* and *Miss*. In this respect, *Ms* cannot be an unmarked, neutral form in the way that *Mr* is, until it is the only form used for women.

In fact, with developments towards gender fluidity and other social changes, it is more likely that address forms as a whole will change more radically or be dropped altogether.

mass noun

A mass noun is a **noun** whose **referent** is treated as not measurable in units, and which cannot therefore be pluralised by the addition of the plural **morpheme** <s> or its **allomorphs** <es> and <ies> (unlike **countable nouns**). For example, *help, foliage, nonsense* and *knowledge* are mass nouns because **helps, *foliages, *nonsenses* and **knowledges* are ungrammatical **forms**. To express the plural of a mass noun, we instead need to use a **quantifier** such as *some, a lot of, less* or *more*; for example, *some help, a lot of foliage, less nonsense* and *more knowledge*. Some nouns can be both mass nouns and countable nouns. *Television* is an example. If used to refer to television as a medium, then it is a mass noun, as in '*Television* nowadays is excellent.' If used to refer to individual television sets, however, it is countable, e.g. 'We have three televisions in our house.' Sometimes a mass noun can be pluralised by the addition of <s> if the unit of measurement is implied (e.g. 'Two beers please', where *beers* implies *pints of beer*). And some mass nouns can be pluralised with <s> in particular contexts only – for instance, *persons* is acceptable in legal contexts, whereas in everyday **language** the more common plural of *person* is *people*. Whether a noun is a mass noun or a countable noun can also be dependent on the **variety** of the language. In Hong Kong and Singapore English, for example, the noun *staff* may be countable (e.g. 'our department has ten staffs') while in British English it is a mass noun ('we have ten members of staff').

meaning

This term can have different meanings in the study of **language**. We can talk about semantic meaning, as in '*Happiness* means "the state of being happy"', or we can talk about meaning in terms of translation, as in '*Gladje* means *happiness* in Swedish.' What is generally agreed on among those who study lexical **semantics** is that **word forms** are arbitrary and do not have intrinsic meaning.

For instance, it is an accident of history that *cat* means a four-legged feline in English, with the written and spoken forms of the **word** just happening to be associated with the animal in question. Other aspects of language also have their own specific types of meaning. For example, the **pragmatics** of a language refers to the meanings that arise from the use of language in particular contexts, such as the fact that, in a railway station, a sign saying 'Trains' can probably be interpreted as meaning 'This way to the trains', rather than being a simple denotational **reference**. We could also talk about textual, or literary, meaning in relation to the meaning conferred upon words and structures by being arranged in particular ways and with particular social roles to play. The word is, therefore, both useful as a general term at times, and also too vague to be used for the kind of precision needed in **linguistics**.

meronymy

This refers to a **sense relation** between **words** that refer to parts and wholes. A meronym is a word that refers to a part of a whole. So, *branch* is a meronym of *tree*, *wheel* is a meronym of *car*, and *string*, *tuning peg* and *bridge* are meronyms of *guitar*. The converse relation is **holonym**: *tree* is the holonym of *leaf*. Meronyms can be used in **metonymy**.

mesolect

A mesolect is a **variety** of a **language** that is considered to be midway between an **acrolect** and a **basilect** in terms of **syntax** and **semantics**, as well as **prestige**. The term is used particularly in relation to the **creole** continuum, where the acrolect represents the standard **form** of the language on which the creole is based, and the basilect the creole form.

metalanguage

This is the language that we use to talk about language. The associated adjective is *metalinguistic*. So, terms such as **clause**, **sentence**, **noun**, **adverbial**, **affix** and so on are metalinguistic terms. In effect, *The Babel Lexicon of Language* is a book about metalanguage. The **prefix** *meta* comes from Greek and means 'at a higher level'.

metonymy

This is a figure of speech in which a **word** is used to refer to something related to the word's usual **meaning**. For example, the word *dish* refers to a piece of crockery, but it can also be used to stand for a particular example of prepared food (because the food is typically served in a dish). If you ordered the *dish of the day*, and the waiter brought you an empty ceramic dish, then you would probably feel cheated, as you would have assumed that *dish* here was standing for something like stew or pasta. Think also of all the different words for body parts that can be used in place of *person* or *people*. For example, you might want some *hired muscle* to help when moving house, or a football manager may bring on *a fresh pair of legs* before a match goes into extra time. Metonymy is a common source of **polysemy** and meaning change.

Middle English

Middle English (ME) refers to the English language as it was spoken in the British Isles between approximately 1100 and 1450. Middle English differs from **Old English** (approximately 450 to 1100) by virtue of its relative lack of **inflections** and its growing dependence on **word order** to indicate **sentence meaning**. Middle English is also characterised by its significant borrowing of Norman-French **vocabulary** – **words** such as *government, parliament, defend, guard, feast, sculpture* and *courageous*. In fact, the influx of words from French during the Middle English period is partly the reason why **Present Day English** has such a large number of **synonyms**. Perhaps the most famous exponent of Middle English is Geoffrey Chaucer, whose unfinished work *The Canterbury Tales* tells the story of a medieval pilgrimage and describes and satirises Middle English society at all levels. 'The General Prologue' to *The Canterbury Tales* is indicative of Chaucer's poetry: 'Whan that Aprill with his shoures soote / The droghte of March hath perced to the roote [...] Thanne longen folk to goon on pilgrimages' ('When April with its sweet showers / Has pierced the drought of March to the root [...] Then folk long to go on pilgrimages').

mind style

This is a term from **stylistics** coined by Roger Fowler to describe the
distinctive linguistic representation of idiosyncratic (i.e. distinctive and
unique to an individual) fictional minds. One of the most famous
examples of mind style in fiction occurs in William Faulkner's *The
Sound and The Fury*, where the first person narrator, Benjy Compton,
describes watching a game of golf: 'Through the fence, between the
curling flower spaces, I could see them hitting.' Benjy's intransitive use
of the **verb** *hit* (as opposed to saying 'I could see them hitting a ball') is
suggestive of both a lack of understanding of what he is observing and
a degree of cognitive limitation (for example, does Benjy understand
cause-and-effect relations?). Mind style can be represented through
a wide range of linguistic devices. In J. M. Barrie's *Peter Pan*, for instance,
the narrator uses the conceptual metaphor (*see* **conceptual metaphor
theory**) CHILDREN ARE COMMODITIES to suggest an unusual mind style
on the part of Wendy's parents, Mr and Mrs Darling. Following
Wendy's birth, they discuss dispassionately whether or not they can
afford to keep their daughter, in much the same manner as discussing
whether or not to return an item to a shop:

> For a week or two after Wendy came it was doubtful whether they
> would be able to keep her, as she was another mouth to feed. Mr
> Darling was frightfully proud of her, but he was very honourable,

and he sat on the edge of Mrs Darling's bed, holding her hand and calculating expenses, while she looked at him imploringly. She wanted to risk it, come what might, but that was not his way; his way was with a pencil and a piece of paper.

Mind style can be conveyed at all **levels of language** and is usually the result of some form of linguistic **deviation**. Current work on mind style is examining the linguistic representation of autistic minds with a view to improving our understanding of this complex condition.

minimal pair

This term from **phonetics** describes a pair of **words** that are differentiated only by one **phoneme**, e.g. *bed/bad*, *wet/met* and *speak/spook*. What minimal pairs demonstrate is that although phonemes don't carry **meaning** themselves, they nevertheless allow us to differentiate words. One of the writers of this book once made a minimal pair-related mistake when attempting to write a text message in Hungarian. Instead of *Hol vagy?* ('Where are you?'), the unfortunate academic mistakenly wrote *Hal vagy* ('You are a fish').

minor sentence

A minor sentence is a structure with no main **verb** and thus no **clause** structure. It may be a single **word** (*Yes*) or resemble a **phrase**, such as a **noun phrase** (*the middle drawer on the right*), and in everyday speech is often part of a longer sequence of interaction (e.g. in answer to the question 'Where is the cutlery?').

minority language

Minority languages are **languages** that are spoken by a minority among a population. For example, Welsh is considered a minority language in Wales, although attempts at language revitalisation may see this change in time. Minority status, in this sense, does not mean that a language is in any way negligible – Welsh has official-language status in Wales. Minority languages can also be (largely) used in just one region of a particular nation – Cornish is a minority language in England.

modal verb

A modal verb is a type of **auxiliary verb**. In English, there are nine modal verbs: *can, could, may, might, must, shall, should, will* and *would* (plus, sometimes, *need* and *dare*). Modal verbs indicate likelihood, permission, obligation or ability. In this respect, modal verbs reveal something about the speaker or writer's attitude to the **proposition** they are expressing. For example, 'You *can* go to the party' expresses permission, while 'You *must* go to the party' expresses obligation. Note that modal verbs can express multiple modal **meanings**. For instance, while the modal verb *can* can express permission (as in 'You *can* go to the party'), it can also express ability (as in 'I'm so glad you can go to the party'). *See also* **semi-modals, boulomaic modality, deontic modality** and **epistemic modality**.

modality

This refers to both the system of **verbs** (in English) that produce modal **meaning**, and the wider capacity of **language** to produce these meanings. Modality refers to the introduction of some kind of doubt or hypotheticality into the **proposition** of a **sentence** or **utterance**. The prototypical way to introduce this in English is to use a **modal verb** (*can, could, may, might, must, shall, should, will, would* – and sometimes *need* and *dare*) in front of the main verb, as in 'He might come' or 'She could arrive.' But there are many other ways of achieving the same effect, using **adverbs** (e.g. *possibly, certainly, hopefully*) or **adjectives** (*possible, certain*) – or even using **intonation** (e.g. rising **tone** to indicate uncertainty) or non-verbal cues (a shrug). There are two main categories of modality: **epistemic modality** and **deontic/boulomaic modality**. Epistemic modality refers to the certainty (or uncertainty) of something happening (or not). It can be strong ('He'll certainly come') or weak ('He might possibly come'). Deontic modality refers to what the speaker wishes would be the case ('I hope he comes'), and boulomaic modality refers to what the speaker thinks ought to happen ('He should come'). These latter are related in being linked to the speaker's own wishes and desires, rather than some concept of reality. *See also* **categorical assertion**.

modifier

A modifier is a **word**, **phrase** or **clause** that restricts the **reference** or enhances the **meaning** of another part of the clause or **sentence** in which it occurs. For example, in the **noun phrase** *the eminent* *linguist with the young son who lives in Russia*, the **head noun** *linguist* is premodified by the **adjective** *eminent* and postmodified by the **prepositional phrase** *with the young son* and the **relative clause** *who lives in Russia* (*see* **premodification** and **postmodification**). In the sentence 'Matt spoke very excitedly', the **verb** *spoke* is modified by the **adverb** *excitedly*, which itself is modified by the adverb *very*. Sometimes, a modifier can introduce ambiguity into a sentence. For example, in the sentence 'I saw the cat with the binoculars', it is not clear whether the prepositional phrase *with the binoculars* is postmodifying the head noun *cat* or whether it is functioning as an adverbial that is modifying the **verb phrase** *saw*. Ambiguous modifiers like these are known as *dangling modifiers*. Whatever you do, don't let your modifiers dangle.

monolingual

This term refers to both the person who speaks only one **language**, and the condition of being such a person. Although there is a tendency for some to see this as the natural condition of human beings (to speak the language of their community and only that language), this is unrepresentative of how most humans on the planet live their lives, as only 40 per cent of the world's population is monolingual. *See also* **bilingual**, **multilingual**.

monophthong

A **vowel** that has a single, stable quality with no obvious changes in the movement of the **tongue** during its production can be described as a monophthong. Monophthongs are considered to be pure vowels as they have the same quality at the beginning of their production as they do at the end of their production. Monophthongs can be contrasted with **diphthongs**, where the vowel quality changes during the production of the vowel sound. Monophthongs are easy to spot in **spectrograms** as their first and second **formants** will be relatively flat; you should not see upward or downward **glides** in the formants. In West Yorkshire (Northern England), it is very common for the vowel from the **word** *face*, /eɪ/, to undergo the process of monophthongisation. As a result, the two-quality vowel sound becomes a single, quite stable vowel quality that is often produced as something close to a long [e] or [ɛ].

mood

This is a grammatical **category**. In many **languages**, mood is indicated through **inflections** on **verbs**, which indicate whether a **sentence** (or **utterance**) is, for example, a statement, a command or a desire. For example, questions are in the **interrogative** mood, while statements are in the **declarative** mood, and commands are in the **imperative** mood. Mood can be difficult to recognise in English though, as the **form** of the verb does not always change. For example, the form of the verb in the imperative 'Enjoy!' is the same as in the declarative 'I enjoy good food.' There are many different grammatical moods and not all languages have all of them. The use of grammatical mood can also change over time. For example, the **subjunctive** mood is used much less frequently in English than it used to be. The subjunctive indicates something that the speaker or writer wishes for. Compare, for instance, the following statements: 'Dan insisted that Hazel works all day' and 'Dan insisted that Hazel work all day.' The former can be paraphrased as 'Dan insisted he was right in saying that Hazel works all day.' The latter, on the other hand, is different in **meaning** because the verb *work* is in the subjunctive mood. Consequently, it can be paraphrased as 'Dan insisted that Hazel should work all day.' Because the subjunctive is arguably dying out in English (using it can sound rather formal), some speakers do not recognise it and may even assume a verb in the subjunctive mood to be incorrectly conjugated. This lack of awareness of the subjunctive can also lead to misunderstandings of what particular **phrases** mean. For example, the line 'God save the Queen' in the British national anthem is hard to interpret unless you know that the verb is in the subjunctive mood, meaning that the line can be paraphrased as 'I hope that God will save the Queen.'

morpheme

A morpheme is the smallest meaningful grammatical unit in the structure of a **language**, – i.e. morphemes cannot be further divided into meaningful units. Note that the smallest meaningful speech sound – the **phoneme** – has the capacity to change **meaning**, but doesn't carry it. The study of morphemes and how they combine is called **morphology**. Morphemes can be free or bound. **Free morphemes** are those that can stand alone (e.g. *establish, run, sing,* *table, moon*). A free morpheme is often referred to as the ***root, stem*** or **base form**. A **bound morpheme** is a morpheme that is not a **word** on its own (e.g. the *-ed* on *established* or the *-s* on *moons*). Below is an example of how bound and free morphemes can combine to create words:

Bound morpheme (prefix)	Free morpheme (root)	Bound morpheme (suffix)
un	feel	ing
	unfeeling	

The two grammatical **Categories** of morpheme are ***derivational morphemes*** and ***inflectional morphemes***. Derivational morphemes are those that change the **semantic** meaning of a word, and often the **word class** of the word, e.g. *chair* (**noun**) → *chairing* (**verb**). Inflectional morphemes are those that indicate grammatical information such as the **tense**, **number** or **case** of a word – e.g. *chair* → *chairs* (number), *prove* → *proven* (tense) and *I* → *me* (case) – but don't change the semantics of the free morpheme itself. The number of morphemes a language has is indicative of whether it is **fusional**, ***isolating*** (*see* **synthetic language**) or ***agglutinative*** (*see* **agglutination**), although most languages have features of each of these types. *See also* **affix**, **prefix**, **suffix** and **derivation**.

morphology

This is the study of the grammatical structure of **words**. It focuses on **morphemes**, the smallest units of **grammar** in **language**. For example, the **verb** *talked* consists of two morphemes: <talk> and <ed>. <Talk> might strike us as the more meaningful morpheme here since it can be a word on its own. The morpheme <ed> also has its own **meaning**, though, which we might summarise as 'in the past' – it's just that it only has meaning when combined with other morphemes. <Talk> is an example of a **free morpheme**, while <ed> is a **bound morpheme**. Even if we don't have particular expertise as morphologists, our familiarity with the structure of words, and the patterns we recognise in how words are structured, means that we can easily construct or understand the meanings of words that we may never have heard before. For instance, if you are familiar with Facebook, or similar social networks, then you were probably able to pick apart the meaning of *unfriended* when it first came into common usage, simply by recognising that it consisted of the free morpheme <friend> and the bound morphemes <un> and <ed>. Likewise, even if we come across an unfamiliar and extremely lengthy word such as *antidisestablishmentarianism*, we are able to use our awareness of the structure of words in English to figure out its rough meaning.

WILL YOU STOP TALKING ABOUT *MORPHOLOGY?* I'M FED UP OF HEARING ABLAUT IT!

motherese
See **baby talk**.

multi-word unit
Multi-word units are strings of multiple **words** that cannot be separated without a loss of **meaning**. In this way, we can see them as equivalent to individual words. **phrasal verbs** are an example of multi-word units – the meaning of *hang up* (to end a phone call) cannot be worked out by simply adding together its constituent

parts *hang* + *up* (at least, not unless you have specific knowledge of what phones originally looked like and how they operated). Similarly, someone whose **L1** (i.e. first language) is not English is unlikely to be able to figure out the precise meaning of *throw up* based only on their knowledge of the meaning of the constituent **verb** and **adverb**. **idioms** are also multi-word units and can be much lengthier than phrasal verbs. Common examples are *as cool as a cucumber* or *kick the bucket*, each of which has a different meaning from its constituent words. Often, these multi-word units are synonymous with single **lexical items**, e.g. *cool* or *relaxed*, and *die*. Idioms in **languages** that we are not familiar with can often be mystifying and intriguing. French *avoir les dents longues* literally translates as 'to have long teeth', but it would take an L1 French speaker to explain that this idiom means 'to have ambitious goals'. Idioms can also cause confusion between speakers of a single language. For instance, there have been many reports of cases where misunderstandings have resulted from literal interpretations of the idiom *Netflix and chill* (a **euphemism** for sexual activity).

multilingual

This is a term used to refer to any individual who speaks more than one **language** – so, anyone who is **bilingual** or speaks even more than two languages is multilingual. Regardless of their particular languages, multilinguals have a first language (sometimes referred to with the abbreviation **L1**) and second or other languages (L2, etc.). Perhaps unsurprisingly, not everyone agrees on the matter of degree. Are you multilingual if German is your L1 and you can also ask for a bottle of wine in French? Different people view *multilingual* as signifying different levels of command over the languages involved, but most would agree that you need not have a **native-speaker** level of competence in your L2 in order to consider yourself multilingual.

N

n-gram

An n-gram is a sequence of **words** in a **corpus**. *N* simply stands for any number – i.e. a 4-gram is a 4-word sequence, a 5-gram is a 5-word sequence, and so on. For example, in a corpus of fairy tales *once upon a time* would constitute a 4-gram. N-grams are sometimes referred to as **lexical bundles** or ***clusters***, though some corpus analysis software packages use the terms slightly differently. For instance, AntConc, a corpus analysis tool, distinguishes between n-grams (repeated sequences of words) and clusters (repeated sequences containing a particular word; e.g. 4-word sequences that contain the word *animal*).

narrowing

This refers to a particular type of **meaning** change. In the UK, Christmas is often a time to eat mince pies, which are made of sweet pastry with mincemeat inside. These are sweet treats, and we might ask why the mincemeat inside consists of dried fruit rather than actual meat? Well, the use of the **word** *meat* to refer to food that isn't animal flesh stems from an earlier meaning of *meat* that meant food in general. In **semantic** terms, *meat* has undergone a process of narrowing. That is, its meaning has become more restricted and specific over time. This earlier **sense** of *meat* also explains the **Early Modern English** word *sweetmeat*, which was equivalent to *confectionery*. Other examples of narrowing include the word *liquor* (which originally meant liquid of any kind, rather than alcohol specifically, though the older meaning survives as a term in cookery). There's also the verb *to starve*, which comes from the **Old English verb** *steorfan*, which simply meant 'to die'. Over time, its meaning has narrowed so that it now means 'to die through lack of food', though in the **Middle English** period it meant 'to die as a result of cold'. (You can still hear the Middle English **sense** in some regional **dialects** of British English.)

nasal

This refers to the **manner of articulation** used for producing a particular set of **consonants** and nasal **vowels**. *Nasal* describes a group of sounds that are produced when air flows out of the **nasal cavity**. Nasal **phonemes** include /m/ and /n/. In order to articulate a nasal sound, the **velum** must be lowered in the oral tract to allow the air to flow through the nasal cavity. It is also important to add that nasal sounds are typically **voiced**; however, it is also possible to produce **voiceless** nasal sounds.

nasal cavity

The nasal cavity is the space just above the palate and behind the nose/nostrils. So far as we know, everyone's nasal cavity is of a different size and shape. However, the complex internal structures and large surface area inside the nasal cavity means that nasals sound 'dampened'.

native speaker

This term, denoting someone who was born into a particular **language** user group, is now seen as problematic for a range of socio-political reasons, but is still used on occasion, for want of a better option. The stereotype of the **monolingual** speaker of a language, where everyone in the nation-state speaks the same language, is clearly not close to representing most human beings' experience, which is more often one of multilingual speakers using their various languages for different functions. There is also an unspoken, but pervasive, tendency to perceive native speaker competence as superior to other **varieties**, whereas the reality, particularly in the English-speaking world, is that second language speakers are very often as fluent as first language speakers, but speak their own regional varieties of the language. *See* **L1** for a more neutral term.

Natural Language Processing

This is known as NLP for short. Much research in NLP is aimed at using computers to analyse vast quantities of natural language data more quickly and accurately than human analysts could. The term *natural language* refers to **languages** used to communicate among humans, as opposed to programming languages, which are used by humans to communicate with computers. A core component of NLP is the development of parsers. These are programs that automatically detect the structure (grammatical or otherwise) of constituent **sentences** of the natural language data set. NLP-derived technology can now be found in many areas of life, including internet search engines and predictive texting.

naturalisation

This refers to the process by which ideologies become embedded in social attitudes, to the extent that they are no longer seen as optional but become assumed as common-sense. Not strictly a linguistic term in itself, *naturalisation* is used extensively in **Critical Discourse Analysis** (CDA) and **critical stylistics** to link **language** choices in **texts** to the kinds of ideology that they are taking for granted.

negation

This refers to the linguistic process by which **words, phrases** and **utterances** can be either denied or inverted in **meaning**. The delivery of negation is prototypically by negative **particles** (*no, not*), but there are many other ways to negate at different levels of structure. Thus, we can include negators in **noun phrases** (*no two cakes*), to negate processes ('they do not live there') and at **sentence** level ('I will never write another novel'). In some **languages**, there is also morphological negation (*disinfectant, anaerobic*), as well as some **lexical items** that seem to include negation as part of their **semantics** (*miss, lack, fail*). Some grammarians would include only structural negation in a strict definition of the process, but these types of negation share a textual-pragmatic effect, which is to conjure up simultaneously both the negative and positive polarities in the reader's mind. Thus, to say 'Erica doesn't have a dog' is to produce the potential mental image of Erica with a dog, as well as the image of her without a dog. This can be a powerful tool for persuasion and influence, so it is included in the **critical stylistics** list of textual features that can carry ideological meaning.

neologism

In Roald Dahl's children's novel *The BFG*, the eponymous big friendly giant is a major propagator of neologisms. These include *babblement, whizzpopper, scrumdiddlyumptious* and *snapperwhippers*. A neologism is a newly invented **word**. Neologisms can be formed through numerous processes, e.g. acronymisation (*radar* from 'radio detection and ranging'), **blending** (*pixel*, a blend of *picture* and *element*), **clipping** (*exam* from *examination*) and **conversion** (*ask* as a **noun**, as opposed to *ask* as a **verb**). Some neologisms become absorbed into the mainstream **language**. Others (like some of the BFG's) don't, and remain as **nonce formations** – that is, words that are used only on single occasions.

Nim Chimpsky

Nim Chimpsky was a chimpanzee who was born in 1973 (d. 2000) and who became the subject of a study at Columbia University on animal **language** acquisition. Project Nim was led by Herbert S. Terrace and Thomas Bever who were interested in whether Noam Chomsky's hypothesis that only humans have language could be disproven. Nim was raised by a human family, in a home environment, from the age of 2 weeks old, and was taught American Sign Language. There was a lot of controversy surrounding Project Nim and the extent to which Nim was able to learn 'language'. However, it was generally accepted that Nim was able to learn fragments of American Sign Language to communicate, but lacked any real **grammar**.

nominalisation

This is the process by which **verbs** (and sometimes **adjectives**) can be made to function as **nouns** by the addition of an **affix** (*continuation, pursuance*) or by **zero derivation**, which means simply using a **word** as though it belonged to a different **word class**, without any additional structure. In English, the uninflected **infinitive** and present participles of verbs can readily be used as nouns, identified as such by their positioning in the **syntax** and by any modification suitable for the noun class ('Loud singing always makes me sad'). Although nominalisation is a common process in all **language** use, there are times when it can have the effect of

obscuring the identity of the **Actor** in the process ('Reduction in benefit payments is unavoidable'). It is therefore of particular interest to **Critical Discourse Analysis** and **critical stylistics** as it can be used to slant the presentation of a message without mentioning those responsible.

non-finite

This describes **verbs** (or **clauses** containing such verbs) that are not fully inflected according to the norms of the **language** concerned. Thus, in English, a fully inflected verb would be inflected for **number**, **tense** and **person**, but many non-finite verb **forms** occur in **subordinate clauses** with no such **inflections**:

Juggling work and family was a challenge for Lesley.

Here, the **subject** of the **sentence** is a non-finite clause (*Juggling work and family*) containing a non-finite **-*ing participle*** which indicates continuous **aspect**. *See also* **finite**.

non-fluency

This refers not to a lack of knowledge of the **vocabulary** or **grammar** of a **language** but to the inability to produce speech quickly and continuously. Stammering is a typical example of non-fluency, but there are others too, such as the inability to control the rate at which you speak, which can lead to speech that is too rapid to be easily comprehended. The Michael Palin Centre for Stammering Children (stammeringcentre.org) is a charity based in London that provides support and specialist services to children and young people affected by stammering, and training for speech and language therapists working in this area. Non-fluency, however, is something that affects everyone when they are speaking. Features of everyday non-fluency include **hesitation** and false starts, and these can be exacerbated by particular situations, such as giving a speech when you're not used to public speaking.

nonce formation

Like **neologism**, nonce formation is the invention of a new **word**, usually through the normal morphological processes of the **language** concerned. However, nonce formations are intended to be used only once in the context in which they are created, reflecting the **Middle English sense** of *nonce*, which derives from *anes*, meaning 'for the occasion'. That is, a nonce word is one formed for the specific occasion. In the British political comedy *The Thick of It*, the spin doctor Malcolm Tucker insults the Secretary of State, Nicola Murray, by describing her as an *omnishambles*, a nonce formation designed to express his intense level of irritation with her. Despite its origins as a nonce formation in the TV series, the word has since gained considerable traction in both spoken and written British English in relation to the world of politics itself.

noun

A noun is a **part of speech** that functions as the head of a **noun phrase**, as in *The bright blue racing car*. *Car* is the head of this **phrase**; without the **word** *car*, this phrase is incomplete. However, the head of a noun phrase is not always the final word. Sometimes the head word can be post-modified (as opposed to the **premodification** in the above example). Consider *The bright blue racing car that won the race.* Also, some noun phrases can be just one word long, as in the following **sentence**:

Noun phrase	Verb phrase	Noun phrase
Cows	*eat*	*grass*

A good test for a noun is to see whether you can put the **definite article** (*the*) before it. If you can, it's likely to be a noun. Typical **suffixes** for nouns include: *leader, racism, station, happiness, prosperity*. Some nouns (**countable nouns**) can also be pluralised by adding either *-s, -es* or *-ies*. Nouns often refer to physical things – e.g. people, places, objects, substances. These are concrete nouns. However, nouns can also refer to abstract concepts. Abstract nouns include: *happiness, love, anniversary, pain, thought*. Defining nouns by their form (e.g. what kind of suffixes or **prefixes** they can take) is difficult, since this can vary between **languages**. Defining nouns by their **meaning** (whether it is the name of a person, a place or a thing) is also difficult, since there are many cases where these **categories** don't adequately cover what a noun refers to (e.g. 'sadness', 'atmosphere'). Focusing on function, then, is the best way to explain what a noun is. What this means is that a noun is simply any word that behaves like a noun. *See also* **form and function** and **mass noun**.

noun phrase

Noun phrases have a **noun** as their **head word**. For example (head noun underlined):

- *a young dynamic lecturer*
- *the bright Huddersfield morning*
- *the beautiful garden with a Japanese maple*

Noun phrases can function as the **subject**, **object**, **complement** or **adverbial** in a **sentence**. *See also* **SPOCA**.

nucleus

In **phonology**, the nucleus is a component part of a **syllable**. Syllables are made up of **segments** (i.e. **vowels** and **consonants**) and it is the vowel that constitutes the nucleus. The preceding consonant (if there is one) is called the **onset**, and the consonant that follows the nucleus (again, optional) is called the **coda**. For example, the **word** *sleep* is composed of on onset consonant cluster /sl/, a nucleus /iː/ and a coda /p/.

number

This refers to the grammatical **category** that is associated with **nouns** and **pronouns** and the form of **verbs** that they require. Most **languages** distinguish between singular and plural versions of **countable nouns** (e.g. *dog/dogs*), and many have verb **inflections** that also reflect whether the **subject** of the verb is singular or plural (e.g. *the dog is black / the dogs are black*). Number in nouns is often marked by a **suffix** (as with <s> in English). Note that some languages have more than singular and plural number and can include dual number (e.g. early Slavic and Baltic languages, and some aspects of Russian and Arabic) and/or greater/smaller plurals (e.g. Austronesian languages of Sursurunga and Lihir).

object

The object in a **sentence** is the person or thing on which the **subject** acts. In the sentence 'Linguists adore books', *Linguists* is the subject (the entity doing the adoring) and *books* is the object (the entity being adored). The object is not as crucial an element of an English sentence as the subject and **predicator** (or **verb**), which are obligatory. Objects divide into direct objects and indirect objects. In 'The lecturers gave some students good marks', the direct object is *good marks* (the entity affected by the verb 'gave') and the indirect object is *some students* (note that the information provided by *some students* is more dispensable than that provided by *good marks*). *See also* **Goal**, **SPOCA**, **complement** and **adverbial**.

obstruent

Obstruent **consonants** are those that cause some kind of significant obstruction to the **airflow** between the **larynx** and the **lips**. They can be **voiced** (i.e. with the **vocal folds** vibrating) or **voiceless** (with no such vibration), but they involve **turbulence** (in the case of **fricatives**) or a complete stoppage (in the case of **plosives**) of the air leaving the **lungs**. They are differentiated phonetically from the **sonorants**, which include all the **vowels**, **nasals** and **approximants**.

Old English

Old English (OE) is the term given to the earliest form of English spoken in Great Britain, between approximately 450 and 1100. Old English was an offshoot of Germanic and is an **analytic language**. That is, **word order** is of less importance in Old English than it is in **Present Day English** because the function of a **word** in OE (whether it is, say, a **subject** or an **object**) is indicated by an **inflection** on the **noun**, rather than by its position in the **sentence**.

Old English is sometimes referred to as *Anglo-Saxon*, after its speakers, though the term *Anglo-Saxon* is more commonly used to refer to the culture as a whole, rather than the language specifically. **Linguists** have identified four **dialects** of Old English: West Saxon, Kentish, Mercian and Northumbrian. West Saxon was spoken in the area south of the River Thames and, by the late 800s, had emerged as a kind of literary standard, primarily as a consequence of it being the dialect used by King Alfred in his translations of Latin **texts**. Kentish was spoken by the Jutes, in Kent, in south-east England. Mercian was spoken in the area between the Thames and the River Humber in the north of England. Northumbrian was spoken north of the Humber. Mercian and Northumbrian exhibit a number of similarities which leads to them sometimes being grouped together and referred to as Anglian. Our knowledge of Old English and its dialects is gleaned from a relatively small amount of data. Only around 3 million words of Old English writing have survived, so it is perhaps not surprising that linguists have only been able to determine four dialects with any confidence, especially when we consider that Anglo-Saxon culture was largely oral. It is, of course, likely that there were more than these four dialects in use at the time (*see* **Uniformitarian Principle** for an explanation of the reason we are able to assume this).

onomatopoeia

This refers to the ability of speech to directly represent the sounds that it refers to. Although most **reference** is arbitrary in form, all **languages** nevertheless have a small subset of **words** which are recognised as being onomatopoeic, though their **phonetic** detail is conditioned by the language in which they occur, which is why dogs go *woof, woof* in English but *ouah, ouah* in French. It is not only animal noises that are onomatopoeic, though. Many sounds reflect their **meaning**, whether these are resonant as in *clang* or *bang*, or more sharp and definite sounds such as *clap* or *thud*. More interestingly, perhaps, the individual sounds of a language can be used for similar effects when they are concentrated into a small amount of **text**. This happens commonly in poetic language, as in the famous poem 'Anthem for Doomed Youth' by Wilfred Owen, which bemoans the loss of so many young lives in the First World War. His lines 'Only the

stuttering rifles' rapid rattle / Can patter out their hasty orisons' contain a concentration of sharp **plosive** sounds (/t/, /p/, /d/, /k/) and short **vowels**, particularly /æ/, which evoke the repeated sounds of distant but insistent rifle fire on the front line of the war. While the alliteration of the /ɹ/ at the beginning of three words in a row ('rifles' rapid rattle') could be seen as adding to this effect (particularly if they are pronounced with a **flap** or a **trill**, rather than a softer **approximant** version of /ɹ/), this sequence of initial **consonants** may be seen more as symbolising the repetition of the shooting rather than the sounds themselves. A subtler and yet still noticeable effect is found in the non-initial **consonants**.

onset

This is the term used in **phonology** to describe one of the parts of a spoken **syllable**. Syllables are considered to have two main parts, the onset (which will be consonantal) and the **rhyme**, which in turn is made up of two parts, the **nucleus** (i.e. the **vowel** component) and the **coda** (more **consonants**). So, a one-syllable **word** such as 'spilt' has two consonants /sp/ making up the onset, a short vowel /ɪ/ as its nucleus, and two further consonants /lt/ as its coda. The description of the possible combinations of consonants in the onset (and coda) of syllables in any one **language** is known as the *phonotactics* of that language.

open class

Most **words** are open-class words. Open-class words carry the most **meaning** in a **sentence**. Using words from this class, we can coin new words. Here are some examples of open-class words:

Open class	Common abbreviation	Examples
noun	N	*dog, sun, happiness, future, shock*
verb	V	*walk, knew, believe, did, falls, left*
adjective	Aj	*small, bright, friendly, red, furry*
adverb	Av	*slowly, well, very, happily*

To identify open-class words, there are three criteria we can consider:

1. **Meaning** What kind of meaning does the word have? What does it express or refer to? If you learned any **grammar** at school, then this is probably the criterion you concentrated on. You may remember **verbs** being referred to as 'doing' words, **nouns** as 'things', and **adjectives** as 'describing' words. These definitions are descriptions of the meaning of these words. The problem, though, is that not all verbs are 'doing' words (consider *is, believe* and *know*), not all nouns are things (what about *love* and *sadness*?) and not all adjectives are describing words (think about *main* and *principal*). Its not enough, therefore, to concentrate on the meaning of a word in order to work out its **word class**.
2. **Form** We can identify the word class that a word belongs to in part by looking at its **form**. Certain words have **suffixes** that are characteristic of particular word classes – e.g.:

    bounciness (N), *clarify* (V), *electrical* (Aj), *inexcusably* (Av)

Suffixes that can be added to words can also indicate the word class to which a word belongs – e.g.:

bottle + *s* (N), *walk* + *ed* (V), *short* + *er/est* (Aj)

These suffixes are called **inflections**. Unlike some **languages**, English doesn't have many inflections (the main ones are *-s/es, -ed, -ing, -er, -est, -'s*). Notice too that some inflections in English are irregular, and involve either a change in the **vowel** in a word (compare *man* and *men*) or a complete change in the word (e.g. *went* as the past tense form of the verb *go*).

3. **Function** We can also look at the function that a word has in a sentence – that is, the role that it has relative to the other words. This is by far the most reliable indicator of word class. The importance of function in deciding which class a word belongs to can be seen in the following sentence:

'Can you *fool* a *fool*?'

The first *fool* in the sentence above is a verb and the second *fool* is a noun. But we can't tell this distinction from the meaning of the word, nor from the form of the word, as both are exactly the same. Instead we have to look at the function of the words in the sentence to determine their **part of speech**.

Open-class words are also known as **lexical words** or **content words**.

See also **form and function**.

opposition

This refers to the **sense relation** between **lexical items** that differ significantly in one aspect of their **meaning**. Lexical items that are *opposites* usually share most of their *semantic components*, apart from the one that distinguishes them. Thus, *long* and *short* are both **words** describing measurement along one dimension, but they differ in which end of that dimension they refer to. *Lexical semantics* recognises a number of (logically) different types of opposition. These include **complementaries, gradable antonyms, converses, relational opposites, reversive opposites** and **directional opposites**. Because opposition is a relation between **senses** (or possibly uses) of words, a single word may have several different opposites. For example, *black* is often the opposite of *white*, but when thinking about wine, the opposite of *white* is *red*, and when thinking of traffic signals, the opposite of *red* is *green*. Oppositions can also be created locally in context, as in 'That's a cowpat, not a roundabout!', said about a village road junction that is smaller than the speaker is accustomed to. These contextual opposites rely for our understanding on the idea of lexical opposition in general. These created opposites can create a binary view of the world which has ideological implications, and are therefore part of the framework of **critical stylistics**. *See also* **antonym**.

oral cavity

The oral cavity refers generally to the mouth. The oral cavity includes everything from the **lips** to the cheeks, **teeth, alveolar** ridge, **hard palate, tongue**, underneath the tongue (the floor of the mouth), **velum** and uvula (*see* **uvular**). The oral cavity plays a vital role in the production of the majority of the world's speech sounds.

overextension

This is a common phenomenon in children's speech. When they acquire **language**, children often learn a **word** and use it correctly, but also use it for things that the word does not fit. For instance, a child might point to the family cat and use the word *cat*, but also use *cat* when pointing to a dog at the park. And many of us may once have been embarrassed when calling a teacher *mum* in class. **Underextension** is the opposite phenomenon.

overt prestige

This refers to the **prestige** associated with **forms** of **language** that are generally assumed by non-linguists to be socially desirable. This sometimes stems from a misapprehension that certain forms of language are correct, while others are not. An obsession with overt prestige can in some cases lead to **hypercorrection**, such as pronouncing /h/ where it is not required ('Hi habsolutely love horse-riding'), or ignoring the norms of **connected speech** in favour of full pronunciations. *See also* **covert prestige**.

oxymoron

This is a term used to refer to apparent contradictions in **texts**, where the juxtaposition of two **words** or **phrases** appears incongruous. These can be common, everyday phrases, as in *open secret* or *deafening silence*, but they may also be more creative as in *splendidly awful* or *fascinatingly boring*.

paradigmatic

This refers to a relationship between members of the same linguistic **category** – for example the grammatical category of **verbs**. If you take the **sentence** 'The linguist swam', then we can see a paradigmatic relationship between the chosen verb – *swam* – and all the other possible verbs that were not selected, e.g. *ran, sang, meditated*. We can think of it as a vertical relationship – imagine a sort of mental dropdown box when you get to the verb position, from which you choose the verb you want. Paradigmatic relations are different from **syntagmatic** relations, which we can think of as being horizontal. That is, the **word class** of one **word** determines the possible word classes to which the next word in the sentence can belong. For example, in the sentence 'The linguist swam', the initial **definite article** determines that the next word must be an **adjective** or a **noun** (in this case, it is a noun), since to put, say, a verb in the next slot would be **ungrammatical**.

parallelism

This is a term from **stylistics** and, along with **deviation**, is one of the causes of **foregrounding** in **language**. Parallelism involves repetition – but not just of **words**. Parallelism can occur at every level of language. This tongue twister, for instance, contains simple phonological parallelism in its repetition of /p/: 'Peter Piper picked a peck of pickled peppers.' This repetition of /p/ is unusual, and therefore foregrounded. But parallelism can be much more complex, as in this example from E. E. Cummings's autobiographical novel *The Enormous Room*, in which Cummings's father writes to the US President, Woodrow Wilson, to ask for help in freeing his son, who had been arrested by French authorities (**sentences** are numbered):

(1) The mothers of our boys in France have rights as well as the boys themselves. (2) My boy's mother had a right to be protected from the weeks of horrible anxiety and suspense caused by the inexplicable arrest and imprisonment of her son. (3) My boy's mother had a right to be spared the supreme agony caused by a blundering cable from Paris saying that he had been drowned by a submarine. [...] (4) My boy's mother and all American mothers have a right to be protected against all needless anxiety and sorrow.

(E. E. Cummings, *The Enormous Room*, 1922)

Sentences 2 and 3 in the above extract are syntactically parallel. That is, they each have the same underlying grammatical structure, consisting of a **subject** made up of a pre-modified **noun phrase** (*My boy's mother*), a **predicator** made up of a single-word **verb phrase** in the past **tense** (*had*), and an **object** consisting of a post-modified noun phrase whose **head word** is *right*. Sentence 4 varies only slightly, by extending the subject noun phrase and shortening the **post-modification** of the object. The effect of parallelism (apart from a general foregrounding effect) is to push the reader to see the parallel components either as similar in terms of propositional content (*see* **proposition**), or as opposites. Here, the sentiment expressed in sentences 2, 3 and 4 is essentially the same. The parallelism helps to build a rhetorical effect that reinforces the **meaning** being conveyed. For this reason, parallelism is extremely common in both advertising and political speeches.

parole

Parole is the French **word** for *speech*, and in **linguistics** is a piece of specialist terminology that was introduced by Ferdinand de Saussure as a contrast to the term **langue**. While *langue* refers to the underpinning **rules** and conventions of **language**, *parole* refers to the external realisation of language – that is, speech or writing. The concept of *parole* is similar to Noam Chomsky's **performance**. *See also* **E-language**.

parser

A parser is a piece of software used in **corpus linguistics** and **Natural Language Processing** that automatically identifies the **clause** elements in a **corpus** of **texts**. That is, a parser will automatically work out whether a **noun phrase** is functioning as, say, a **subject** or a **complement**. The decisions that parsers make are often based on statistics about **language**. For instance, the parser will consider how frequently noun phrases tend to be used as subjects, as opposed to complements, in **sentences**, and thereby work out the probability that the noun phrase is a subject. Parsers can also be rule-based – that is, decisions are made on the basis of descriptive **rules** about the structures that are allowed in an acceptable sentence in a given language.

part of speech

Part of speech (POS) is the term used in some **grammar** books to refer to **word class**. It has also been adopted in some areas of **linguistics** (e.g. **corpus linguistics**) to refer to the tags (*POS tags*) added to electronic databases of **texts** to identify the **verbs**, **nouns**, etc. Essentially a part of speech or word class (e.g. **determiner** or **preposition**) is a group of words that function in similar ways in the **syntax** of a **language**. Traditionally derived from knowledge of Latin grammar, these classes are now systematically discovered in the process of linguistic description.

participant

This is a useful term that has a number of different applications in **linguistics**. In the most straightforward usage, it refers to people who may be participating in some research, by being interviewed or recorded, taking part in an experiment or answering a questionnaire. The more technical usage refers to the role that is taken by someone in an interaction (*see* **participant roles**).

participant roles

The influential sociologist Erving Goffman developed the concept of participant roles to explain the various roles that a participant can fulfil during an interaction. Goffman observed that the terms *speaker* and *hearer* do not fully capture the range of roles that participants can take in a conversation. For instance, with regard to speakers, we can make a distinction between an *animator* (the person who articulates the message; i.e. literally speaks it), an *author* (the person responsible for putting together the content of the message) and a *principal* (the person who is responsible for the message being conveyed). In some cases, a speaker may fulfil all of these roles at once, but it is also possible for these roles to be taken by different people. For example, imagine a speech being given by a politician (the animator), which was written by a speechwriter (the author) on the instructions of the Chair of the political party in question (the principal). With regard to hearers, these can be divided into **ratified** and **unratified** participants. A ratified participant is one who is expected to hear the message being conveyed (note, of course, that a ratified hearer may not actually be able to hear the message, or may choose not to pay attention to it). Ratified hearers include the **addressed recipient** (the person to whom the message is being directed – sometimes called the **addressee**) and the **unaddressed recipients** (people who are not specifically being addressed but who are intended to hear the message – think, for example, of a teacher asking a child a question in front of the rest of the class). All of the above participant roles are part of what Goffman calls a **participation framework**.

particle

This refers to **words** that don't belong in the main **word classes** (**noun**, **verb**, **adjective**, **adverb**, **preposition**, etc.) and, as well as being invariable in **form**, have little **semantic** (i.e. denotative or connotative) **meaning**. They usually have a grammatical function, such as marking an **infinitive** form in English (e.g. *to sing*, *to dance*) or forming part of a **phrasal verb** (e.g. *bring up*; *set out*) where the particle does not contribute a separate identifiable part of the meaning of the whole **phrase**. Other types of particle, such as *oh* or *well* have a **pragmatic** function, usually as a **discourse marker**. Particles are related to **interjections**, which are words or sounds that convey emotional meaning rather than semantic meaning (e.g. *grrr*, *ugh*).

passive

A passive structure is one which reverses the normal focal position of the **Actor** and **Goal** in a **clause** – in English, by using the passive **auxiliary** *be* followed by the past participle, as in 'The roof was mended by the builders', 'Turkey is eaten at Christmas' and 'The car had been damaged'. These structures are implicitly paired with equivalent **active** structures. They have useful potential in textual **meaning** for focusing on a different clause element from the active structure – and for omitting the Actor when they are not known, or when it is convenient to background them.

pattern grammar

This is an approach to **grammar** that is based on the **idiom principle** that we form **sentences** (or **utterances**) primarily by using fixed patterns of **language** (as opposed to constructing sentences word-by-word). The corpus linguists Susan Hunston and Gill Francis explain this by using the expression *I must confess* as an example. Under the terms of the idiom principle, *I must confess* operates as a single **lexical item** and means something like 'I'm going to tell you something that I'm embarrassed about or that I regret.' We can see this in the following example from the **British National Corpus** (BNC): 'I must confess that I tend to go and make a pot of tea whenever election coverage starts.' However, the expression can also be interpreted using the *open choice principle*, in which case it means something like 'I am obliged to own up to something that I've done wrong', as in this example from the BNC: 'Before I die I must confess what I've done wrong.' One test for whether an expression constitutes a pattern (i.e. an **idiom**) is whether its **meaning** changes if we alter the **words** in it. For example, if we change the **pronoun** in *I must confess* (e.g. 'She must confess that she tends to go and make a pot of tea whenever election coverage starts'), the idiom principle meaning is lost and we are left instead with the open choice interpretation. Pattern grammar differs from, for example, structuralist grammar (*see* **structuralism**) by suggesting that speakers form sentences by combining patterns rather than by filling syntactic slots with individual words.

pejoration

This is a process by which a **word** begins with a neutral or positive **meaning** and, over time, is downgraded to a more negative meaning (*see* **amelioration** for the opposite of pejoration). Unfortunately, there are many more examples of pejoration taking place than amelioration, and there is no stopping the process of pejoration. As **language** is always changing, this means that some words will continue to develop more negative meanings over time. You may think of pejoration as good words going bad – below is a list of words in English that are known to have gone south in their meaning.

- *Awful* once meant something that inspired or created awe. Now it describes something that is bad or not very nice.
- *Bitch* was originally used to denote a female dog, eventually being applied to any female of another species (with four limbs). Now it is more commonly used to describe an unpleasant woman, and is often used as an insult to women.
- *Bully* was originally used to refer to a close friend or used as a term of endearment. Now it refers to a person who tries to intimidate or harm another.
- *Idiot* was originally used much more generally to describe a private, more introverted person. Now it is used to describe someone of low intelligence, and is often, like *bitch*, yelled as an insult.
- *Nazi* is a shortened version of German *Nationalsozialist*, and was originally a reference to the National Socialist German Working Party. During and after the horrors of the Second World War, for which the Nazi party were largely responsible, the word underwent pejoration. From being a purely descriptive term in 1930s Germany, *Nazi* is now indubitably associated with fascism. Its meaning has also broadened, such that it is now sometimes used in a more general sense to refer to any person who is obsessively dedicated to a cause or specific activity. Even then, its pejorative meaning makes it a very contentious word to use as a descriptor of someone.

percussive

A *percussive* is a sound produced by striking two **articulators** together; for example, this may be the **lips** smacking together, or the **tongue** making a click-like sound in the **oral cavity**. Percussives do not necessarily involve an airstream, and are not intended to create **meaning** in speech; rather, they are seen more as artefacts of the articulators beginning to move or coming to rest. Humans produce a lot of percussive sounds, and many commonly sound similar to click sounds. However, you will find that these percussive sounds will typically lack two complete closures (which are needed for the articulation of true clicks), yet they still produce a sound similar to a click. *See also* **airstream mechanism**.

performance

This is a term introduced by Noam Chomsky that is best understood in relation to Chomsky's other term, linguistic **competence**. *Competence* refers to your internalised knowledge about your first **language**, which provides you with the ability to judge whether a **sentence** in that language is grammatical or not, as well as the ability to produce grammatically acceptable speech. However, competence can be affected by performance, which can be thought of as the externalisation of your language ability. That is, our performance is not necessarily a good indicator of our competence. If you are tired or drunk, for instance, this may well affect your speech – but it does not indicate that there is anything faulty about your competence. The concept of performance is derived from Ferdinand de Saussure's concept of **parole**. Chomsky's view is that the proper object of study for **linguists** is linguistic competence. Many linguists would disagree with this, though. The entire premise of **sociolinguistics**, for instance, is that variation between speakers in terms of linguistic performance is fundamental to the function of language. *See also* **E-language**.

performative

This is a term from the work of the language philosopher J. L. Austin (1911–60), whose work was the forerunner of **Speech Act Theory**. Austin's most well-known work is the book *How to Do Things with Words* (1962), based on a series of lectures he gave at Oxford and Harvard in the 1950s. In it, Austin observes that we use **language** not just to make statements (such as 'Linguists love language') but also to perform actions (like naming a ship or pronouncing two people married). What's more, certain actions can only be achieved through language. Take the action of making a bet, as in 'I bet Lesley will love that jazz concert.' We can make this bet in speech or in writing or in **sign language**, but the point is that we can't do it at all without using language of some form. Austin called statement-like uses of language **constatives**, and action-like uses of language, *performatives*. Constatives are either true or false. For instance, the constative 'Linguists love language' may be true or it may be false – it depends whether **linguists** do indeed love language. But performatives don't work in this way. For example, truth or falsity doesn't come into the naming of a ship. You either name it (e.g. 'I name this ship *Titanic*') or you don't. Even if something goes wrong in the naming of a ship (perhaps the bottle doesn't smash against the hull), this still doesn't make the performative false. It just means that it is *infelicitous*. That is, the performative doesn't work because it has not been carried out properly. Austin introduced the concept of **felicity conditions** to explain what needs to be in place in order for a performative to work properly. For instance, to successfully name a ship, you have to have a certain status and ceremonial role and you have to carry out the procedure properly. Austin's work on performatives is important because it laid the groundwork for modern **pragmatics**. However, the concept of performatives turns out to be flawed. For example, you don't always need a performative **verb** in order to do something with language. Imagine a sign that says 'No loitering'. We know that this is a command but it is not achieved via a performative verb. Neither do performatives always perform the actions they specify. Consider the **utterance** 'I promise you'll regret taking advantage of me!' Although the performative verb is *promise*, this sounds much more like a threat. Because of this problem with the concept of performatives, Austin later introduced the concepts of **locution**, *illocution* (*see* **illocutionary force**) and *perlocution* (*see* **perlocutionary effect**). *Locution* refers to the actual **words** used, *illocution* refers to the force of an utterance (e.g. whether the locution is a question, a command, a promise, etc.), and *perlocution* refers to the effects arising from the speech act (for instance, the locution 'I order you to stop' has the illocutionary force of a command and, if successful, would result in the addressee stopping doing whatever it is that was annoying the speaker).

periodic

This is a term used in **acoustic phonetics** to describe regular cycles in the **waveform** (*see* **aperiodic** for irregular speech sounds). Repeated cycles allow for the calculation of **fundamental frequency**, which means that periodic sounds, by definition, are **voiced**. **Vowels** and **nasals** are two types of voiced sounds that typically display clear, periodic cycles in the waveform.

perlocutionary effect

This follows from the **locution** and **illocutionary force** of an **utterance**. It is the effect that an utterance has on the person addressed. If someone asks you whether you can give them a lift to the shops, then the perlocutionary effect will be your acceptance or rejection of the request. If we misinterpret the illocutionary force of what someone says, then it may bring about a perlocutionary effect that was not desired. You might point out to a friend that 'There are sharks in that water', intending it as a warning – but if your friend misinterprets your utterance as a dare, then the perlocutionary effect may be dangerous! *See also* **Speech Act Theory**.

person

This is a grammatical **category**, along with **number, gender** and **case**. Person is usually expressed through ***personal pronouns*** (*see* **pronoun**), which can be first person, second person or third person. First person refers to the speaker and anyone that they are grouped with (e.g. 'I / we like linguistics'). Second person is the **participant** being spoken to (e.g. 'You like linguistics, I hear?'), and third person includes all other participants ('Sadly, she/he/it doesn't like linguistics', 'They do like linguistics though'). Person can affect the form of the **verb** in a **sentence**. In English, for instance, irregular verbs require different **forms** for first, second and third person (e.g. 'I am a keen linguist', 'You are a keen linguist', 'She is a keen linguist', 'They were keen linguists'). Regular verbs, on the other hand, require a different form for the third person singular in the present simple (e.g. 'I run for the bus but Matt runs marathons'). In some **languages**, person is indicated in the verb. In Italian, for example, personal pronouns are routinely dropped in conversation because the verb form indicates these. For instance, we can say

'Guida una macchina' (She drives a car) rather than '*Lei* guida una macchina', and 'Spero vi piaccia' (I hope you like it) rather than '*Io* spero vi piaccia'.

pharynx

The pharynx is part of the **vocal tract** anatomy and can be found just behind the mouth and **nasal cavity** – but before the **larynx**. The pharynx is not the easiest place to see if you open your mouth and look in a mirror, so it may help to think of it as the back of the throat. While the pharynx provides important support in the digestive process, it also plays a role in speech production. There are a set of speech sounds that are referred to as pharyngeal sounds, and, as their name implies, they are produced with the pharynx. Arabic uses pharyngeal sounds.

phonation

This term can have slightly different **meanings** depending on the area of **phonetics** in which it is being used. *Phonation* is generally used to refer to the process by which the **vocal folds** produce sound (or **voicing**) through the vibration or the contact being made between the vocal folds. When working with **voice quality** descriptions, phonation has a broader definition insofar as it considers how the vocal folds are producing sound. Phonation within voice quality research can look at types of phonation/voicing (e.g. **creak**, falsetto), types of laryngeal friction during phonation (e.g. whisper, breathy, murmur), or whether there is laryngeal irregularity in the phonation (e.g. harshness or tremor).

phoneme

This is a term used to describe the smallest contrastive unit of sound that can distinguish one **word** from another in any given **language**. Phonemes are placed between slashes, like /p/ for a **voiceless bilabial plosive** or /z/ for a **voiced alveolar fricative**. Phonemes are generally established through the use of **minimal pairs**; for example, /p/ and /z/ occur in the minimal pair of *pit* and *zit*. The phonemes /p/ and /z/ contrast in identical environments and are considered to be separate phonemes. That is, /p/ and /z/ constitute phonemes because they distinguish the words *pit* and *zit*.

phonetics

This is the study of speech sounds and can be broken down into a number of sub-areas. **Articulatory phonetics** is the study of the physical production of speech sounds, **acoustic phonetics** focuses on the physical properties of speech sounds, and **auditory phonetics** examines how people perceive speech sounds.

phonology

This is the study of the sound systems of **languages**, and how sounds are organised systematically. Whilst **phonetics** is concerned with the production and reception of speech sounds, phonology is concerned with the function of speech sounds and how these encode **meaning**.

phrasal verb

This refers to a **category** of **verbs** consisting of a standard verb plus a **particle**. *Hang on* is an example, as in 'Lesley hung on for a while.' Here, *hung* on its own would not have the same **meaning**, and we could replace the unit *hung on* with a non-phrasal verb, such as *waited*. This demonstrates that *hung on* is a phrasal verb in this **sentence**, rather than a verb plus a **preposition**. Phrasal verbs have subtly different meanings from their constituent parts – 'The student threw up the pancakes' has quite different meanings depending on whether we treat *threw* as a verb and *up* as an **adverb** (the tossing pancakes interpretation), or whether we treat *threw up* as a phrasal verb (the less pleasant interpretation!).

phrase

A phrase in **syntax** is a group of **words** that forms a **component** within a **sentence**. Its head defines the type of phrase that it is – for example, *the linguist* is a **noun phrase**, as the crucial element is the **noun** *linguist*. If we take the sentence 'The linguist played football in the garden', then we can see the different **categories** of English phrase working together to form a grammatical sentence. The **subject**, as is standard in English, consists of a noun phrase: *The linguist*. We then have a **verb phrase** – *played* – which functions as the **predicate**, followed by another noun phrase which functions as the **object** of the sentence: *football. In the* *garden* is slightly more complicated – it is a **prepositional phrase** that functions as an **adverbial** in the sentence, telling us more about how/where/why the action took place. This prepositional phrase is headed by the **preposition** *in*, and is postmodified by another noun phrase, *the garden*. *See also* **adjective phrase** and **adverb phrase**.

pidgin

What do you do if you meet someone from another country and you don't share their **language**? One possibility is to use a **lingua franca** – a language that you both have in common. But what happens if you don't have a lingua franca? In such cases, you (or, more realistically, the two or more groups of people who are aiming to communicate with each other) might develop a pidgin – a rudimentary language that develops from a combination of your respective languages. Pidgins have a number of features: they have fewer **lexical items** than fully developed languages, less complex grammatical **rules** (for example, no **inflections**), fewer forms of the **verb**, and fewer *functions* than an established language. They also tend to have fairly low **prestige**. And they don't have **native speakers** (when they get to the stage of having native speakers, **linguists** then refer to the language not as a pidgin, but as a **creole**). The Tok Pisin language of Papua New Guinea began life as an English-based pidgin that drew on local **vernacular** languages such as Tolai. Evidence of its early simplicity can be seen in the fact that, in the following examples, **person** is marked only by the **pronoun**, not by the verb that follows: *mi go, yu go, em go* (I go, you go, he/she/it goes).

pitch

This refers to the auditory perception of how high or low in **tone** a sound might be. Pitch is specifically used in **auditory phonetics** to describe whether a voice is perceptually high or low without acoustically measuring the **fundamental frequency**.

place of articulation

In **articulatory phonetics**, *place of articulation* refers to the place in the mouth where a sound – specifically, a **consonant** – is produced. The **International Phonetic Alphabet** divides consonants into eleven different places of articulation: **bilabial**, labiodental, **dental**, **alveolar**, post-alveolar, **retroflex**, palatal, **velar**, **uvular**, pharyngeal and glottal.

plosive

Plosives are **consonant** sounds that are sometimes referred to as stops, though the latter term focuses on the restriction of **airflow** through the mouth and can therefore sometimes include the **nasal** consonants. Examples of plosives include /p/, /b/, /t/ and /d/. *See* **stop** for a fuller explanation of how plosives are articulated.

polysemy

This refers to the relationship between different **senses** of a single **word**. *Bright* is an example of a *polysemous* word. Its senses of 'full of light' and 'cheerful' are clearly different, but related, illustrating how we can often see a relationship of metaphorical extension between polysemous senses. A bright lightbulb is literally 'full of light', and the 'cheerful' **meaning** extends from the literal meaning because happiness is often associated with light (and despair with dark). Words also often take on new senses due to technology – think of how the computer sense of *mouse* stems from the animal sense. Polysemy is useful for humour, as it allows us to make puns. Think of the man who asks a taxidermic dog whether it would like a bone to chew on, only for the dog to say, 'No thanks, I'm stuffed!' Polysemy is different from **homonymy**, where two words share the same form, as for *bank*, which has different meanings ('the side of a river' / 'an establishment that looks after your money') stemming from different **etymology**. In some cases, it's difficult to decide whether senses are related by polysemy or homonymy. For instance, think of as many senses as you can for *wave*, and consider whether you think they are all related polysemous senses of a single word, or whether they demonstrate that the form *wave* represents different words.

portmanteau

This refers to a **word** that is a blend of two or more other words (also known as a *blend*). Examples include *sitcom* (formed from *situation* and *comedy*), *smog* (*smoke* and *fog*) and *brunch* (*breakfast* and *lunch*). Sometimes, we are so accustomed to examples such as these, that we forget (or never notice) that they are based on pre-existing words. Note that a portmanteau is different from a **compound** – the former takes parts of existing words, while the latter joins existing words in their entirety (e.g. *greenhouse*). An episode of the tricky TV quiz show *Only Connect* also once suggested the idea of *reverse portmanteaus* – can you see what is going on with examples such as *foke* and *leakfast*? (Look at the earlier examples.) *See also* **blending**.

postmodification

This refers to the process of *qualifying* a **head noun** (i.e. further describing it) by adding additional information after it, in the form of a *postmodifier*. A postmodifier is a **phrase** or **clause** that follows the head noun in a **noun phrase**. In English, postmodification is achieved mainly through **prepositional phrases** (e.g. '*The linguists on the hill* watched the clouds') and **relative clauses** (e.g. '*The linguists who were interested in nephology* gazed skywards'). As with **premodification**, there is no strict limit to the extent of postmodification in English, though for reasons of comprehensibility, speakers usually limit this. This example from the **British National Corpus** is one of the longer postmodifications found in English (the head noun is *evidence*):

> ... the United States actually wanted *evidence* of the fact that funds that had been transferred to the UK Treasury, were being so to speak properly used by the Bank of England. (File KRT)

Praat

Often considered to be the best friend of your resident phonetician, Praat is an open-source software package that was first developed in 1992 to allow for the scientific analysis of speech. The software package, identifiable by its lips and ear icon, was developed by Paul Boersma and David Weenink of the University of Amsterdam in the Netherlands. Pronunciation of the software's name varies, but you typically find [pɹat̺] used in North America and [pɹɑt] in the United Kingdom. *Praat* is actually the Dutch **imperative** for 'speak' – a fitting name for a tool that allows you to analyse speech. Praat is available on a number of operating systems, and new versions of the software are frequently provided. Praat supports a variety of functions, including: speech analysis, labelling and segmentation, learning algorithms, graphics, speech synthesis, listening experiments, speech manipulation, and statistical analysis. When opening the software, you are met with an objects and picture window. The objects window will get you started, and allows you to open files or record new ones, and then view your content in the form of a **waveform** and **spectrogram**. As with many new pieces of software, it takes some time to learn to navigate Praat, but once you get the hang of things the possibilities for speech analysis are endless. Why not download the (free) software and see for yourself: www.fon.hum.uva.nl/praat?

pragmatics

This is the study of how context affects **meaning**. Imagine being stuck in a boring meeting on the hottest day of summer. The person next to you says 'Phew, it's hot in here!' What do they mean? Well, they might simply be making a comment about the temperature. Or they might intend something else – perhaps 'Can you open a window?', or even 'I can't believe you didn't bother to use some deodorant this morning.' How do we know? This is the central question that pragmatics is concerned with. Or, to put it another way, 'How do we infer meaning in context?' *See also* **face**, **Cooperative Principle** and **Speech Act Theory**.

predeterminer

This refers to a **category** of **words** that can come before the **determiner** in a **noun phrase**. For example, *all* is a predeterminer in *all my favourite things*. The determiner *my* specifies the favourite things in question, and *all* makes the **referent** that bit more precise (not just *some* of my favourite things, but all of them). Predeterminers play a quantifying role, e.g. *all the young dudes*, *many of my best friends*. *See also* **quantifiers**.

predicate

This is a linguistic term that has slightly different **meanings** for different approaches to **grammar**. Across approaches, though, a predicate is one of the two main parts of a **sentence**. In English, it follows the **subject**, contains a **verb**, and tells us something about the subject. In the sentence 'Linguists love words', *Linguists* is the subject and the predicate consists of the verb *love* and the **object** *words*, giving us a complete statement about linguists (note that 'Linguists love', with just a subject and a verb, is also grammatically OK). A sentence requires a predicate in order to be complete. The US hip-hop group NWA showed that they realised the essential nature of subject plus predicate in their 'Express Yourself': 'When you got a subject and a predicate / Add it on a dope beat and it'll make you think.'

predicator

In some **grammars**, *predicator* describes the function of a **verb phrase** in a **sentence**. While **noun phrases** can function as **subjects**, **objects** and **complements**, verb phrases can only ever function as predicators. There are a number of different types of predicator. These are *transitive*, *intransitive* and *copular* (*see* **copula**).

Transitive predicators need a direct object after them in order for the sentence to be complete. Consider the following examples:

1. Dan took a tablet.
2. *Dan took

Example 1 is OK but example 2 sounds strange. That's because the **verb** *take* is a transitive verb – it has to have a direct object after it.

Intransitive predicators do not need a direct object after them in order for the sentence to be complete. Consider the following examples:

3. Lesley smiled.
4. *Lesley smiled the student

This time, example 3 sounds OK but example 4 sounds odd. That's because the verb *smile* is intransitive – it does not need a direct object after it. If we do put a direct object after it (as in example 4), it is **ungrammatical**. Sometimes a predicator is neither transitive nor intransitive. These are known as copular or linking predicators. A typical case is the verb *to be*. Consider example 5:

5. Dan is very happy.

In this example, *is* is the verb, but *very happy* is not an object. *Very happy* is an **adjective phrase** and is telling us something about the subject of the sentence, *Dan*. Therefore, the verb *is* is linking the noun phrase *Dan* to the adjective phrase *very happy*. The verb *to be* is the most common linking – or copular – verb. Other copular verbs include *seem*, *become*, *feel* and *look*. You may come across others too. To decide whether a verb is a copular verb or not, look at what comes after it. If this refers back to the subject of the sentence and gives you more information about it (as opposed to being a separate entity) then you know that you're dealing with a copular verb. The following sentences all contain linking verbs:

6. Matt seemed honest.
   (*Honest* refers to a perceived quality of the subject, *Matt*.)
7. Erica felt tired.
   (*Tired* refers to the way that the subject, *Erica*, was feeling.)
8. Dan looked stupid.
   (*Stupid* describes how the subject, *Dan*, looked.)
9. The problem became clear.
   (*Clear* refers back to the subject, *The problem*, and describes how it was perceived.)

See also **SPOCA** and **adverbial**.

prefix

A prefix is a **morpheme** added to the front of a **word** in **languages** with morphological structure (*see* **agglutination**) where morphemes are added to a **base** or root **form** to produce different versions of a **lexical item**. English has some morphological structure of this kind and uses prefixes in the process of **derivation**, particularly for negating the **meaning** of the base (e.g. <u>un</u>kind, <u>dis</u>obedient, <u>non</u>-responsive). *See also* **affix**, **infix** and **suffix**.

premodification

This refers to the process of *qualifying* a **phrase** (i.e. further describing it) by adding additional information in the form of a *premodifier*. A premodifier is a **word** or phrase that precedes the **head word**. For example, in the **noun phrase** *the seven diffident grammarians*, the head **noun** *grammarians* is premodified by a **determiner** (*the*), an **enumerator** (*seven*) and an **adjective** (*diffident*). In the **adverb phrase** *very slowly*, the head word *slowly* is premodified by the **adverb** *very*.

preposition

Prepositions introduce **prepositional phrases** and express relations of place, time, possession, etc. They are always followed by a **noun phrase** to complete the prepositional phrase.

prepositional phrase

Prepositional phrases have a **preposition** as the **head word**, which is followed by a **noun phrase**. The grammatical role of prepositional phrases is as **adverbials**, as in 'Dorothy travelled _over_ the rainbow' and 'I parked the car _outside_ the house', or as **postmodifier** to the head noun in noun phrases, as in 'the dog _in_ the living room' or 'those potatoes _on_ the table'. _See also_ **SPOCA**.

prescriptivism

Do you think that splitting the **infinitive** in English is tantamount to a sin? Do you believe that some **accents** are better than others and that people should learn to talk 'properly'? If so, you're a prescriptivist (and you've clearly not read enough of _The Babel Lexicon of Language_!). Prescriptivism involves telling people how they should use **language**. This is closely linked to **proscriptivism**, which involves telling people what they should _not_ do. **Linguists** are not interested in prescriptivism or proscriptivism (except for what they reveal about people's attitudes towards language). This is because, linguistically, there is nothing intrinsically better or worse about any particular **variety** of a language. That is, all varieties of a language are equally good for communicating ideas and identity. Any perceptions that this is not the case are the result of purely social prejudices. So, prescriptivism is out. The real business of **linguistics** is describing language and language use. This is not to say that anything goes when using language. It is important, for instance, to understand what variety of language is most appropriate in any given context, and skilful users of language are adept at moving seamlessly between varieties. But this judgement is a social issue, rather than a linguistic one. _See also_ **rules** and **prestige**.

Present Day English

Present Day English (PDE) is a general term to describe contemporary English, in the same way that **Old English** describes the **language** of the Anglo-Saxon period, and **Middle English** describes the language of the Middle Ages. In this respect, it is used to talk about a language type (i.e. the fact that contemporary English is an **analytic language**), rather than a language **variety** (such as, for example, British English or Singaporean English).

prestige

This is a sociolinguistic concept that refers to the differing levels of respect given to different **languages** or **dialects** within a community of speakers. More often than not, the recognised standard **form** of a particular language is the prestige form. For example, in the UK, **Standard English** has prestige as the written form of the language – it is the written form that you would use when filling in a job application or writing an essay, even though you may not use it in more natural day-to-day communication. **Received Pronunciation** (RP) is the **accent** that is seen to have the greatest level of prestige. This was especially the case in the past, when, for example, it was obligatory for a BBC news reader to speak RP. While attitudes have changed in more recent decades, there is often still pressure on people in positions of influence to speak RP – teachers, for instance, may be encouraged to modify their own regional accents towards RP, in order to seem more credible. Note that, while **linguists** will observe and study notions of prestige, the majority take a descriptive, rather than prescriptive, approach – describing the forms that are seen to have prestige, but not suggesting what forms ought to be viewed as prestigious. *See also* **descriptivism** and **prescriptivism**.

presupposition

A presupposition is an assumption inherent in a particular piece of **language**. For example, the **sentence** 'Lee Harvey Oswald assassinated President Kennedy' contains two **existential presuppositions**. That is, the **noun phrase** *Lee Harvey Oswald* assumes the existence of someone called Lee Harvey Oswald, and the noun phrase *President Kennedy* assumes the prior existence of someone called President Kennedy. A presupposition differs from an **entailment** in that the presupposition remains even when the **proposition** is negated – e.g. 'Lee Harvey Oswald did not assassinate

President Kennedy.' By contrast, the entailment (i.e. President Kennedy died) is only present in the non-negated sentence.

pro-forms

These are **words** or **phrases** that take the place of another word or phrase in a structure. Most often, these forms are a way of the **language** being economical, as they are shorter than the material that they replace. They also help to avoid repetition of detailed information. The most common type of pro-form in English is the **pronoun**, which replaces a **noun phrase**, usually one that has already occurred earlier in the **co-text**. In the following example, *she* and *her* occur in the second **sentence**, and both pronouns refer back (*see* **anaphora**) to the person introduced in the first sentence:

'On the back row of the photograph you can see *my great-grandmother, Emily Watkins*. *She* was very old when I was little, but I remember *her* well.'

Note that pro-forms make communication much smoother because we don't have to repeat whole phrases (e.g. *my great-grandmother, Emily Watkins*) over and over. Note that pronouns can point forwards as well as backwards in the text (*see* **cataphora**):

'*She* was very old, but I remember *her* well. She was *my great-grandmother, Emily Watkins*.'

Note that this (cataphoric) kind of use of pro-forms, before we have encountered the **referent**, has the stylistic effect of creating tension and intrigue. There are other pro-forms that work in similar ways. These include **forms** that can replace a **verb phrase**: 'I went to school that morning and so <u>did</u> Dan.' Here *did* is a **verb** that is used as a pro-form, indicating that we are meant to understand the same verb (*went*) operating in both **clauses**. There are also **adverbs** which can represent whole clauses as being understood. For example, in the following, the clause is replaced first by *so* and then by *not*:

- 'Matt might win the London marathon, but I don't think *so*.' (= I don't think he will win)

A: 'Hazel has lost her car keys again.'

B: 'I hope *not*.' (= I hope she has not lost her car keys)

Pro-forms do not always behave exactly like the **text** they replace. If you say 'Erica's car was green and mine was too', at first sight *too* seems to replace an adjective (*green*) and you could therefore see it as a pro-adjective. However, there is really a 'space' or 'gap' where the adjective should be, as we can see from 'Erica's car was green and mine was green too.' The adverb *too*, then, is the trigger that helps us fill in the **ellipsis**, but it doesn't itself replace the missing word.

prominence

This is a term used in **phonetics** and **phonology** to describe a sound that stands out from others due to some form of **stress**, sonority, length, quality or **pitch**. A prominent sound is one that will appear to have an emphasis (over other sounds) to a listener.

pronoun

Pronouns can be used in place of a **noun phrase**. For example, in the **sentence** 'The exceptionally handsome actor smiled warmly', we can replace the noun phrase ('The exceptionally handsome actor') with a pronoun – e.g. '*He* smiled warmly.' Sometimes, pronouns are needed to avoid awkward (even **ungrammatical**) **utterances**, e.g. 'Dan admitted to *himself* that he was a terrible cook' (compare 'Dan admitted to Dan that he was a terrible cook'). Unlike **head nouns**, pronouns can't be modified with **determiners** or **adjectives**. *See also* **pro-form**.

propagation

This is the process of spreading a linguistic innovation throughout a **speech community** and thereby causing linguistic change to become widespread. The causes of propagation are social. In essence, propagation depends on contact between speakers. Often, whether a speech community adopts a linguistic innovation or not is partly down to how close-knit it is. The sociolinguist Lesley Milroy's concept of *social networks* is useful here. People in closed social networks (that is, networks of people who all know each other) are more likely to accommodate to each other and thereby rebuff linguistic change. People in open social networks (that is, networks of people who do not all know one another) are likely to be much more open to change, simply as a result of being exposed to a wider variety of **forms**. Propagation is therefore easier in open social networks. This is the reason why linguistic change often originates in urban centres and stems from the middle classes (*see* the **Great Vowel Shift** for an example). Sometimes, linguistic changes are propagated as a result of speakers aspiring to the linguistic forms they hear produced by speakers they believe to be of a higher social status than them. This is what the sociolinguist William Labov has called 'change from above'. **Prestige** is often a driver of propagation as speakers attempt to emulate forms to which they attach high social value. Alternatively, a linguistic change might be propagated simply as a result of a large number of speakers choosing to adopt it. This is what Labov calls 'change from below'. Over time, the speed at which linguistic innovations can be propagated has been increased by the development of technologies for communication. These include now archaic technology such as the landline phone, as well as more recent developments such as video chat facilities. In essence, any technological development which facilitates closer contact between people (such as innovations in transport, for example) is a potential driver of propagation. *See also* **accommodation** and **actuation**.

proposition

This term is borrowed from logical philosophy, though it is used somewhat differently in **linguistics**. It indicates the core **meaning** of an **utterance** or **sentence**, irrespective of the function it is performing in the situational context. Whilst **language** does a lot which is not propositional (hints, assumes, presupposes, shows solidarity or the reverse, etc.), most utterances also contain a proposition upon which the other functions of language are hung. A sentence such as 'It's going to rain today' has the proposition that matches the surface **text** (it will rain on the day in question) but there may be all sorts of other meaning swirling around in addition, including the implication that you should cancel the picnic, take an umbrella, listen to the speaker in future, take more notice of weather forecasts and so on. The propositional content is the product of the whole **clause**, including the relationship between the process (**verb**) and the participants (usually **noun phrases**). Note that the everyday meaning of *proposition*, which is close to *proposal*, is not what is intended in this technical use of the term.

propositional content

This refers to the identifiable message of any **utterance** or **sentence**. It is the **meaning** that can be deduced straightforwardly from the **grammar** and *lexis* without having to make any **inferences**, and not including any assumed meaning (such as **presuppositions**), though these underlie the **proposition** itself.

proscriptivism

This involves telling people what they shouldn't do when they use **language**. For example, many proscriptivists say that you should never use a **split infinitive**, or that you should never end a **sentence** with a **preposition**. Proscriptive **rules** are almost always entirely arbitrary and matters of personal preference. Proscriptivism is closely related to **prescriptivism**, which involves telling people how they *should* use language. Indeed, the term *prescriptivism* is often used to describe attitudes which, strictly speaking, are proscriptivist. Needless to say, professional **linguists** have no interest in proscriptivism (or prescriptivism), except for what it reveals about people's attitudes to language. Instead, **linguistics** is based on **descriptivism** – that is, describing how people actually use language.

Proto-Indo-European

Proto-Indo-European (or PIE as it is sometimes abbreviated) is a linguistic reconstruction of a supposed common ancestor **language** of the Indo-European languages that are used today. (The Indo-European language family includes most of the languages of Europe and many Asian languages.) The existence of PIE was first postulated by Sir William Jones (1746–95), the scholar of Sanskrit, who first observed the similarities between Sanskrit and classical Greek and Latin. It is assumed that PIE would have been in use around 3500 BCE, though estimates vary.

prototype

The notion of a prototype is an important concept in **cognitive linguistics** and can be used to account for how we store **semantic** knowledge. Prototype theory suggests that **categories** are not discrete but **fuzzy** (that is, they blend into one another), and that for any category we will have central, secondary, and peripheral members. For example, if you're asked to think of a fruit and you live in the UK (prototypes are culturally determined), the first example that springs to mind is unlikely to be a kumquat. You're much more likely to think of an apple or banana. It's not that a kumquat isn't a fruit, it's just that it's a peripheral category member for most British people, while apples are central category members. But if you live in Japan, say, or India, a kumquat might well be a central category member for you. What about a tomato? Again, probably peripheral to most people, but if you're asked to choose the most fruit-like between a tomato, a parsnip and a sweet potato, you'd be more likely to go for the tomato. Basic-level concepts such as *bird* are basic precisely because they constitute a prototype category (in effect, they are **hypernyms**), as opposed to, say, *penguin* or *emu*.

psycholinguistics

This is an interdisciplinary subfield of **linguistics** that combines linguistics and psychology research in order to consider the mechanisms in which **language** is processed and represented in the brain. Psycholinguistics can also be referred to as the psychology of language, but within linguistics there is the preference to use the term *psycholinguistics*. The term was first used in 1936 by J. R. Kantor, a psychologist, in his book *An Objective Psychology of Grammar*. Psycholinguistics was later popularised by Kantor's student Nicholas Pronko. As psycholinguistics is an interdisciplinary field, not just between linguistics and psychology, researchers will come from a variety of backgrounds which also include cognitive science, speech and language pathology, and **Discourse Analysis**. Despite the varied backgrounds, researchers will generally be interested in answering similar questions, like those listed below.

- How is language acquired?
- How is language processed?
- How is language comprehended?
- How do we produce language?

Within psycholinguistics, you will also find subdivisions of research which fall in line with the linguistics subfields: **phonetics, phonology, morphology, syntax, semantics** and **pragmatics**. Researchers will consider more specific questions like how we process specific sounds, how we understand **word** structures, whether certain grammatical patterns are processed faster or slower than others, and how we comprehend semantically unpredictable word **meanings**. Many different methodologies are employed to answer these questions, and psycholinguists will often use eye tracking, production errors, behavioural tasks, computational modelling, and various forms of neuroimaging techniques.

Q

qualifier

This is a term that is sometimes used instead of ***postmodifier*** to refer to **phrases** that occur after **head nouns** in **noun phrases**. Thus, for example, **prepositional phrases** such as *in the car* or *over the bridge* can be added after a head noun, as in *the dog in the car* or *the field over the bridge*. **Relative clauses** also postmodify head nouns, as in *the dog that I bought* or *the field [that] he's just ploughed*. Such phrases occur within the boundaries of the noun phrase and do not signal the start of a new **clause** element. Thus, *the dog that I bought* could be the **subject** of a clause, as in 'The dog that I bought has run away', and could be replaced by a single **pronoun**, as in '*He* ran away.' These replacement tests demonstrate the extent of a phrase, by showing that it works as a unit in the higher level of structure.

qualitative research

This refers to an approach to research in the social sciences in general, and **linguistics** in particular, whereby the investigation relies not on numerical findings but on other kinds of descriptions of the data. This could involve, for example, producing a categorisation framework, or attempting to predict the nature of future additions to the data. It is rare for research to be solely qualitative, and it can provide hypotheses that may be tested quantitatively. For example, early child **language acquisition** research was based on broadly based longitudinal studies of a very small number of children. Whilst the results from these studies were highly influential, they could not be generalised to all children without support from short-term studies of a larger number of children, focusing on narrowly defined aspects of their acquisition.

quality

This is one of the four maxims in Grice's **Cooperative Principle**. It recognises the fact that interaction runs smoothly based on the assumption that people will say what they believe to be true, and not say anything that they believe to be false. If someone says something which does not seem to fit with this maxim, then we will assume that they are doing so wittingly and communicating some sort of implied message. An early hit by The Beatles features a nice example, in which they declare that 'I ain't got nothing but love girl, eight days a week.' Clearly, this cannot be the case since there are only seven days in a week. So, unless the protagonist is trying to mislead, then presumably what they're trying to implicate is that they are prepared to offer an unusual amount of love.

quantifier

This is a term used to refer to the premodifiers within a **noun phrase** that indicate the amount or **number** of the head being referred to. This includes the **enumerators** (i.e. numbers), both *cardinal* (1, 2, 3, etc.) and *ordinal* (1st, 2nd, 3rd, etc.), and also more general quantifiers such as *much, some, more, many, a lot of,* and so on. *See also* **premodification**.

quantitative research

This refers to an approach to research in the social sciences in general, and **linguistics** in particular, whereby the investigation relies on numerical findings to test hypotheses and provide generalised descriptions of large amounts of data. It is rare for research to be solely quantitative, and it usually relies on some qualitative investigation to support the statistical findings. For example, **corpus linguistic** investigations of very large amounts of **text** (**corpora**) provide broad-ranging descriptions of the data, but it is often important to check that these generalisations are accurate through a close investigation of a sample of the data, usually in **concordance** form.

quantity

In relation to Gricean **pragmatics**, this refers to one of Grice's conversational maxims. The maxim of quantity refers to our general expectation that our **interlocutors** will provide sufficient information in their contributions to the conversation, but not too much. Flouting this maxim may result in an **implicature**: that something is being hidden, either through verbosity where too much is being said (and which may confuse and overwhelm the addressee(s)) or by the impression that the speaker is being too reluctant to impart sufficient information where too little is said. Here is an example:

Erica: Do you like cheese and wine?
Hazel: I like wine.

Here, Erica's question anticipates a response that deals with Hazel's feelings towards both cheese and wine. Hazel's response, by just focusing on one of these elements, seems to implicate that she is less fond of cheese.

question forms

In English, question forms divide into two distinct groups. These are known as Y/N or **yes/no questions**, on the one hand, and **wh-questions** on the other. They are logically distinct because the Y/N questions presuppose a binary one-word answer of *yes* or *no*, whereas the wh-questions indicate which part of the information is missing. Thus, *where, when, who, why* and *how* ask for the place, the time, the participant(s), the reason(s) and the means, respectively. The significance of question forms for grammatical theory is that the English **forms** require certain other changes in the order and structure of the remaining **sentence**. So 'Where is the house?' demonstrates that the wh-word is fronted (brought to the front), and then the **verb** (or the first **auxiliary verb**) is brought forward, in front of the grammatical **subject**, after the wh-word. Likewise, in Y/N questions, the first auxiliary (or the **dummy auxiliary** *do*) is fronted to realise the question form, as in 'Have the parcels arrived?' Such structural differences between **declaratives** and **interrogatives** were part of the original evidence that Noam Chomsky used to argue for his model of **generative grammar**, which hypothesised that speakers *transform* the **base form** of a simple declarative to produce interrogative, **imperative** and emphatic structures. It is worth noting that some **languages** (e.g. Czech, Bulgarian) front all the wh-words, irrespective of their role in the underlying structure, so that you get sentences that would translate literally as 'Who what ate?' It is, of course, also possible to ask a question by other means, including a change in **intonation** (a rising tone) or non-verbal cues (a shrug); lots of languages (e.g. French) don't have to have (overt) movement in questions, so their normal question forms look like our echo questions, or they use **particles** to form questions, as with Chinese *ma*.

quotative

This is a term used in **Discourse Analysis** to refer to what is also sometimes called the *reporting clause*. This is the **clause** that introduces direct quotations from someone's speech, such as 'He said' or 'She shouted'.

R

Received Pronunciation

Sometimes referred to as BBC English or the Queen's English, Received Pronunciation (RP) describes the pronunciation or **accent** typically associated with Southern Standard British English, though it is not uncommon to find RP speakers throughout England and Wales, making it a social rather than a regional accent. The term *received* means 'accepted'. Received Pronunciation is often taught to learners of English as a foreign language. Like all accents, RP is ever changing and adapting. One only has to listen to the Queen's Christmas broadcasts over the years to notice that the monarch's own accent has changed. Received Pronunciation from the 1960s is definitely not the same as Received Pronunciation in 2019.

reconstruction

The **language** known as **Proto-Indo-European** is generally accepted by **linguists** as the single common ancestor of all other Indo-European languages. But we have no direct written evidence of Proto-Indo-European, so how do we know it existed? The answer lies in linguistic reconstruction. This is a technique in **historical linguistics** that involves comparing known languages in order to identify similarities between them, and then working backwards to determine what the language from which they developed must have been like. One way of doing this is to compare **cognate** terms between languages and establish, say, phonological similarities between them. In Latin and Greek, for instance, the word for *foot* begins with a [p] (*pod-* and *ped-*, respectively), while in English and German it begins with a [f] (*foot* and *Fuss*). Each of these four languages belongs to the Indo-European family, but to explain why English and German uses [f] rather than [p], we have to postulate that, at some point, Indo-European must have developed another branch, as indeed it did (Germanic). Through processes such as this, we can identify the **rules** that govern particular linguistic developments, and from these we can set about reconstructing languages for which we have no surviving written evidence.

recursion

This refers to the capacity of the **syntax** of human **languages** to embed structures within other structures repeatedly, the only limit being the speaker's or hearer's ability to comprehend this. Thus, **noun phrases** in English can have postmodifying **prepositional phrases** that are in turn made up of a **preposition** plus a noun phrase, which in turn can contain a prepositional phrase. Here's one example: 'the dancer on the stage in the theatre by the river in the capital city'. This feature of recursion can be used playfully in songs and children's stories such as 'This is the House that Jack Built', where it is often **relative clauses** rather than prepositional phrases that are being repeatedly applied.

reference

This is the other side of the coin to **sense**. While the sense of a **word** is (essentially) its definition in relation to the rest of the words in the **language**, the reference of a word is all the objects that the word could belong to. The word *cat* has a sense something like 'a feline animal', but the potential **referents** of that particular sense are many and varied, from the sprightly young kitten at home to the wild tiger in the jungle. **phrases** and **sentences** also refer – for instance, 'You are reading this book' refers to what's happening right now. Abstract words, too, have reference. Just because you can't see *curmudgeonliness* doesn't mean it doesn't exist and can't be referred to. *See also* **denotation**.

referent

A referent is what a **word** or **phrase** refers to in the real world when the word/phrase is used in a particular context in speech or writing. For example, the **noun** *cat* in its **sense** 'feline animal' has one definition, but many different possible referents in different contexts. While we can look up the sense of a word in a dictionary, we depend on context to help us work out the referent of a particular use of *cat*. *See also* **denotation** and **reference**.

reflexive pronouns

These are used when the **object** in a **sentence** is the same as the **subject** – e.g. 'Hazel is teaching *herself* to play the clarinet.' They can also act as indirect objects, as in 'Dan cooked *himself* dinner', in which case they can sometimes function as **intensifiers** (i.e. 'Dan cooked dinner for himself and no-one else').

register

This refers to **language** variation as determined by particular social contexts. For example, we would use a different register when in a meeting at work from that which we would use when talking to friends informally. There are three components to register: *medium* (i.e. speech or writing), *domain* (e.g. science, religion, advertising, education) and *tenor* (i.e. level of formality and politeness).

relation

This is the maxim in Grice's **Cooperative Principle** concerned with whether what we say is relevant. It states that, ordinarily, we assume that people will only say things that are relevant within the interaction. If someone says something that is not obviously relevant, then we assume they are trying to imply some other message that is relevant, as in the example below:

Dan: Did you enjoy your run at the weekend?
Hazel: The beer at the end was nice.

Here, Hazel's response does not provide a clearly relevant answer to Dan's straightforward **yes/no question**. However, Dan understood the correct answer: Hazel's answer is only relevant to one small (and not usually obligatory!) part of the running experience – if she is focusing on her enjoyment of that one aspect, then presumably she is implicating that she did not enjoy the run itself.

relational opposite

This refers to one of the **opposition sense relations** that hold between **lexical items** in a **language**. Similar to **converse** opposites, relational opposites such as *teacher–pupil* or *father–son* are mutually dependent, but are more variable in their partnerships than the more restricted converses. For instance, for the converse pair *parent–child*, if Harry is the *parent* of Mary, then we know that Mary is the *child* of Harry, but for the relational pair *father–son*, Harry being the father of Mary doesn't entail (*see* **entailment**)that Mary is Harry's son (since she could instead be his daughter).

relative clauses

These are a type of **subordinate clause** (i.e. a **clause** which cannot stand alone as a **sentence**) that typically provides more information about a preceding **noun** or **noun phrase**, as in 'The very hungry caterpillar who had eaten four strawberries'. In English, as in many other European **languages**, relative clauses can be introduced by a relative **pronoun** such as *who, whose, when, which* or *that*, or by no relative pronoun at all, as in 'The person [that] I spoke to'. In other languages, the relative clause may be marked by a morphological **inflection** on the **verb**, or by other means such as **word order**.

repair

This is a term from **Conversation Analysis** that is used to describe instances where a speaker notices a speech error that either they or their conversational partner has made and corrects this to clarify what should actually have been said. This can be done by, for instance, lexical replacement (e.g. 'I need a thingy . . . screwdriver') or a clarifying statement (e.g. 'I mean . . . '). Repairs can be self-initiated and self-repaired, self-initiated and repaired by someone else (other-repaired), other-initiated and self-repaired, or other-initiated and other-repaired.

reported speech

This is a commonly used term to refer to the presentation of the speech of someone else. In actual fact, ***presented speech*** is a more accurate term, because when we present what someone else has said we don't always report it accurately or in full, as the term *reported speech* might suggest. For example, in 2017, the then President of the European Parliament, Martin Schulz, said: 'I refuse to imagine a Europe where lorries and hedge funds are free to cross borders but citizens cannot.' As we have presented it here, this is ***direct speech*** (DS). That is, we have presented the exact **words** that Schulz used. But there are lots of other options for presenting this speech. We could, for instance, use ***indirect speech*** (IS), where the reported **clause** ('Martin Schulz said') becomes subordinate to the main clause, and where there is a backshift in **tense** and a change in **pronouns** that reflect the change in speaker: e.g. 'Martin Schulz said that he refused to imagine a Europe where lorries and hedge funds were free to cross borders but citizens were not.' Alternatively, we could choose to present only the speech act (*see* **Speech Act Theory**) that Schulz used: 'Martin Schulz made a statement about his beliefs on the future of freedom of movement within Europe.' This **form** is known as the ***narrator's presentation of a speech act*** (NPSA). The other possibility is to use an even more minimal form known as the ***narrator's presentation of voice*** (NV), where we simply report that speech happened but say nothing about the content of the speech, e.g. 'Schulz spoke briefly.' There is one further **category** available to us, and this is ***free indirect speech*** (FIS). This is an unusual category in that it gives the impression of blending elements of direct speech with elements of narration. An example would be: 'Martin Schulz refused to imagine a Europe where lorries and hedge funds are free to cross borders but citizens cannot.' Here, there is no reporting **verb** like *said* or *opined*, and so in one sense the report looks like a simple stretch of narration. On the other hand, the level of detail concerning what Schulz refused to imagine is such that it would seem unlikely that this is simply the narrator's summary of what Schulz said. Hence, FIS appears to be a blend of two categories. The speech presentation categories summarised here can be thought of as existing on a cline:

NV	NPSA	IS	FIS	DS

At one end of the cline is the most minimal form of speech presentation (NV), while at the other end is the category that give us the exact words that were originally uttered (DS). The other categories lie at midpoints in between. As we move along the cline, each category offers an additional claim to faithfulness with regard to the speech presentation. For example, NV tells us only that speech occurred, while NPSA tells us that speech occurred *and* the speech act that was used. IS tells us that speech occurred, what the speech act value was, and gives us some indication of the words that were used (it is often possible to reconstruct the original direct speech from the indirect presentation of it). Finally, DS tells us that speech occurred, what the speech act value was, and gives us the exact words that were used. FIS is an unusual category in that its exact position on the cline is not clear (research is currently underway investigating how readers understand FIS in relation to the other categories). The options for presenting other people's speech are similar to those for presenting other people's thoughts and writing. Recent large-scale **corpus** analyses of reported speech, writing and thought in written English have shown that practices have changed considerably over the years. In **Early Modern English**, for instance, direct speech was much less common than in **Present Day English**. *See also* **reported thought**.

reported thought

This refers to the presentation of another person's thoughts in speech or writing. The **categories** of reported thought (or *thought presentation*) are essentially the same as for **reported speech** (or *speech presentation*), except that the term *thought* replaces the term *speech*. For example, 'The linguist thought that a new tower of Babel should be built' is an example of *indirect thought*, while 'The linguist thought, "I'd like to build a new tower of Babel!"' is an instance of *direct thought*. As with reported speech, we can choose to present a detailed report of what someone thought (as in the direct thought example above), or a much less detailed version, e.g. 'They thought for a long time' (i.e. the *narrator's presentation of thought*). We can also use different reporting **verbs** to indicate the *thought act* used – e.g. 'They pondered', 'He considered the matter', 'He decided to act' (these are all instances of the *narrator's presentation of a thought act*). *Free indirect thought* ('The linguist wanted to build a new tower of Babel!') seemingly blends narration and direct thought. As with reported speech, the categories of thought presentation exist on a cline, from least faithful reporting categories at one end, to most faithful reporting categories at the other. The difference between reported speech and thought is that, while direct speech is the norm for speech presentation, indirect thought is the norm for thought presentation. This is because thought, unlike speech, is an internal activity, therefore it would seem appropriate that the norm for reporting it should be indirect rather than direct, since we cannot know exactly what thoughts someone else has – and in what **words** that thought may be couched. The norms referred to here are semantic norms, though corpus stylistic analyses have revealed that these two categories are the most frequent forms of speech and thought presentation too. *See* **reported speech** for more details on the cline referred to in this entry.

retracted

This refers to the horizontal position in the **vocal tract** of a sound being articulated. A retracted sound is one that is articulated farther back than might be expected (see **advanced** for the opposite of *retracted*). Both **vowels** and **consonants** can be described as being retracted, but it is slightly more common to see vowels being described as retracted. There is a specific **diacritic** assigned to the term *retracted*, whereby a short horizontal line is placed under the sound being transcribed: [a̠]. It can be especially helpful to transcribe vowels with such specific descriptions as *retracted* when a **language** might not contrast /a/ and /ɑ/, but the **linguist** wants to capture the fact that the speaker has a tendency to produce a sound that is like [a̠], such that /a/ is not as far forward in the mouth as it is depicted in the **International Phonetic Alphabet**. It is important to note that a retracted diacritic is not used on back vowels, as they are thought of as already lying on the extreme periphery of the vowel quadrilateral (a schematic representation of the arrangement of the vowels; see the IPA chart at the front of the book for an example). If back vowels were to be retracted any further, they would in essence no longer be vowels as some form of frication or approximation would occur with another **articulator** (and at that point they would be more consonant-like in their production).

retroflex

Curl the tip of your **tongue** back and place it just behind your **alveolar** ridge. Now try making a /t/ or a /d/ sound. Congratulations, you've just produced a retroflex **consonant**.

Compare this with a /t/ or a /d/ produced with your tongue resting on your alveolar ridge. You should be able to hear a clear difference. Retroflex consonants are particularly common in the **languages** of the Indian subcontinent.

reversive opposite

This is one of several **opposition sense relations**. Reversive opposites indicate a dynamic process, in which each of a pair of terms reverses the action of the other. For example, the **verb** pairs *unbutton–button* and *raise–lower*. See also **directional opposite**.

rhyme

A *rime* or *rhyme* is contained within a **syllable**. A rhyme consists of a necessary **nucleus**, and may also include an optional **coda**. The rhyme usually begins with a **vowel** sound, and may end with a vowel sound or a **consonant**. In some **languages**, the nucleus does not necessarily have to be a vowel, therefore a rhyme may start with a consonant. The rhyme of a syllable is generally the portion of the syllable that is used in poetic rhymes, like that of nursery rhymes. Consider the *Three Blind Mice* nursery rhyme below. You will notice that the rhyme in the final words of the third through fifth lines forms a rhyming triplet.

1. Three blind mice. Three blind mice.
2. See how they run. See how they run.
3. They all ran after the farmer's wife,
4. Who cut off their tails with a carving knife,
5. Did you ever see such a sight in your life,
6. As three blind mice?

rounding

Rounding accompanies those **vowel** sounds that involve changing the position of the **lips** into a rounded shape. If you look in the mirror when pronouncing the **word** *boot*, you may notice that your lips form a circular shape when moving from the /b/ **consonant** sound to the /u:/ vowel sound. This depends on your **accent**, of course. If you don't pronounce *boot* with lip-rounding, which words do you use lip-rounding for?

rules

Linguists are sometimes accused of an 'anything goes' attitude when it comes to language use, presumably because most linguists avoid prescribing how **language** ought to be spoken and written (*see* **prescriptivism**). But this misses the fact that there *are* rules that govern how languages work, and that linguists are interested in discovering these rules. The difference is that what linguists are interested in are descriptive rules, not prescriptive ones. A descriptive rule is a statement that explains a particular aspect of how a language works. For example, in English, a **sentence** can be composed of a **noun phrase** plus a **verb phrase** (NP + VP), but it can't be composed solely of an

adjective phrase plus a noun phrase (*AjP + NP). NP + VP is thus a simple descriptive rule for the formation of sentences in English. It has nothing to do with taste or personal preference, as most prescriptive rules do. Instead, it is based on the objective observation of how speakers form English sentences.

S

Sapir–Whorf hypothesis

The Sapir–Whorf hypothesis is named after the **linguists** Edward Sapir (1884–1939) and Benjamin Lee Whorf (1897–1941), whose work examined the concept of *linguistic relativity*. Linguistic relativity is the view that **language** affects thought. There are commonly held to be two forms of the hypothesis: a strong form and a weak form. The strong form suggests that language determines thought (this is also known as **linguistic determinism**), while the weak form suggests only that language can influence thought. For example, the strong form of the Sapir–Whorf hypothesis would suggest that a speaker of a language which has numerous terms to denote shades of purple (e.g. *purple, indigo, violet*) would be able to perceive more shades of purple than the speaker of a language which has only one term to refer to all shades. Numerous experiments to test this have been carried out with the result that most linguists nowadays would reject the strong version of the hypothesis (i.e. linguistic determinism). There is some empirical support for the weak version of the hypothesis, however, which some proponents of **conceptual metaphor theory** subscribe to, arguing that the metaphors we use influence the way we see the world. Strictly speaking, the term *Sapir–Whorf hypothesis* is inaccurate, since neither Sapir nor Whorf ever formulated a hypothesis from their work (nor did they ever work together). The term is actually attributed to one of Sapir's students, who used it in reference to Sapir's and Whorf's research.

schema theory

This is a concept derived from psychology. It attempts to explain how it is that we are able to communicate in the absence of full information. So, for example, when a friend tells us that they went to a restaurant, the story will not usually include the information that they were shown to a table, given a menu and asked what they would like to drink/eat, and so on. These regular patterns of behaviour in restaurants are part of our 'schema' about eating out and we do not need to repeat them all the time. This kind of schematic knowledge fills in gaps every time we communicate, and only becomes problematic when there is a difference in schemas between the originator of a **text** and the recipient, because of either cultural difference or some other social distance such as age, social class or gender.

schwa

In **phonetics** and **phonology**, schwa is a mid-central **vowel** /ə/ that is located in the centre of the vowel space and is sometimes referred to as the neutral vowel. Schwa is the only sound to get its own entry in this book, simply because it receives a lot of attention and even non-linguists have sometimes heard of it. Perhaps its popularity is due to its pleasing name, its appearance in memes ('Be a schwa; they're never stressed'), or the fact that it appears in so many **languages** and is one of the easiest sounds to produce. Whatever the reason, schwa in English is found in unstressed **syllable** positions (e.g. the beginning of the word *about*).

segment

This refers to a discrete unit that can be identified auditorily in the speech stream, or physically identified in the **waveform/ spectrogram**. *Segment* is used to refer to the smallest building block of language and is sometimes used interchangeably with the term *phone*. Segments are often referred to as being discrete, because they are generally thought of as being separate or individual units that can be ordered. However, in reality, in speech production and perception, segments are much more dynamic, as natural speech contains *coarticulations* where the segments overlap. **Suprasegmental** features exist in all languages.

segmentation

This is the identification of the boundaries between sounds, **syllables** or **words** in spoken **language**. This is not necessarily as straightforward as it sounds and yet it is something we are able to do intuitively through our familiarity with a language. Listen to someone speaking (preferably quite a fast talker) and try not to focus on the actual words being spoken. You'll probably notice that many stretches of speech are like one long stream of sounds, with no clear boundaries between individual words. This is especially the case, for instance, when adjacent words end and begin with the same speech sound, like in *linguists' secrets*. This is why we can often feel the need to ask a **native speaker** of a language that we are learning to slow down. Research in speech segmentation looks at subjects such as children's acquisition of language. Young children will struggle to segment speech into individual words in the more or less instant way that adults do. If they cannot consistently make matches between the sounds that they hear in a stream of speech and the words stored in their mind, then how are they able to segment the sounds that they hear, and make sense of what they are being told? Infants' abilities in spite of these limitations may be due to their budding recognition of the prosody of a language, and how **stress** is used. This also helps explain why, as adults, we struggle with learning a new language since we have to do this sort of learning at a much later stage and in spite of the language(s) we already know, at a point when our brain is less malleable.

semantic field

This refers to a set of related **meanings** (e.g. parts of animals or types of weather) which may or may not be lexicalised (i.e. labelled by **words**) in a particular **language**. The way that words interact in such a field of meaning is referred to as a **lexical field**, though the two terms are sometimes used interchangeably. Semantic fields may be very general (e.g. emotion) or more specific (e.g. anger) and we refer to any concept within a field that is not lexicalised in a language as a **lexical gap**. *See also* **lexicalisation**.

semantic prosody

This is a concept from **corpus linguistics**. It refers to a type of **meaning** that arises as a result of **collocation**. For example, the expression *get away with* tends to collocate with negatively charged **words** such as *murder, fraud, crime* and *carelessness* (you can check this by searching for collocates in the **British National Corpus**). *Get away with*, therefore, can be said to have a negative semantic prosody. What this means is that even when the expression is used with words that do not appear to have any intrinsic negative meaning (e.g. 'The Prime Minister thought she could get away with her policy on education'), the negative meaning that is commonly associated with it (as a result of its collocates) will still be perceived. That is, the negativity of the common collocates of *get away with* seems to bleed over into the expression itself. The *semantic* element of the term relates to meaning. The *prosody* element is because the term is formed on analogy with a similar phenomenon in **phonology**. For example, compared to the **vowels** in the word *cart*, the vowels in the word *barman* have a **nasal** quality because they are surrounded by nasal **consonants**. In the same way, the meaning of a word is affected by the surrounding meaning in its usage.

semantics

This is the name given to the study of **meaning** in **language**. It is used to broadly cover all sorts of meaning, including lexical (i.e. **word**) meaning and the meaning of structures (**phrases**, **clauses**, **sentences**). The way that semantics is perceived depends on the larger theory of language that the **linguist** follows, but it is generally agreed that there is some kind of meaning associated with words and structures in human language which can be studied, at least partly, in isolation from other aspects of language (**phonetics**, **grammar**, etc.). Many linguists also differentiate between semantics and **pragmatics**, with semantics being the linguistic contribution to meaning, and pragmatics being how meaning arises in the specific linguistic, social and situational context. Semantics has a complex history, in which linguistic theories interact with *philosophy of language* and are affected related to whichever theories of **lexicon** and grammar are at play. Recent developments in grammatical theory tend to integrate semantics more closely with structural considerations (i.e. grammar). These include **construction grammar**, *cognitive grammar*, *Systemic Functional Grammar* (*see* **Systemic Functional Linguistics**) and newer models of **generative grammar**.

semi-modals

In English, there are some **verbs**, known as semi-modals, which historically were **modal verbs**, but are increasingly used as main verbs in **Standard English**. These are *dare, need, ought (to)* and *used (to)*. You might like to test them as auxiliaries by trying them out in **negation** (do they carry the reduced negative **form,** such as in *daren't?*); questions ('Need I go?'); emphatic **phrases** ('I *ought* to go'). You may remember older members of your family using such structures, even if you don't. Or these may be modal for you in your **dialect**. *See also* **dummy auxiliary** and **auxiliary verb**.

sense

This refers to the **meaning** of a linguistic expression, i.e. a **word**, **phrase** or **sentence**. A word's sense is the kind of meaning you would find in a dictionary. In essence, the sense of a word is the set of conditions under which the word can refer to something (*see* **reference, referent**). For example, the word *linguist* has the sense of 'a person who studies linguistics', and so, if we know someone who is studying **linguistics**, we know we can apply the word *linguist* to them. While senses may change over time, in cases like *linguist*, they are likely to remain relatively stable within the community of language users so that communication can work. Theories of **semantics** try to determine the nature of senses: e.g. whether they break down into smaller parts or if they have to be treated as wholes. Note that a single word can have more than just one sense (*see* **polysemy**). If you look up the word *linguist* in a dictionary, you are likely to find that it has one sense similar to the one outlined above, and another concerning 'a person who speaks many languages'. Note that this latter sense could also be attributed to the word *polyglot*. (If this sense was attributed only to *polyglot* and not to *linguist*, it would save a lot of misunderstandings in social introductions!) *See also* **connotation** and **denotation**.

sense relation

This refers to semantic links between the individual **meanings** (**senses**) of **lexical items** of a **language**. Take, for example the **word** *heaven*. It is related by *antonymy/oppositeness* to *hell*, by *synonymy* with *paradise*, by *metonymy* with *the Pearly Gates*, by *hyponymy* with *place*, and so forth. Examples like these are relatively stable within and between speakers of the same **variety** of a language, but sometimes sense relations can be devised within a particular context. *See also* **antonym, opposition, synonym, metonym** and **hyponym**.

sentence

This refers to one of the levels of structure in human **language**, which can contain a single **clause** (*see* **simple sentence**) or more than one clause (*see* **compound sentence** and **complex sentence**). Whilst we do sometimes speak in sentences, they could be seen as an 'idealised' structure influenced by the written language, where we use fully formed sentences more frequently than we do in speech (though social media usage is beginning to erode this distinction). In fact, much of the time in everyday life, we speak (and sometimes also write) in fragments and minor sentences.

sibilant

This refers to speech sounds that are a particular type of **fricative**. As well as constricting the **airflow** so that they make white noise (as fricatives do), sibilants funnel the outflowing air through a focused gap in the **articulators** (like a whistle rather than a draughty window). This causes the white noise to be acoustically clearer and often louder, as well as concentrated in higher frequency bands, in the sibilant fricatives (such as /s/, /z/, /ʃ/ and /ʒ/) than in the non-sibilant fricatives such as /f/ or /θ/ (**voiceless** *th* in English). The sibilant sounds, then, are made by forming a groove along the middle of the **tongue**: this is what produces the whistling effect. A narrow groove produces the **alveolar** sibilants /s/ and /z/, while a wider groove produces /ʃ/ and /ʒ/. You can feel the effect of this by preparing to say a long *sssss* sound or a long *shhhhh* sound and then, instead of saying the sound, breathing in sharply. You should feel a strip of cold air travel up your tongue, in either a narrow band or a wider one.

sign language

This is a type of **language** that is not dependent on the vocal and aural apparatus for communication, but uses the hands and facial expressions to replace spoken language. Whilst there is some relationship between, for example, British Sign Language and British English, there are significant differences in the way that the language expresses ideas, and the delivery mode results in different ways of combining the language units. For example, **adjectives** may be represented within the sign for a **noun**, rather than as a separate sign. A small ball and a large ball may simply have the same sign but using smaller or larger gestures. Sign languages are the first language of many people who are deaf or hard of hearing, and can be used for the same full range of functions as any spoken language.

simple sentence

This is used to label those **sentences** that are made up of a single **clause**. This means that there is only one **verb phrase** and one or more other elements in the sentence. Examples of simple sentences include:

- Dan blinked. (**subject** and **predicator**)
- Erica strolled along the beach. (subject, predicator and **adverbial**)
- Matt ran a marathon. (subject, predicator and **object**)
- Hazel brought some cakes to the meeting. (subject, predicator, object and adverbial)
- Lesley was excited. (subject, predicator and **complement**)

Other forms of sentence are **complex sentences** and **compound sentences**. *See also* **SPOCA**.

social meaning

This concerns those **meanings** of **words** that have to do with the context in which we would expect to find them. We can see social meaning in action with a set of words like *father*, *dad*, *daddy* and *papa*. The denotative meaning of each of these words is more or less identical ('male parent'), while the connotative meaning of each may vary slightly (perhaps we picture a slightly more old-fashioned paternal figure for *father* than for the others?). But the main way in which the meanings of these words differ is in their social meanings. For instance, we would usually expect younger speakers to use *daddy*, and we might well find the way in which children address their parents as 'father' in a period drama oddly formal and stiff. A word's social meaning is less precisely defined than other types of meaning. Nonetheless, we are all likely to see differences in social meaning between *farewell*, *ta-ta*, *Godspeed* and *laters* –probably relating to the age of those who are likely to use each word. Social meaning also comes to mind any time we notice differences between regional or national **varieties** of a **language**. Take, for instance, the example of a Canadian friend thanking his host for the use of *a clutch double protector*. (In some varieties of American English, *clutch* is roughly equivalent to *cool*, and *double protector* to *thick duvet*.) Social meaning also applies to sounds. That is, particular pronunciations index particular aspects of identity. *See also* **denotation** and **connotation**

sociolect

A sociolect is a **language variety** associated with a particular social class of people (**dialect**, by contrast, tends to be used to refer to a variety of a language associated with a particular geographical region). The sociolinguist William Labov's famous 'fourth floor' study is an investigation of how language varies according to social class, and may therefore be seen as a study of sociolects. The most well-known part of Labov's study involved him asking shop assistants in three Manhattan department stores where he might find a particular item. The stores were chosen as representative of the upper middle class (Macy's), lower middle class (Saks) and working class (Klein's). Labov's questioned was designed to elicit the response 'fourth floor'. The reason for this was Labov's hypothesis that rhotic /ɹ/ (i.e. the sound you produce if you pronounce the /r/ at the end of *floor*) was a marker of **prestige** and might therefore be produced most frequently in the upper-middle-class store. However, Labov found that the sales assistants who produced /ɹ/ most frequently were those at the lower-middle-class store, Saks. Through this and a variety of other tests, Labov established that it is was the lower middle class who were most aware of the prestige associated with rhotic /ɹ/, and that they used it as a means of projecting an identity of themselves as being of a higher social class than they actually were. Similar findings were reported in other variationist studies, such as Peter Trudgill's study of Norwich speech. The importance of these findings is that they begin to shed light on why language changes over time. For example, one of the likely motivators for the **Great Vowel Shift** is the middle classes aiming to emulate the speech of those to whose social class they aspired. In effect, the middle classes have a tendency to be the drivers of linguistic change. *See also* **overt prestige** and **covert prestige**.

sociolinguistics

This is the sub-discipline of **linguistics** which investigates how **language** interacts with social **variables**. There are two main branches of sociolinguistics. The first is variationist sociolinguistics which developed out of traditional *dialectology*, applying systematic linguistic methods of description and experimentation first to different regional **dialects**, and then to the dialect features observed amongst speakers from different social classes. The earliest sociolinguistic studies followed dialectology in recording variant forms of pronunciation, **grammar** and *lexis* according to place or social class. Following this, variationist sociolinguistics also began to investigate other social variables such as gender, sexual orientation, ethnicity, etc. Studies of social and regional varieties of languages continue to be carried out, some based on interview and questionnaire data and some more experimental. Most of these produce quantitative as well as qualitative results. A famous example of the latter is Labov's 'fourth floor' study (*see* **sociolect**). The other strand of sociolinguistics reflects an approach which owes more to **ethnography** and considers the wider contextual influences on language variation, focusing on variation as an expression of identity. Examples include the work of Lesley and James Milroy who developed the concept of social networks in relation to language use by investigating the linguistic habits of three communities in Belfast, Northern Ireland; and Penelope Eckert's in-depth approach to studying the variation in the different communities of practice in a US high school.

sociophonetics

This is a sub-discipline of **linguistics** that combines the study of **sociolinguistics** and **phonetics**. Sociophonetics, unlike sociolinguistics, refers more specifically to the area of study that considers how sound systems may vary in line with social factors. The field of sociophonetics (and sociolinguistics more generally) is often noted as being led by Professor William Labov of the University of Pennsylvania, whose early studies in the 1960s and 1970s found relationships between certain pronunciations and social identities. However, the first recorded use of the term *sociophonetics* is believed to have been in the 1974 dissertation by Denise Deshaies-Lafontaine that used phonetic methods and data to answer sociolinguistic questions.

sonorant

This is a phonological term that refers to a class of **consonants** that are produced with a relatively low degree of obstruction to the **airflow** through the **oral** or **nasal cavity**. Air is able to flow freely with little restriction. Sonorant sounds include **vowels, glides, liquids**, and **nasals**.

source domain

In **conceptual metaphor theory** (CMT), the source domain is the object that the **target domain** is compared to. For example, in the conceptual metaphor IDEAS ARE FOOD (linguistic instantiations of which include 'That's a half-baked idea' and 'Did he swallow your explanation?'), FOOD is the source domain, as this is the area of life being drawn upon when discussing IDEAS (the target domain).

spectrogram

A spectrogram is a visual representation of the speech signal, with time represented on the horizontal axis, and frequency represented on the vertical axis. **Amplitude** is indicated by the darkness, such that the darker the representation of the energy, the more intense or loud the sound. Spectrograms can be produced using software for phonetic analysis such as **Praat**.

Speech Act Theory

Speech Act Theory has its roots in the work of J. L. Austin (*see* **performative**), who had aimed to explain how we use **language** to perform particular actions (such as promising, requesting, warning, etc.). Austin introduced the concept of *illocution* to describe the intention behind the use of particular words. Austin's student, John Searle, later attempted to further explain the properties of so-called *illocutionary acts* in his 1969 book *Speech Acts: An Essay in the Philosophy of Language*. Searle suggested that, for a speech act (his term for an illocutionary act) to be successful, it had to meet a number of conditions. There are four basic conditions that need to be met in order for a speech act to be *felicitous* (*see* **felicity conditions**). These are best explained with reference to a specific example. Consider the speech act of promising. This can be described as follows:

PROPOSITIONAL ACT:	The speaker says that he/she will carry out some act (A) for the hearer.
PREPARATORY CONDITION:	The speaker believes that he/she is capable of carrying out A, and that A will be good for the hearer.

SINCERITY CONDITION:	The speaker genuinely intends to carry out A.
ESSENTIAL CONDITION:	The speaker undertakes to carry out A for the hearer.

What this means is that for a promise to work (that is, for it to count as *felicitous*), all of the above conditions must be met. If they are not, the speech act is ***infelicitous***. For instance, saying 'I promise I'll bake you a cake' is a felicitous speech act. Saying 'I promise you'll regret taking advantage of me!' isn't, because the relevant preparatory condition (that A will be good for the hearer) is not in place. In effect, what Searle was trying to do with his conditions for speech acts was explain how it is that we understand each other when we don't always say what we mean. In this respect, his aim was very similar to that of Austin's other student, H. P. Grice. The difference is that Searle's approach was to try and identify formal **rules** that governed how implied **meaning** is conveyed. Grice, by contrast, thought that implied meaning was best explained by a series of malleable principles, summarised in his **Cooperative Principle**. *See also* **illocutionary force** and **perlocutionary effect**.

speech community

This is the term used to refer to a group of people living, working or socialising near (or virtually near) to each other, where there is a considerable amount of interaction and where there is some kind of shared **language variety** in use. The term can therefore be used to refer to a community sharing a regional or social **dialect** (**sociolect**), a **register** associated with particular activities (work, leisure, etc.) or even the language shared by closer-knit groups such as families or religious or political groups. The flexibility in application of this term to larger or smaller communities is deliberate, and helpful in establishing what level of grouping a linguistic description is aimed at.

split infinitive

This refers to a supposed error of usage in English, a **language** which has two versions of the **infinitive verb**; one of them is the version that would be listed in the dictionary (e.g. *sleep, sing, dance, eat, watch*) and the other is the **to-*infinitive*** which is preceded by the

particle *to* (e.g. *to sleep, to sing*, etc.) There are some contexts in which the *to*-infinitive is required by the grammatical structure (e.g. following a catenative verb – e.g. 'Matt wanted to go home' – or where the verb is part of a **subordinate clause** in a nominal position – e.g. 'To dance is to live'). Because the particle (*to*) doesn't really carry any separate **meaning**, except to indicate that the verb is infinitival, and also because the *to*-infinitive translates as a single **word** in many languages, early grammarians of English decided that the two words should always occur side by side and never be separated by an **adverb**. Henry Alford, the Dean of Canterbury, wrote a book called *The Queen's English* in 1864, in which he consolidated this supposed **rule**, which can be found mentioned in earlier sources too. There remain many people, educated to consider Latin **grammar** as the standard by which to measure other modern languages, who would still insist that the *to*-infinitive should not be interrupted. However, no **linguist** would subscribe to this view, and most would simply point out that usage dictates that the *to*-infinitive can be interrupted on occasion. In addition to usage, they would appeal to meaning. If the hearer (or reader) can understand perfectly well what is being said with no experience of ungrammaticality, then the structure is acceptable. Moreover, there are certain circumstances in English where choosing not to split the infinitive results in a very different meaning. Consider the differences of meaning between the following sentences:

- I urge you to quickly give up smoking.
- I urge you quickly to give up smoking.
- I urge you to give up smoking quickly.

What these examples demonstrate is that it is perfectly acceptable to boldly split an infinitive if it suits the message you are trying to put across.

SPOCA

This is an **acronym** that stands for **subject, predicator, object, complement, adverbial**. *SPOCA* is a shorthand term for a descriptive **grammar** in which the components listed in the acronym are **clause** elements. S, P, O, C and A are known as *constituents* of a clause. They can be *realised* by particular types of **phrase**. That is, the phrases listed below can function as the following clause constituents:

Clause constituent	Realised by
Subject (S)	noun phrase
Predicator (P)	verb phrase
Object (O)	noun phrase
Complement (C)	noun phrase or adjective phrase
Adverbial (A)	adverb phrase or prepositional phrase

There are seven basic clause structures in English. These are:

SP	Erica lied.
SPO	The three kings forgot their lines.
SPC	The journey was a nightmare.
SPA	Lesley went to London.
SPOO	Hazel sent me a present.
SPOC	My teacher made me a linguist.
SPOA	Dan placed his book on the desk.

The only additions that can be made to these clause structures are more optional **adverbials**. For example:

On the whole, the journey was a nightmare from start to finish.

The relationship between clause constituents and their phrasal realisations can be seen by using a **tree diagram**. The branches in a tree diagram divide a higher level of structure into lower-level units (e.g. clauses into phrases and phrases into **words**), as in the following example:

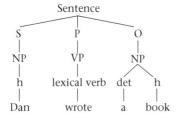

See also **simple sentence, compound sentence** and **complex sentence**.

spoken grammar

For a long time, spoken **language** was viewed as the poor relation of written language. That is, speech was considered **ungrammatical** and less fluent – somehow messier – than writing. In reality, speech can appear this way simply because it does not follow the same principles of **grammar** as written language. Consequently, it makes little sense to compare speech and writing in this way. Spoken language clearly must have a grammatical structure to it, otherwise it would be impossible to interpret. It just happens to be the case that the **grammar** of spoken language is somewhat different from that of written language, and much of this is down to the fact that speech takes place in real time. The results of the largest study of the grammar of spoken language to date can be found in *The Longman Grammar of Spoken and Written English* (1999). In it, it is suggested that there are three underlying principles of the production of spontaneous speech that affect the grammatical structure of spoken language. These are:

- the need to keep talking
- the fact that there is limited time to plan ahead
- the need to qualify what has been said

These three principles help to explain the apparent **non-fluency** of much spoken English, as in the extract below from the spoken section of the **British National Corpus**:

A: Well, oh isn't he, I can see when she looking at him was looking at him, that's what
B: Yeah
A: Oh! And he, and he
B: Mind you, you know
A: No!
B: Yeah, but you do forget sometimes, you sa you still think they're
A: Yeah!
B: You know and what do you think I am? An and and things like that and yo it's automatic
A: Mm

B: And if want to check quickly in a car and I'm driving
I automatically put the hand
A: Now you know
B: I've done that to Pam and she couldn't stop laughing!

(File KST)

In spontaneous speech, then, it is common to observe normal non-fluency, **ellipsis**, **hesitations** and pauses, repetitions, *reformulations* (saying the same thing but in a different way), *attention signals* (e.g. *hey*, *yo*, *say*) and what in written language would be thought of as grammatical incompleteness. The diagram shows another example from the BNC that contains a number of these features.

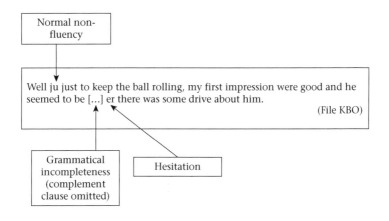

See also **C-unit**.

spoonerism

The spoonerism is named after the Reverend William Spooner (1844–1930) and refers to the habit of exchanging sounds to produce either nonsense or, more often, a completely different **phrase**. Spooner himself is credited with some of the following:

• 'our queer old dean' (dear old Queen)
• 'go and shake a tower' (take a shower)
• 'you have tasted a whole worm' (wasted a whole term)

There is no linguistic pattern that predicts when such phonological alteration is likely to produce an amusing alternative phrase, though it is noticeable that many of the examples that survive or are observed in everyday life tend to swap initial **consonant clusters**, leaving the **nucleus** of the **syllable** (i.e. the **vowel** element) intact.

Standard English

The concept of a standard **language** may seem familiar and simple to define at first sight. We can see it as a shared **variety** or **dialect** of a language, which is used in government, the courts, education and other public settings in order to minimise the potential disruption to society resulting from people not understanding each other. This is a positive view of the value of a **lingua franca**, which sees language as having a mainly functional role, to smooth the path of business, government, education and civil society in general. Standard English, in particular, has developed, for historical reasons relating to the colonial era, as the variety that second language speakers are often encouraged to learn. It has greater prestige than other dialects as a result of both its dominance in English-speaking countries and also as the lingua franca par excellence throughout the world.

However, there are a range of ways in which one could challenge the very existence of Standard English, as well as many reasons why one might want to do so. First of all, there is the linguistically sound argument that all dialects are equally suited to communication for all purposes, and the standard language is no better for public roles than any regional or social dialect. Most **linguists** would subscribe to this viewpoint on the linguistic evidence, but they are also very practical people and would often concede too that learning Standard English if you speak a different dialect is going to help you communicate in the wider world, with potential consequences for success and wealth. However, there are arguments about how this attitude can still cause speakers of nonstandard dialects to be disadvantaged, compared to those for whom Standard English is their first language. Children who grow up in Standard English households have a head start when they go to school, compared with children who need to acquire another dialect of English in order to succeed in examinations and other life challenges, such as job interviews. There follows the question, then, of whether – and how – one might educate children in their own dialect (at least to start with) and what the practical challenges are of this approach, given the mobility of both families and teachers in the contemporary world.

Another challenge to the concept of Standard English is whether one should talk about standard *Englishes*, rather than asserting that there is a single standard. This is also the dominant view amongst linguists who spend their time observing language in use. They note that, although modern communication systems mean that English speakers from all backgrounds and regions of the world can largely communicate with each other successfully, there is also the opposing tendency, for local versions of English to spring up in response to local conditions, in particular to incorporate some of the features of local indigenous or other common languages. This may be as simple as lexical **borrowing**: the need to add **words** to English to refer to natural phenomena or human-made artefacts. However, the local standard may also reflect structural aspects of the surrounding linguistic context or pragmatic (interactional) features of local social customs. One of the consequences of this variation is that we also talk of other Standard Englishes, such as Standard Indian English, Australian English, etc. Thus, it is necessary to make clear when we are talking about Standard English in its international sense, and when, for example, we mean Standard British English. (The concept of Englishess brings its own problem, of course, since the notion of languages in some sense belonging to nation states is problematic). In essence, like so many other linguistic concepts, Standard English is what is sometimes called a convenient fiction, by which we mean that it is not a well-defined entity with absolute boundaries, but a concept with **fuzzy** edges, which we nevertheless find helpful in some aspects of everyday life, as well as in some research contexts in **linguistics**.

standardisation

This is the process by which a **language variety** comes to be accepted as a standard. Sociolinguists recognise at least four stages that a variety goes through as it becomes a standard form. The first stage is *selection*. That is, members of a **speech community** have to select a variety for use as a standard (or select elements from a number of **dialects**). Next comes *codification*. This is the process by which the **rules** (ideally descriptive, but often prescriptive) of the selected variety are written down. The outcomes of codification are books like dictionaries, grammars and guides to usage. The next stage is *elaboration*. This is what happens when the selected and codified variety is used for purposes associated with high cultural value. For example, if the selected variety is used for writing literature or for making speeches in parliament, then it can be said to have undergone elaboration. Finally comes *acceptance*: members of the speech community have to accept the selected variety as a viable and useful standard **form** of their language. Standard varieties often emerge from the region where the most powerful people (in terms of wealth, status and cultural capital) live (e.g. London and the south-east Midlands in the case of England), and there usually follows a social as well as a linguistic shift towards valuing the standard language as a sign of superiority, and thus **prestige**. This is partly because the variety chosen to be a standard becomes associated with the law, with political power and with education, but also because it simply confers on first language speakers of this dialect a status that is largely accidental.

A variety of a language can have a written form or a spoken form (or both), and these forms do not necessarily emerge at the same time. Consider the case of English. In the **Old English** period, the West Saxon dialect emerged as a kind of written literary standard. By contrast, the **Middle English** period lacked any standard form at all. In the period of **Early Modern English**, a standard variety emerged from the 1450s onwards as a result of selections from a number of southeast dialects, including the variety known as *Chancery Standard*, a form associated with the work of government clerks. However, this was a written rather than spoken standard. A spoken standard did not arise in Britain until the advent of radio in the 1920s, which enabled the promulgation of so-called *BBC English* as a spoken variety associated with high prestige. In the USA, by contrast, a spoken standard English emerged before a written standard, as a result of dialect levelling among the early settlers (who spoke a range of regional British English dialects). A written standard did not arise until much later, as a consequence of the publication of

Noah Webster's *An American Dictionary of the English Language* (the forerunner of today's range of *Merriam Webster* dictionaries).

In the case of American English, the development of a standard variety was closely tied to efforts to assert an 'American' identity as part of a process of distinguishing the United States as a country in its own right (not simply an ex-colony of Great Britain). A standard variety of a language, then, has the contradictory power of bringing people together through mutually intelligible communication while simultaneously restricting people's access to power if they do not acquire that standard.

stop

Often used interchangeably with **plosive**, a stop is a **manner of articulation** used for producing a particular consonantal sound. A stop is a sound that creates a complete closure between two **articulators**. *Stop* is typically used to refer to an oral closure such that the two articulators creating the closure will be within the *oral tract* (and the **velum** is also raised). However, **nasal** sounds are also classified as stops because they also create a closure in the oral tract, but there is no plosion because the velum is also lowered to permit **airflow** through the **nasal cavity**.

stress

A stressed **syllable** is the syllable (or syllables) in a **word** with the most prominence. A stressed syllable is often identifiable through a relatively greater length than other syllables in the word, or it may be louder than other syllables, or it may have a higher **pitch** than other syllables. Some **linguists** may also refer to stressed syllables as *accented syllables*. Some linguists argue that **languages** divide into those which give each syllable equal weight (*syllable-timed* languages) and others (*stress-timed* languages), including English, where the timing between word stresses is relatively equal, meaning that the unstressed syllables in-between are hurried over.

striation

The term *striation* is used to describe the dark vertical lines that appear in the **spectrogram**. Striations are indicative of the **vocal folds** opening and are a sign of **voicing** occurring. A **voice quality** that has very marked **creak** will have wider spacing between its striations than are seen with a modal voice quality.

structuralism

This is the term which refers to a theory of **language** originating in the work of Ferdinand de Saussure, who is often seen as the founder of modern **linguistics**. Although it has since been appropriated by literary and cultural theorists, its original more practical insights remain fundamental to linguistic endeavours. Thus, for example, the now obvious assumption that most language (with the exception of some iconic forms, such as **onomatopoeia**) is arbitrary was first made explicit by Saussure, as was the still powerful idea that languages form systems of items and arrangements of those items that are partly closed. In other words, when one thing changes in the system, it has a knock-on effect on other parts of the system. One clear example of this would be the loss of the familiar form of the second person **pronoun** in English (i.e. *thou* and *thee*), which is only residually still used in the liturgy of churches. Though other European languages (e.g. French, Spanish and Italian) retain the distinction between two types of second person, English doesn't. The effect on the system of English is that *you* has to cover all types of second person address and is thus wider in meaning than its European counterparts.

style

This is not associated solely with literary **language,** nor with supposed good style. These may be some of the ways that the **word** is used in everyday language ('she has real style'; 'the style of Shakespeare'), but in **linguistics** it is a neutral term relating to the choices that language users make when they are speaking or writing – and the potential effects of those choices. So, for example, we can indeed talk about the style of Shakespeare, by describing the choices he made in his plays and poems, and then explaining what the literary (aesthetic, characterisation, plot) consequences of those choices are. We may also talk about the style of a popular detective genre to the extent that all writers in that genre share some stylistic choices (e.g. avoiding internal monologue in favour of observations of the physical world), but we may also decide to investigate the detailed variation represented by individual writers of that genre. Style includes those elements of literary, political and other **texts** (e.g. advertising or preaching) which stand out (*see* **foregrounding**), but also those which are in the background and often characterise a genre or register by being regular and repetitive choices. The development of computational **corpus linguistics** has enabled stylisticians (i.e. **linguists** who investigate textual choices) to study the regular, backgrounded features of texts in more depth. Note that the effects of stylistic choices may well be literary, but they can also be ideational, and even ideological too. Thus, a similar textual feature (for example, creating a one-off opposition in context) may produce a literary binary (such as the distinction between wizards and muggles in the Harry Potter novels) or an ideological division (such as the remain/leave binary in the debate about whether the UK should leave the EU).

stylistics

This is a sub-discipline of **linguistics** concerned with the study of **texts** and the relationship between linguistic choices and functional effects. Whilst stylistics originated in the application of descriptive linguistics to the study of literary **meaning** and effects, it has now developed to be a fully fledged sub-discipline with its own theories and models, as well as productive links to other disciplines (e.g. psychology) and sub-disciplines (e.g. **cognitive linguistics**). Stylistics has established a number of important concepts relating to the meaning of texts, including the concepts of **foregrounding**, **deviation** and **parallelism**, all of which help to explain the effects of textual choices.

subject

The subject in a **sentence** is (prototypically) the agent of the action. For instance, *Hazel* is the subject in 'Hazel baked a cake for Lesley', while *Lesley* is the subject in 'Lesley tooted a trumpet solo for Hazel.' In English, the subject has a tendency to come at the start of the sentence. Nonetheless, it is not always as straightforward as this might suggest. In some cases, it is hard to

think of the subject as 'doing' something. For example, in the
sentence 'Grammar lessons are fun', it is hard to think of *grammar
lessons* as doing something – nonetheless, it is the thing that the
proposition is about, and controls the **verb**. Subjects, also, are not
always simple **noun phrases** such as *Hazel* or *grammar lessons*.
Take the sentence 'What the syntacticians discovered was
amazing.' Here we have a much more complex subject – a **noun
clause** (*What the syntacticians discovered*) rather than
a straightforward person or thing. Nonetheless, we can tell that it
is the subject, because it controls the verb (*is*) and can be
substituted by a **pronoun**: *it*. *See also* **SPOCA**, **predicator**, **object**,
complement and **adverbial**.

subordinate clause

A subordinate clause is one that is dependent on a main **clause** to
be grammatical. For example, 'The linguist said that she loved
linguistics' is a **sentence** that is composed of two clauses: a main
clause and a subordinate one. The main clause is 'The linguist said
that she loved linguistics.' It is a composed of a **subject** (the **noun
phrase** *The linguist*), a **predicator** (the **verb phrase** *said*) and an
object. Notice, though, that, unlike the subject and predicator,
the object is not a **phrase** but a clause: *that she loved linguistics* (we
know it is a clause because it has clause elements, i.e. a subject *she*,
a predicator *loved* and an object *linguistics*). And that clause
cannot stand on its own as a grammatically acceptable sentence.
That is, in order to be grammatical, it needs to be part of (i.e.
embedded within) a main clause. The effect of embedding
subordinate clauses within a main clause can produce **recursion**,
as in this lyric from The Killers' song 'Somebody told me':
'Somebody told me that you had a boyfriend who looked like
a girlfriend that I had in February of last year.' *See also* **relative
clause**, which is a type of subordinate clause, and **embedded
clause**.

substitution test

A substitution test is a technique used in descriptive **linguistics** to
support the analysis being proposed, whether that is at the
phonological, morphological, syntactic or semantic level. If you can

substitute one element of a **text** (spoken or written) by either a **proform** or another similar element without making the result **ungrammatical**, then you can be sure that they belong in the same **category**. So, if you are wondering how to show that *the poor hungry orangutan* is a **noun phrase** in the **sentence** 'The poor hungry orangutan saw the loggers cut down his trees', you can try substituting with the **pronoun** *he*, or by another noun phrase, *the old opossum*. (This sentence will work for most of the world's threatened species!) Likewise, if you wonder whether [v] is a **phoneme** in Spanish, as distinct from [b], try substituting it in a **word** like *verdad* (truth) and you will find that whichever sound you use produces the same **meaning**, so the two must be linked in a single phoneme for that **language**, unlike in English where *van* and *ban* mean rather different things.

suffix

This is the term for an inflectional or derivational **morpheme** occurring after the **base form** of a **word**. The plural inflections in French (*chaises*) or Spanish (*sillas*) or English (*chairs*) all happen to add <s> in the written form of the **language**, and they therefore share the suffix <s> for **noun** plurals. An example of a derivational suffix would be <er> in English which can indicate 'a person who does the activity named in the base verb' (e.g. *baker*, *footballer*). *See also* **affix**, **infix** and **prefix**.

superlative

This is the term used to denote the most extreme form of a gradable **adjective** or **adverb** in a sequence (*good, better, best; bad, worse, worst; strong, stronger, strongest; quickly, quicklier / more quickly, quickliest / most quickly*). There is nothing evaluative about this term, despite its use in everyday colloquial usage to mean that something is really good ('that was a superlative meal'). *See also* **comparative**.

superordinate

This can be used in both lexical **semantics** and in **syntax** to indicate a relationship between linguistic forms. In lexical semantics, the term is used to refer to a **lexeme** which is more general in scope than one or more other lexemes which are termed **hyponyms** – another common term for *superordinate* in this sense is **hypernym** or *hyperonym*. For example, dog is a superordinate term whose hyponyms include *poodle* and *terrier*. The superordinate can always be used in place of the more specific lexeme, but not vice versa. This is because the meaning of the superordinate is contained within its hyponyms, but their specialist features are not contained in the superordinate. That is, all poodles have the qualities of dogs, but not all dogs have all the qualities of poodles. In syntax, superordinate is normally used to describe the higher-level **clause** structure within which you find **subordinate clauses**. Sometimes the term is replaced by *main clause*, but note that a clause can be superordinate to another clause without also being a main clause. The following **sentence** illustrates: *Dan told Lesley that the milk that was in the fridge was sour*. Here, the main clause is *Dan told Lesley X*, where *X* stands for the subordinate clause *that the milk that was in the fridge was sour*, which is playing the role of *grammatical object*. However, there is also a subordinate **relative clause** within this clause (*that was in the fridge*) and this means that the object clause is both subordinate to the main clause and superordinate to the relative clause.

suprasegmental

This is an **adjective** that describes a group of phonetic features that are not the properties of individual **segments**, but are associated with multiple segments, **phrases** or **utterances**. Suprasegmentals include features such as speaking *tempo* (i.e. speed), *tone*, **intonation**, **voice quality** and **stress**.

syllable

Syllable is a term used to describe the organisation of speech sounds into different units – and these are often referred to as the building blocks of **words**. A syllable can be made up of an **onset, nucleus** and **coda**. Syllables can be made up of different combinations of **vowels** and **consonants**, but it is also possible to have syllables that are just a single vowel or single consonant. Different **languages** can have preferences for different types of syllable structures, and, as a result, this can influence the *prosody*, *rhythm* and **stress** of a language.

synchronic

This describes the analysis of **language** as it is at a particular point in time. It can be contrasted with **diachronic** analysis, which involves the study of language over a particular period of time. The two terms can be attributed to Ferdinand de Saussure, the Swiss **linguist** whose *Cours de linguistique generale* (*Course in General Linguistics*), published posthumously in 1916, paved the way for the emergence of modern **linguistics** as a discipline. Doing a synchronic linguistic analysis is like taking a snapshot of a language at a particular point in time. For instance, we might want to know how French teenagers use language in the second decade of the twenty-first century, or what the characteristic features of the Yorkshire **dialect** were in the early 1950s. And, according to Saussure, synchronic analysis is of primary importance in linguistics. For example, in order to determine how language changes over a particular period of time, we need to have a clear sense of what the language was like at the beginning of our period. That is, we need to undertake a synchronic linguistic analysis first. Only after we have done this can we start to compare forms of the language at particular points in its development. In essence, synchronic analysis must precede diachronic analysis.

synecdoche

This is a traditional *figure of speech* (i.e. a form of expression, often used for rhetorical effect, that relies on figurative as opposed to literal language). *Synecdoche* is still referred to in **linguistics** and denotes the use of a part of something to refer to the whole, and sometimes also the use of a whole entity to refer to only part of it. For example, *hands* was often used in the nineteenth century to refer to factory workers. Note, too, how in this example, the synechdoche dehumanises the workers, revealing the exploitative mindset of their employers. By contrast, the use of *America* to refer to the USA, rather than the whole of the continent (including central and south America, as well as Canada), takes the word for the whole landmass and applies it to only one part of it. This reinforces the global dominance of the United States and makes the other countries relatively invisible. There is some overlap with **metonymy**, though the latter is broader in concept and does not necessarily depend on a part–whole relationship between the **word** and its **referent**. **meronymy** is another term used to denote part–whole reference of the kind found in synecdoche.

synonym

A synonym is a **word** (or sometimes a **phrase**) that means the same as another word in the same **language**. There are different definitions of *synonym*, but the most common one holds that synonyms have the same **denotation**, but they might differ in other aspects of **meaning** or use, such as **connotation**. If we were to restrict the meaning of *synonyms* to words that were exactly the same in all aspects of meaning, we would find no true synonymy in language, since words with similar meanings tend to specialise to different uses. For example, the words *dog* and *hound* both denote the same creature, though *hound* has connotations of a hunting dog whereas the former is a more general term. Differences in connotative meaning between synonyms are often related to **register** (i.e. degrees of formality). Synonyms often arise when a language borrows words from another language. For example, English is a Germanic language and yet it has acquired many words from French as a result of the influence of French over many years (not least the fact that, during the **Middle English** period, French was the language of the royal court, religion and the law in England). Examples of this phenomenon in English include *abandon* or *forsake* (Germanic) and *abdicate* or *renounce* (Latinate), where each of these words, meaning approximately the same thing in terms of their denotation, nevertheless have specialised their usage to particular contexts (e.g. *abdicate* now being almost exclusively used to refer to someone giving up a position of power) or, through their grammatical patterning, have developed stronger connotations (e.g. *abandon* and *forsake* are often followed by a human or animal **Goal**, as in 'He abandoned his children', with the result that these actions acquire a ***pejorative*** tone). Sometimes, synonyms reflect different **dialects** – for example, different parts of the UK call the passageway between houses a *ginnel* or a *snicket* or a *twitten*. We may also perceive differences between synonyms based on connotations or social meaning. For instance, we may deem *lies* to be bigger and more serious than *porkies*, and in polite company we are more likely to ask for directions to the *bathroom* than to the *crapper*. There are many such examples to be found, and there is almost always a slight difference of emphasis or usage or connotation, to the extent that it is very difficult to argue that there are any true and exact synonyms in English or any other language. Indeed, nuances of meaning between synonyms develop to avoid the redundancy of having two terms that mean exactly the same. For instance, *defecate* (from Latin) is a formal synonym for the more informal Germanic word *shit*.

syntagmatic

Syntagmatic relationships hold between items (sounds, **words**, **phrases**) that are used together. Thus, there is a syntagmatic relationship between the **subject** (*The dog*), the **predicator** (*ate*) and the **object** (*my cake*) in the **sentence** 'The dog ate my cake.' This type of relationship is sometimes thought of as horizontal, whereas **paradigmatic** relationships (e.g. between the options that could fill the space occupied by *dog* in this sentence – including *cat*, *rabbit* and *baby*) are seen as vertical.

syntax

This is related to the idea of **syntagmatic** relationships, as it investigates the way in which **words** and **phrases** are put together into **sentences** and larger structures. Although *syntax* is sometimes used interchangeably with **grammar**, it usually excludes the grammar of word structure (*see* **morphology**), so that syntax and morphology together make up the wider field of grammar. Morphology could be said to have a more paradigmatic focus, too, which is why the term *syntax* is less well suited to cover this area of grammar.

synthetic language

A synthetic language is one which relies primarily on a system of **inflection** rather than **word order** to convey **sentence meaning**. *See* **analytic language** for a full explanation.

Systemic Functional Linguistics

Systemic Functional Linguistics (SFL) is a field of **linguistics** associated with the **linguist** M. A. K. Halliday (1925–2018). It is based on the belief that linguistics should be able to explain how people exchange **meanings** through **language**. When we communicate, we make choices from the language that we are speaking, which can be seen as a *system*. The *function* element of the term stems from Halliday's perception that the system serves three different functions – ideational, interpersonal and textual – which he calls **metafunctions**. The ideational metafunction concerns the relationship between language and how we perceive and construct our experience of the world. The interpersonal metafunction refers to how we use language to interact with others – whether it be to attempt to persuade someone of our point of view, or just to establish and maintain relationships with people. Finally, the textual metafunction relates to how we use language to organise our thoughts and meanings into messages, be they **turns** in conversation, poems or text messages. SFL is distinct from other approaches to language (such as the generative approach that originates in the work of Noam Chomsky) in the way it looks at language as a system, rather than as a structure. While approaches such as Chomsky's are more concerned with the **rules** that govern how syntactic structures pattern together in language, SFL is more concerned with the choices we make when faced with alternatives, and the functional significance of these. For example, structuralist **grammar** is concerned with uncovering the rules that determine which **parts of speech** could be inserted into the gaps in the following **sentence**: 'Dan ___ the ___ book'. SFL, though, is more concerned with the choices we make when we select the units that would fit in those slots, e.g. '[Dan/Lesley/Erica] [wrote/read/discussed] [the/a/their] [red/stylistics/great] [book/novel/epic]'.

taboo

Taboo language, or **linguistic taboo**, refers to **words** or **phrases** that are deemed socially inappropriate or offensive. Types of taboo language in English include profanities, e.g. words to describe excretion and words to describe sex. What is considered taboo language varies between cultures, and taboo words can change over time. For example, the word *cunt*, often considered one of the most offensive words in English, was not considered taboo or offensive historically. In fact, it appears in some UK place names as far back as

1230. For example, in the English city of York, there is still a *Grape Lane* in the city centre, which was historically called *Grapcunt Lane* (i.e. *grope + cunt + lane*). In the Middle Ages, it was common practice to name streets according to what they were used for, and Grope Cunt Lane was associated with prostitution. Due to the changing attitudes towards *cunt*, the street name was changed to Grape Lane. Furthermore, *cunt* features in historical medical documents to refer to the vulva, which gives further evidence that the word was not considered taboo or offensive historically. One way that language users have developed the means to talk about taboo subjects is through **euphemism**. An example of a euphemism would be *making love* instead of *having sex*.

tag questions

Tag questions are just great, aren't they? The term refers to statements (*see* **declarative**) or commands (*see* **imperative**) that are turned into questions by the addition of an **interrogative** 'tag' that consists of an **auxiliary verb** followed by a **pronoun**. There's an example at the beginning of this entry (you did spot it, didn't you?). Tag questions are found in many **languages** and are particularly common in speech. In English, they can take the form of a positive statement + negative tag ('Just leave, won't you?!'), negative statement + positive tag ('You won't leave, will you?') or positive statement + positive tag ('I'll just leave, shall I?'). Tag questions have a range of functions. Early research in language and gender claimed that women use more tag questions than men, and that this demonstrates a lack of confidence on their part, the tag being used to seek confirmation for the views expressed. However, as many **linguists** have pointed out, the use of tag questions might just as easily demonstrate a concern for the listener (not to mention the fact that generalising about differences between women's and men's language use has long since been shown to be problematic). Tag questions have also been shown to function as leading questions, pushing the listener to give the response that the speaker actually wants. An interesting recent development in the structure of tag questions can be seen in Multicultural London English, where the tag *innit* can be used in place of an auxiliary and pronoun, and can be appended to any statement, positive or negative (as in 'You need to go, innit?'). Although this might seem unusual to speakers who don't use this form, *innit* just fixes the tag function in a single unvarying lexical item – in exactly the same way as French *n'est-ce-pas*. Interesting, no? *See also* **question forms**.

tap

A tap is the **manner of articulation** used for producing a particular consonantal sound. *Tap* and **flap** are often used interchangeably by **linguists** to describe a **consonant** that is produced when an active **articulator** (such as the **tongue**) is thrown against another articulator. A *tap* is a quick movement that is typically articulated with the tip of the tongue moving in an upward motion towards the roof of the mouth, and then returning to a more neutral position in the mouth.

target domain

In **conceptual metaphor theory** (CMT), the target domain is the object being conceptualised in terms of something else. For example, in the conceptual metaphor TIME IS MONEY (linguistic instantiations of which include 'You're wasting my time' and 'Missing my train cost me an hour'), TIME is the target domain as it is being discussed as if it is MONEY (which is the **source domain**).

target position

In **phonetics**, *target position* refers to an idealised articulatory position. *Target position* is typically used to describe a reference point for producing a specific sound. Phoneticians may talk about a speaker *under-shooting* a target, such that the production does not sound as one may expect (as may happen if the speaker doesn't have time to get their **articulators** in place before the next sound has to be articulated). A speaker who is consistently missing target positions for articulations may be perceived as mumbling, as targets may be approximated, lenited (*see* **lenition**) or elided (*see* **elision**) completely.

tautology

In **linguistics**, *tautology* is used in two different but related ways. The first **sense** of the word relates to rhetoric and, when used in this sense, *tautology* means saying the same thing twice, often creating different

meanings. An example of this type of tautology is the saying 'It is what it is' which means more than its surface form may suggest, i.e. it isn't just a comment on what a situation happens to be, it is a statement about accepting what that situation is. In this sense, a tautologous expression is one that expresses the statement twice using the same, or different, **words**. Related to, but slightly distinct from, this first sense is the sense of *tautology* most often used in the field of **semantics**, particularly logical semantics. Here, *tautology* is concerned with the truth of a statement. For a statement to be a logical tautology, the statement expressed must always be true. For example, 'Matt will come to the party or Matt will not come to the party' is tautologous because the complex statement expressed will always be true.

tense

This is the linguistic term for time reference in **language** (the term *tense* derives from the French **word** for *time*). The most common way of encoding tense in language is through **verbs**. In languages that do this, tense is indicated through specific verb **forms**. In English, tense can be marked by adding an **inflection** to a verb (e.g. *wash* + *ed* = past tense) or by changing the **vowel** in the verb stem (*see* **base form**), a process known as **ablaut** (e.g. *sing* → *sang*). Some people would claim that English has only two tenses: present and past. Future reference is created either by using a present tense form (e.g. 'Lesley *is going* to a gig tomorrow') or by the addition of a modal **auxiliary verb** to the **verb phrase** (e.g. 'Matt *will* meet us at the pub later'). While these methods allow us to refer to future time, the **sentences** are not in the future tense as we have not changed the verb in any way, either by inflection or ablaut (unlike what happens when we form present and past tense). However, some languages do not express tense in the verb at all. For example, Mandarin Chinese expresses tense via **free morphemes** that follow the verb. 过 (guò), for instance, is the **particle** used after the verb to denote that the action has taken place in the past. *See also* **aspect**.

text

A text is a stretch of cohesive and coherent **discourse**. The **word** *text* originally meant 'something woven' (from Latin *texere*, meaning 'to weave'), and, although you might nowadays only associate woven things with material (e.g. woven fabric), text can also be thought of as a woven artefact. The reason for this is that texts contain **sentences** that are structurally related to each other through lexical or grammatical **cohesion**. These structural relations result in our conceiving of the text as being a unified whole. The **linguists** M. A. K. Halliday and Ruqaiya Hasan note that the defining quality of a text is *texture*. And texture is the result of cohesion. Texts do not have to be long. Here is an example of a text (i.e. a product of discourse that has texture) that is composed of a single sentence:

> One fine evening a young princess put on her bonnet and clogs, and went out to take a walk by herself in a wood; and when she came to a cool spring of water, that rose in the midst of it, she sat herself down to rest a while.
>
> (The Brothers Grimm, 'The Frog Prince')

What make this a text is that there are cohesive relations between the elements of its constituent sentence. For example, we know that *her* and *she* relate back to the **noun phrase** *a young princess*. To return to the weaving analogy, this anaphoric reference (*see* **anaphora**) acts as the linguistic equivalent of fastening two pieces of material together with a cross-woven thread. Compare this with the following example, which has no texture and therefore cannot be thought of as a text:

> Check for concrete strengthening. Received from Dan McIntyre the amount of fifty pounds. Crack the eggs into a mixing bowl.

By contrast with the first example, there are no cohesive relations between sentences here. In actual fact, this example is made up of a cryptic crossword clue, a line from a receipt, and an extract from a recipe. Because the definition of a text is a product of discourse that has texture, the term *text* does not have to be restricted to written **language**. That is, we can think of cohesive speech as constituting a text too. Linguists interested in multimodality may go even further – for example, describing movies as filmic texts. *See also* **coherence**.

thematic role
Thematic roles are the semantic relations between a **verb** and the **noun phrases** (or *arguments*) it takes. Thematic roles indicate the

relationship between the different arguments (often realised as noun phrases) in a **clause** or **sentence**. Some examples of thematic roles are *agent* (the doer of an action), *patient* (the thing being affected by the action) and *experiencer* (the thing experiencing something). For example:

Richard designed the magazine	*Richard* is the agent of this action because he is the one completing the action (designing)
Dan praised *Erica*	*Erica* is the patient because she is the thing being affected by the action (being praised)
Hazel thinks *The Sopranos* is great	*Hazel* is the experiencer, as she is experiencing the action (thinking)

Thematic roles are closely related to *theta roles* in **syntax**; however, thematic roles are concerned with the semantic relations between a verb and its noun phrases, whereas theta roles are concerned with the noun phrases a verb can take based on its syntactic properties. Thematic roles are interesting as they offer information about what semantic information the verb encodes. For example, in the sentence 'Dan praised Erica', *praised* requires another thematic role (syntactically realised as a direct **object**), therefore *praised* must take an argument.

tone language

A tone language is one in which the *tone* you use when uttering a particular **word** has an effect on the **meaning** of that word. Tone refers to **pitch** change. For example, in Chinese, the word *ma* has four possible meanings, and the particular meaning you convey is dependent on the tone you use when uttering it. A high and level tone will convey the meaning *mother*. A rising tone will convey *bother*. Use a falling tone and you'll mean *scold*. Adopt a fall–rise tone and you'll convey the meaning *horse*. Tonal languages can be tricky for learners whose first **language** doesn't use tones to convey meaning. Particularly if you're referring to a Chinese friend's mother.

tongue

Your tongue is the most important **articulator** involved in speech production. You use it in most of the sounds you make. The height and position of your tongue (whether it's towards the front or back of your **oral cavity**) determines the **vowel** sounds you produce, while using your tongue in conjunction with another articulator generates **consonant** sounds. The tongue has a tip, a **blade**, a front, a back and a root. To see how the various parts of the tongue have an impact on consonant production, say the **word** *thin*. You should feel that the tip of your tongue is against your front **teeth**. Now say *ship*. The blade of your tongue will be in contact with the back of your **alveolar** ridge. Try *yes*. The front of your tongue will be raised towards your **hard palate**. Now try saying *dog*. Producing the final consonant of this word involves using the back of your tongue in conjunction with the **velum**.

topic

Along with *comment*, *topic* is to do with the information structure of **sentences**. Specifically, *topic* is the label given to the thing being discussed in a sentence. Different **languages** present information in different ways, and one way that **linguists** explore this phenomenon is through looking at how the syntactic structure of a sentence emphasises a topic–comment structure. Many East Asian languages such as Vietnamese, Chinese and Japanese have topic–comment structure.

trajector

This is a term taken from **cognitive linguistics**, particularly the cognitive **grammar** proposed by Ronald Langacker. *Trajector* is the term given to an object or entity that moves across, or changes, in relation to some static object or **landmark**. The way in which a trajector gets to a landmark is sometimes called the *path*. Trajectors and landmarks can relate to concrete or abstract objects and entities. For example:

Trajector	Path	Landmark
Hazel and Erica	ran towards	the university.
The lecturer	worked through	the pile of assessments he had to mark.

Trajector and *landmark* are related to the concepts of **figure** and **ground**.

transformational grammar

This refers to the grammatical theory first proposed by Noam Chomsky, which was inspired by the observation that some **sentences** in a **language** appear to have the same propositional content (*see* **proposition**) whilst being different in their surface structure. Chomsky proposed that, for example, *the green car* and 'the car is green' *must* be related to each other at some deep level of structure and suggested that there was a 'transformational' relationship between all such pairs of structures. The same kind of transformational relationship, he argued, must underlie the pairs of **active** and **passive** sentences, such as 'Dan ate all the pies' and 'All the pies were eaten by Dan.' It seemed unlikely, Chomsky argued, that speakers would construct passive sentences completely in isolation from their active counterparts; rather, they would have an underlying structure in mind where the **Actor** is Dan, irrespective of whether he turns up as the grammatical **subject** of the **utterance** or in the **adverbial** (*by Dan*) of the passive version. In the early stages of this development in grammatical theory, it was linked to **generative grammar**, though the latter has now developed into a separate strand of theoretical thinking not necessarily linked to the idea of transformations.

transient

In acoustics, *transient* refers to a sound with a very short duration, typically characterised by its high **amplitude**. Transients are often described as resembling spikes in the **waveform**. **Plosives** are commonly associated with transient sounds as the initial release of air will often cause a spike in the waveform. Other sounds are also capable of appearing as transients on a waveform – for example, doors slamming, gunshots, a book being dropped, or even some musical sounds.

transitivity

This is a term used to describe whether a **verb** needs an **object** to be grammatical, and, if so, how many objects it needs in order to be grammatical. If a verb does not take a ***direct object*** (Od) then it is described as ***intransitive***; if it can take a direct object, it is described as ***transitive***; if it can take a direct object and an ***indirect object*** (Oi), then it is described as ***ditransitive***. Direct and indirect objects are realised as noun-phrase **complements** which are necessary ***arguments*** of the verb. For example:

Lesley *fell*.	***Intransitive*** because the verb *fell* does not need a direct object to be grammatical
Erica *fixed* the computer.	***Transitive*** because the verb *fixed* needs a direct object to be grammatical: *Erica *fixed*.
Hazel *gave* the book to Dan.	***Ditranstive*** because the verb *gave* needs both a direct and indirect object to be grammatical: *Hazel gave

As well as its traditional use to describe the arguments of a verb, transitivity has also been appropriated by **Systemic Functional Linguistics** to refer in more functional terms to those participants that are semantically necessary when a verb is chosen. This is related to the more grammatical type of transitivity, but explores the semantics of the **subject**, object and complement choices and their relation to the verb. For example, although 'Dan ate the chocolate cake' and 'Dan remembered the chocolate cake' are similar in their grammatical structure (SVO), they nevertheless imply different relationships between the subject (Dan) and the two objects. In Halliday's version of transitivity, the first **sentence** contains a ***material action (intentional)*** verb where Dan is the **Actor** and the cake is the **Goal**. The second sentence contains a ***mental process*** where Dan is the ***Sensor*** and the cake is the ***Phenomenon***. Halliday's transitivity system is made up of three main types of process (material, mental and relational) and three minor types (behavioural, verbal and existential).

tree diagram

Tree diagrams are a type of diagram used in **linguistics** that are used most often to show the hierarchical structure of **sentences** according to a theory of **syntax**. A syntax tree looks a bit like the roots of a tree, hence its name. Tree diagrams are used to model sentence structure. The top of a tree diagram is marked 'S' which stands for *sentence*. The sentence is then broken up into different constituents such as **noun phrases** (NPs), **verb phrases** (VPs) and **prepositional phrases** (PPs). There are different **rules** about which **phrases** can be nested within other phrases. The following are some phrase structure rules. The elements on the left of the arrow (e.g. VP, NP, and so on) are parent nodes, whereas the elements on the right side of the arrow are child nodes – i.e. they are nested within the parent node. Any elements in round brackets are optional elements – i.e. a sentence node has to include a verb phrase and a noun phrase, and a verb phrase (which is a child node of a sentence) has to include a **verb** (which would be a child node of the verb phrase branch) but not necessarily a noun phrase or prepositional phrase:

$S \rightarrow NP\ VP$
$VP \rightarrow V\ (NP)\ (PP)$
$NP \rightarrow (Det)\ N$
$PP \rightarrow P\ NP$

Below is a syntax tree for the sentence 'The cat sat on the mat.' The tree shows that the sentence (S) is made up of a noun phrase (NP), and a verb phrase (VP) which then contains a prepositional phrase (PP), which contains a **preposition** and a noun phrase.

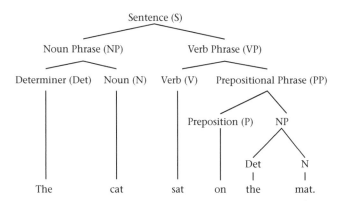

Tree diagrams may look different depending on which model of **grammar** is being used. For example, some theories of **syntax** express a *tense phrase* (TP), whereas other theories of syntax may only refer to a verb phrase (VP). Syntax trees are important in syntactic analysis because they allow **linguists** to discuss the different ways in which internalised knowledge of **language** (what Chomsky calls **I-language**) may be realised in external language (what Chomsky calls **E-language**). Moreover, syntax trees allow linguists to show why the meanings of some sentences are ambiguous. For example, the headline 'British left waffles on Falkland Islands' is syntactically ambiguous because *British left* could be a NP (i.e. left-wing political parties) or *left* could be a VP (i.e. an undefined group of Brits have left some dough-based desserts on the Falkland Islands . . .).

tremor

This is a term used in **voice quality** research, and speech and language pathology more generally, to refer to the shaky-like quality a voice can have. The shaky voice quality is caused by irregular vibrations of the **vocal folds**. Severe vocal tremors are often associated with different neurological disorders, but slight tremors are commonly found across **languages** and **accents** as part of an individual's normal speaking voice. Voice specialists quantify tremor using measures like **jitter** and *shimmer*.

trill

A trill is a specific **manner of articulation** that is produced in a subset of consonantal sounds. A trill is produced when an active **articulator** is held in place, and the **airflow** causes the articulator to vibrate. A trill, unlike a **tap**, involves multiple contacts between two articulators. [r] is an example of a trill. This **alveolar** trill appears in many Spanish **words**, like *burrito*, where the trill is represented orthographically (i.e. in conventional spelling) as a double <r>.

truth-conditional semantics

This is a theoretical approach to the study of semantic **meaning** that asserts that the meaning of a **sentence** should be thought of in reference to the conditions in the world in which the sentence would be true or false. The facts that would need to be the case in order for a sentence to be true are known as **truth conditions**. Take, for example, the sentence *Joe Biden is President of the USA*. In truth-conditional semantics, for this sentence to be true (and therefore meaningful) there must be a person called *Joe Biden*, there must be a person who is President of the USA, and the person who is currently President of the USA must be Joe Biden. Truth-conditional semantics has been heavily criticised, however, for being circular and also for being unable to account for the meaning of sentences whose truth conditions are not met, such as 'Claire Underwood is President of the USA.' Clearly, the President of the USA is not Claire Underwood, but it seems reductive in the extreme to say that this is not a meaningful sentence, especially if you happen to have seen the US television series *House of Cards*, in which the President of the USA is called *Claire Underwood*. **Possible Worlds Theory** emerged to try and solve this problem by suggesting that, while a sentence's truth conditions might not be met in the real world, they might well be met in some alternative possible world, such as a fictional one.

turbulence

This is a term used to describe the quality of the **airflow** that may occur when producing speech. Turbulent airflow is created as a result of a constriction, where a large volume of air is pressed through a very small/tight passage. Turbulent air is perceived as having a hissing quality, and within **phonetics** turbulent airflow is typically just referred to as frication. **Fricative** sounds, by definition, are considered to include turbulent airflow in their productions.

turn

This is a term taken from the sub-disciplines of **linguistics** that study talk-in-interaction, for example **Conversation Analysis** or **Discourse Analysis**. Conversations are made up of a series of coordinated turns, or times when a single person is talking within an interaction. When somebody is speaking, i.e. when they are taking their turn, interruptions are unusual, and instead speakers opt to deploy a series of **turn-taking** strategies to manage conversations on a turn-by-turn basis. Such strategies include signalling a *transition relevance place* (or TRP) in which the turn at talk is passed to another speaker in the conversation. TRPs include silences that indicate that the current speaker has finished speaking, for example at the end of a question or answer. When these silences occur, they typically do so at the end of a **turn-constructional unit** (or TCU) which are the units by which conversation analysts measure turns. For example:

TURN → A: [TCU Are you coming to the party next week?] [TRP]

TURN → B: [TCU I am!] [TRP]

TURN → A: [TCU Great!] [TRP] [TCU I hope they have cake!]

Linguists have found turn-taking to be a universal phenomenon, as people do not generally speak or sign (as is the case in **sign languages**) at the same time as one another. Turns have been the object of study in very many linguistic studies aiming to analyse the conversational differences between different groups – for example, exploring the thesis that men interrupt more than women, or that discursively powerful **participants** in conversations take longer, and more frequent, turns than other less discursively powerful participants. For these reasons, the analysis of turns and their structure is a fundamental part of the study of talk-in-interaction and studies into conversations in different contexts. The terms *turn*, *TRP* and *TCU* are used to label phenomena that speakers already know about and observe (albeit without being conscious that they do). For example, the comedian Steve Coogan exploited the problems that can arise when trying to work out what is a TRP in lagged conversation when he wrote a sketch for his comedy character, the inept TV presenter Alan Partridge. The transcript below is taken from a sketch that parodies British current affairs programmes. In the sketch, Alan Partridge moves from one segment of the fictional show in which he is discussing apple pies to another segment where he introduces the show's newsreader, Ruth, via a (lagged!) video link from Hollywood (overlapping talk is marked using square brackets):

Alan: Ruth I bet you loved your mum's apple pie

((Ruth appears on screen but does not respond to Alan. Alan looks at the camera bewildered and makes a second attempt to get Ruth to talk))

Alan: .hhh first up police raid a house in Cleveland and
        find four dead men in a septic tank. Not the kind of
        story anyone like[s]
Ruth: [I do actually], I love anything
        like that, ha ha. [Absolutely

((Alan looks at the camera out the side of his eye with
furrowed brows))

Alan: [Right]
Ruth: delicious]
Alan: (...) Oh. Um. You mean the apple pie. I'm the same
        though, Ruth. All the pastry turns into a FAT BACK

((Alan grabs the skin on his back and smiles at the
camera))

Ruth: Well quite. It's been described as a truly gruesome
        [sight]
Alan: [°what? °]
Ruth: [A vision of hell

turn-taking

This is a term from **Conversation Analysis**. We follow turn-taking
rules when we engage in conversation. But, like many rules in
linguistics, these are descriptive rather than prescriptive. That is,
they are rules that describe what people have been observed to do, as
opposed to being rules that prescribe what people *should* do. When a
turn-taking system is in place, speakers take it in turns to hold what
conversation analysts call the **floor**. Holding the floor means having
the right to speak and have other participants in the conversation
listen to you. The turn-taking system is made up of the ***turn
allocational component*** and the ***turn constructional
component***. The first of these controls turn change. For example,
the current speaker might select the next speaker, or the next
speaker might self-select – perhaps by disagreeing with a point that
the speaker has just made. The turn constructional component
controls turn length and complexity. For example, if you're
speaking and feel that someone is about to interrupt you, you might
raise your voice to ensure that your turn continues. Needless to say,
some people are better at managing the turn allocational

component than others. What the turn-taking system reveals is that conversation is highly structured. If you've got something to say, there are strategies for getting hold of the floor. You don't just have to wait your turn.

type–token ratio

Consider the following **sentence**: *Hazel went to the shops to buy some eggs to make a cake.* In this sentence, there are 13 **word *tokens*** (that is, 13 words in total) and 10 word ***types*** (that is, only 10 different words because *to* is repeated 3 times). If we divide the number of types by the number of tokens and multiply by 100, we get a type–token ratio. The type–token ratio for our example sentence is 76.92. Type–token ratios can be indicative of **lexical richness** – that is, how varied a text is in terms of its **vocabulary**. This can only ever be indicative though, and you have to be cautious in how you interpret type–token ratios. For example, **Middle English texts** often contain lots of spelling variation (i.e. different spellings of the same word). As a result, the type–token ratio for such texts can be artificially high. You may well find the same to be true of WhatsApp messages and emails.

ultrasound

Like X-ray, ultrasound is a non-invasive technique for seeing inside the body. The difference is that is not dangerous in any way. Ultrasound is used, of course, to monitor foetuses in the womb, but it can also be used to see the configurations of the **articulators** (**tongue**, *teeth*, **lips**, **glottis**, etc.) when we are talking.

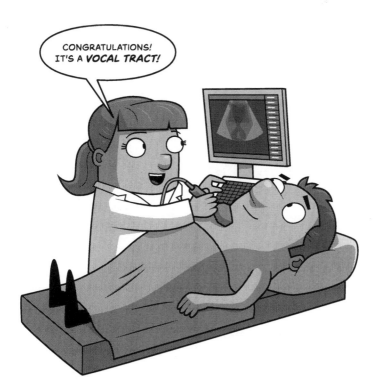

unaspirated

Unaspirated sounds are those where no aspiration occurs – i.e. they are not accompanied by a puff of air when you pronounce them. For example, hold your hand in front of your mouth. While you will feel a puff of air against it when you pronounce the /k/ in *kill*, you won't for the /k/ in *skill*.

underextension

This occurs when someone uses a **word** in a more specific way than usual. Children commonly underextend when they are acquiring **language**. Perhaps you have known a child who recognises that their parents' vehicle is a *car*, but won't use the same word for other similar vehicles – their parents' car is *car*! Or perhaps a child uses *tiger* for their cuddly toy tiger, but other tigers are simply *big cats*. In these examples, the child has acquired a word, and can use it correctly, but does not extend it to other examples of the same thing. *See* **overextension** for the opposite phenomenon in language acquisition.

ungrammatical

Ungrammatical structures are **phrases** or **sentences** that do not conform to the **rules** of a language's **grammar** and would therefore be deemed unacceptable by a **native speaker** of the **language** in question. (*Rules* in this sense refers to descriptive rather than prescriptive rules; *see* **descriptivism** and **prescriptivism**). For example, 'This is a book about language' is an acceptable sentence in English, but 'Book language this a is about' is not. This is not a matter of preference but one of comprehensibility. In **linguistics**, ungrammatical sentences are marked with an asterisk, like '*a on the Cat sat mat'.

Unitary Language System Hypothesis

This idea posits that children who have more than one **language** only have one language system. When a child is acquiring language, they are not aware that certain **words** that they are picking up are from one language, while other words belong to another language. Young children hearing two different languages will not realise that they are hearing more than one language, and it is only later on in their development that they recognise that they possess two different **lexicons**. This may, naturally, mean that sometimes young children produce **utterances** that contain words from their two different languages.

universal language

This refers to a hypothetical **language** spoken by everyone in the world. There have been some attempts to produce an artificial universal language, perhaps most famously Esperanto, which was developed by L. L. Zamenhof in the 1800s. Zamenhof developed Esperanto with a number of aims, including to make international communication easier. While estimates suggest that there are a couple of million speakers of Esperanto language worldwide, it remains a long way from becoming a true universal language.

underlexicalisation

This is the feature of a **language**, **variety** or **text** that has (or in the case of a text, uses) a small range of **words** to refer to things (concrete or abstract) in their worlds. English, as a language, is overlexicalised, because it has borrowed so many words from other languages and developed a rich **vocabulary** as a result, often with many words referring to approximately the same thing, though with subtle differences of **connotation**. Languages in earlier stages of development, such as **pidgin** or **creole** languages, tend to be under-lexicalised by comparison. These are not value judgements, and all languages operate perfectly well in the contexts for which they have evolved. Shakespeare might seem to be a writer whose texts are overlexicalised, because of the wide range of options he appears to have, whereas some writers (e.g. Ernest Hemingway, Samuel Beckett) have made a virtue of working with a very limited vocabulary that has a very different stylistic effect. *Underlexicalisation* has a specific meaning in **stylistics**, where it refers to a character or narrator who has an unusually limited vocabulary. In this sense, underlexicalisation can be an indicator of **mind style**.

Uniformitarian Principle

The Uniformitarian Principle is a principle in **historical linguistics** that states that nothing that is not the case in **language** today could ever have been the case in language in the past. For example, it is not the case that we produce **approximant** sounds by using our **teeth** as **articulators**. Therefore, it cannot ever have been the case in the past that we produced approximant sounds by using our teeth as articulators. The Uniformitarian Principle doesn't just cover language structure though; it also applies to language use. For instance, because language varies according to a wide range of non-linguistic factors today (such as age, social class, region, etc.), we can assume that this would also have been the case in the past. The value of the Uniformitarian Principle is that it helps us to hypothesise about how and why particular linguistic changes might have been actuated and propagated (*see* **actuation** and **propagation**). For instance, we know from research in **sociolinguistics** that the middle classes are often the drivers of linguistic change. The Uniformitarian Principle allows us to speculate that this would also have been the case in the past. Consequently, we can reasonably hypothesise that one possible cause of the **Great Vowel Shift** was speakers trying to emulate what they saw as high-prestige **varieties**.

Universal Grammar

According to the theoretical framework of **generative grammar**, Universal Grammar (or UG) is a set of linguistic principles that human beings are born with. The claim that human beings all share fundamental knowledge about the possible ways in which natural **languages** are structured, whichever language we learn to speak, is widely shared among generativists (though not all **linguists** subscribe to the notion – *see* **design features**, for instance). However, the specific nature of that set of expectations is under debate by those who are trying to identify these language universals by studying the diversity of human languages and how children acquire them. The idea of UG is logically derived from the generally accepted belief that children receive a relatively impoverished input into their language development (i.e. they are not systematically taught the language) but they still manage to acquire a functioning first language. This leads to the conclusion that there must be some kind of internal (mental) set of structures and **rules** – a universal grammar – that the child matches to the language round about. *See also* **I-language**, **E-language**, **competence** and **performance**.

unmarked

This is a term (with its partner, ***marked***) that helps to identify the default **meaning** in a pair of **lexical items** (and the non-default one, by default). Thus, length is indicated in English by an unmarked term, *long* – as in 'How long is it?' – and a marked term, *short* – as in 'How short is it?' The difference is that the latter indicates that you are expecting the thing concerned to be comparatively short, whereas the former has no such assumption – the answer to 'How long is it?' could quite comfortably be 'Oh really short', whereas the answer to 'How short is it?' would normally confirm that the **referent** is, indeed, comparatively short (e.g. 'Quite short'). To answer this question with the news that it is, actually, quite long, would require some additional explanation, because it goes against the expectations of a marked **form** (e.g. 'Well, actually, it's really rather long'). Most **adjective** pairs of this kind have unmarked forms (e.g. *wide*, *tall*, *big*) and some **nouns** also come in marked/unmarked pairs, particularly in the animal kingdom where the male (e.g. *dog*, *lion*) is used for the whole species, and the female (e.g. *bitch*, *lioness*) only for the females.

The origins of markedness are in **phonology** where sounds are made up of phonetic features, some of which may be in their default or unmarked state where there is no meaningful contrast apparent. In lexical terms, it is easy to see that some pairs have a term which is literally 'marked' by the addition of a **suffix** (*lion* – *lioness*) and this has in the past been the case for many pairs of words referring to human activity, including job titles (e.g. *actor* – *actress*; *manager* – *manageress*), though there has been considerable change in this practice as a result of the achievements of feminism and its critique of the 'male-as-norm' society. Of course, there are professions, such as nursing, where the female was traditionally the norm, but since there were simply no nurses who were male at one time, there was no morphological suffix created, so the marked term was a two-word **phrase** (*male nurse*) once men started to take up this profession. A similar situation occurred in the early days of women becoming doctors (*woman doctor*) but this is now less commonly used as the gender of the doctor treating you is not really as important as their skills and knowledge. *See also* **markedness**.

unrounded

Unrounded **vowel** sounds are produced without lip-rounding. When we pronounce a vowel such as the /iː/ in *beat*, the **lips** are spread, rather than rounded. The difference becomes clear if you then change just the vowel sound, switching from the unrounded /iː/ in *beat* to the rounded /uː/ in *boot*.

uptalk

This is also known as *upspeak* or the *High Rising Terminal* (HRT) and refers to the tendency to use a high rising **intonation** pattern at the ends of **utterances** in some **varieties** of English. Many accounts of English intonation, including many textbooks teaching English as a second or foreign **language**, define rising intonation patterns as symptomatic of questions, and assert that a mid-to-low falling intonation pattern is the sign of a statement or **declarative**. A recent rise in HRT, however, has led to a great deal of controversy in the media about the influence of Australian soap operas and/or American-style speech on the intonation of British English. It is clearly a pattern that is being used more by younger speakers, not only in Britain, but HRT is a long-standing feature of some Irish varieties of English, particularly in mid-Ulster and Belfast, so it is not simply a recent phenomenon, though it seems to be growing in popularity, particularly amongst girls and women. This has led to some speculation about its sociolinguistic importance as a signifier of linguistic change, women being more likely in general to innovate than men. However, the pattern is increasingly used across all speakers, including men and women of all ages.

upward convergence

Part of the bigger *communication accommodation theory* (CAT), upward convergence (also called *convergence* and *linguistic convergence*) is a strategy that speakers adopt (often subconsciously) in certain social settings in order to more closely resemble the speech used by their **interlocutor(s)**. An example of convergence would be pronouncing a **word** in the same way as your friend even if the word does not sound the same in your **accent**, e.g. pronouncing *bath* with a short /a/ (as is the predominant pronunciation in northern varieties of British English) rather than *bath* with a long /a:/ sound (as is the predominant pronunciation in southern varieties of British English). There are many reasons why people converge in their speech. Reasons for convergence may be related to social status (e.g. wanting to be approved by a social group) or not wanting to stand out from a social group (e.g. for having a different accent from your friends). Upward convergence is the opposite of *divergence* whereby a speaker adapts their speech to sound less like their interlocutor(s). *See also* **accommodation** and **downward convergence**.

usage-based linguistics

This is an area of language study that looks at how **languages** have developed into their current **form**, as well as the reasons why languages change. The 'usage' bit reflects the idea that every time you hear something in a particular language, your impression of that language will change. Similarly, every time you use a particular language, what you say will influence others' impressions of the language. Usage-based **linguistics** is interested in working out how our perceptions of a particular language change when we hear, speak, read or write in that language.

utterance

linguistics makes a distinction between grammatical structures, such as **clauses** and **sentences**, and spoken units of language, which are known as utterances and may match the grammatical structures. Or not. *See also* **C-unit** and **spoken grammar**.

uvular

This is one of the **places of articulation** that define speech sounds in **phonetics**. The *uvula* is the part of the upper mouth that is farthest back, and is partly made up of the 'dangly' projection you can see if you look in the mirror with your mouth open. There is speculation about its primary function, which may be to provide lubrication to your throat, but, as an **articulator**, it helps to make a number of speech sounds, including the **voiceless** [q] in Arabic and many African **languages**, which sounds like a /k/ but farther back in the mouth and occurs in names like *Qatar* and *Iraq*. In some **dialects** of some European languages, including French, German and a few Scandinavian languages, the uvular **approximant** [ʀ] is the preferred pronunciation of /r/.

V

variable

A linguistic variable is any element of **language** that has the capacity to vary between **dialects**. For example, the /r/ **phoneme** is a variable in that it is pronounced differently in different dialects. In Scottish English, for instance, it may be an **alveolar** trill /r̝/ (i.e. a rolled /r/), while in Lancashire /r/ may be rhotic – for example, the **word** *car* may be pronounced /kaːr/ as opposed to, say, /kaː/. (Note how a **diacritic** can be used to indicate a variant of the phoneme.) Variables can be found at all **levels of language**. A famous lexical variable in the UK is the word used to describe a small bread roll, which may be described variously as a *cob*, *batch*, *breadcake*, *teacake*, *huffkin* and so on. The study of linguistic variables is at the heart of variationist **sociolinguistics**, which often examines how linguistic variables are influenced by non-linguistic variables such as age, gender, social class, etc.

variation

In **linguistics**, variation can be seen in the fact that there are multiple ways of saying any one thing. If you are from the northeast of England, you may pronounce the **word** *cloud* to rhyme with *rude*; if you are from the south of England, you are more likely to pronounce it to rhyme with *loud*. If you are quite young, you are unlikely to describe something cool as *groovy*, whereas if you are older, you are unlikely to use *sick*. These examples demonstrate how different aspects of **language**, such as **accent** and **dialect**, vary according to factors such as region and age. Note that there do tend to be limits to this sort of variation – aspects of language such as **syntax**, for example, are less prone to variation, although note that variation does sometimes occur here too, such as in *because* + **noun phrase** formulations such as 'Because the internet' (for 'Because

I spent too much time on the internet'). **Linguists** study variation from different perspectives. Variationist linguists are interested in how language changes over time, investigating phenomena such as how words for *cool* come and go. Sociolinguists, on the other hand, focus on how social context affects how we use language, investigating, for instance, how a word like *cloud* is pronounced in different parts of the UK.

variety

Non-linguists often assume that **dialects** are sub-standard regional **forms** of a **language**. For this reason, **linguists** often prefer to use the term *variety* when discussing dialects, because *variety* does not have these negatively evaluative **connotations**. *Variety* is also useful as a term because it can be used to discuss many different types of variants of a language. For example, we can talk about **register** variants (formal as opposed to informal, for instance) or social variants (that is, social dialects – or **sociolects** – as opposed to regional dialects). *See also* **lect**.

velar

This describes a group of consonantal sounds that are articulated with the back part of the **tongue** body against the **velum**. In English, the most common velar sounds are /k/, /g/ and /ŋ/ (the last one refers to the sound of *ng* at the end of English **words** like *sing*).

velum

The velum is also referred to as the *soft palate*. The velum is a soft tissue structure at the back of the mouth that can be raised and lowered to allow for air to flow out of the **nasal** or **oral cavity** (or both at the same time). If you run your **tongue** back across the roof of your mouth, you will feel first the **hard palate** and then the bony areas will stop and you will feel the softer velum. Stop there, or you might make yourself sick!

verb

Lexical verbs function as the head of a **verb phrase**. Sometimes the verb phrase will consist of just the main (i.e. lexical) verb, and other times there may be **auxiliary verbs** before it. Here are some examples of verb phrases (italicised), with the main verb underlined:

Cows *eat* grass.

I *was avoiding* work.

The mice *must have eaten* all the cheese!

When you're analysing a **sentence**, always look for the main verb first!

In English, verbs have five different **forms** (see the table below). For regular verbs, the past and past participle form are the same. For irregular verbs, these are different.

	Infinitive	Present	Past	Present participle	Past participle
Regular	walk	walk/s	walked	walking	walked
Irregular	drink	drink/s	drank	drinking	drunk
	give	give/s	gave	giving	given
	fly	fly/flies	flew	flying	flown

Verbs can refer to a wide range of actions and states, including physical actions (*run*, *jump*), states of being (*is*) and mental processes (*think*, *believe*, *understand*).

verb phrase

Verb phrases have a lexical **verb** as their **head word**. For example:

* was sleeping
* had been sleeping
* must have been sleeping

Verb phrases function as the **predicator** in a **sentence**. *See also* **verb** and **SPOCA**.

verba sentiendi

Verba sentiendi are a subgroup of **verbs**. They refer to mental processes and feelings that can only be experienced by the person who uses them, such as *hope* and *feel*. We find plentiful *verba sentiendi*, for instance, in works of fiction. These may be used deliberately by a writer to encourage the reader to share a character's point of view. For instance, in the opening lines of *One Hundred Years of Solitude*, by Gabriel García Márquez, *verba sentiendi* allow us to see things from the character's point of view: 'Many years later, as he faced the firing squad, Colonel Aureliano Buendia was to *remember* that distant afternoon when his father took him to discover ice.'

vernacular

This refers to the **variety** of your **language** that you speak most naturally in informal contexts. We vary our language use considerably, depending on the situation we find ourselves in. In a job interview, for example, you might well adopt a more standard **accent** and **dialect** than you would use in other contexts. When discussing the experience afterwards with family or friends, you'll probably slip back into your vernacular. In everyday usage, vernacular can have a negative evaluation, but in **linguistics**, it doesn't.

Verner's Law

Verner's Law is named after the Danish **linguist** Karl Verner (1846–96) and was formulated to explain what appeared to be irregularities in the operation of **Grimm's Law**. For example, Grimm's Law states that /p/, /t/ and /k/ in **Proto-Indo-European** (PIE, for short) shift to /f/, /θ/ and /x/ in Proto-Germanic. However, Verner noticed that some **words** in Germanic **languages** do not follow this pattern. For example, the Indo-European word for *father* was *pətēr* (from which we get Latin *pater*). The presence of a /t/ would suggest that Germanic words for *father* should replace this with a /θ/. But in English, for example, which is a Germanic language, we find /ð/ instead. That is, the word *father* contains a **voiced fricative** rather than the **voiceless** one predicted by Grimm's Law. Verner's Law basically explains the reason for this. It states that PIE voiceless fricatives only become voiced in Germanic languages if they occur next to a voiceless sound and if the **stress** in the corresponding PIE word is on the preceding **syllable**.

virgule

The virgule, or forward slash (/), was a punctuation mark used in medieval and early modern writing. Early punctuation did not work in quite the same way as contemporary punctuation. While punctuation in present-day writing tends to mark grammatical boundaries (e.g. semicolons distinguish between **clauses**, and full stops differentiate **sentences**), earlier punctuation marks were used more to indicate rhetorical divisions in a **text**. The virgule was used to mark a *caesura* – that is, to indicate where to pause when reading the text aloud. In this respect, while the virgule is the ancestor of the modern comma, in its original form it functioned slightly differently from its modern counterpart.

vocabulary

This refers to all the **words** known by an individual person. This is more specific than **lexicon**, which can refer to the words of a person, **language** or field of expertise. Distinctions are sometimes made between different types of vocabulary. For instance, there is a distinction between *reading vocabulary* (the words you recognise when reading) and *listening vocabulary* (the words you recognise when listening to others talk). This is a handy distinction, as sometimes we might be used to reading a word in books, but not recognise it when we hear it (think of a word like *misled*, where people often imagine it sounding like *mizzled*). We can also think of our *speaking vocabulary* (all the words you use in your own speech) and our *writing vocabulary* (all the words you use in your written language). You may be able to think of words, for instance, that are part of your writing vocabulary, but not of your speaking vocabulary – perhaps quite formal-sounding words like *thus*, *whomsoever* and *notwithstanding*. The same may be true the other way around – you might be more likely to use **Standard English** 'It rained' when writing than a more colloquial equivalent such as 'It chucked it down', or a dialectal equivalent like 'It stotted it down.' In even more general terms, we can distinguish between *active vocabulary* (words we commonly use) and *passive vocabulary* (words we don't use, but recognise).

vocal folds

Vocal folds (commonly referred to as the *vocal cords*) are two pieces of muscle that stretch horizontally across the **glottis** and which can be adjusted according to the particular sound we want to produce (*see* **voicing**, below). In effect, they can be used to close off the glottis.

vocal tract

The **larynx**, **pharynx** (commonly known as the *throat*) and **oral** and **nasal cavities** are collectively known as the *vocal tract*. When producing (most) speech sounds, we expel air from the **lungs**, which then passes through the *trachea* (windpipe) and, depending on the sound we are producing, is set in vibration by the **vocal folds** in the larynx. The sound that is ultimately produced depends on the shape of the vocal tract. Humans can alter their vocal tracts considerably in order to produce a wide variety of speech sounds.

vocative

In **languages** that use **case** marking, a **noun** that is in the vocative case is one that has an **inflection** (or, in some cases, zero inflection) to indicate that its grammatical function is to name or address someone or something. In Hungarian, for example, the **sentence** *Nem szeretem Lászlót* means 'I don't like László.' In this case, *László* is the direct **object** of the **verb**, and its inflection consequently marks it as being in the accusative case. The sentence, *László, nem szeretlek!* ('László, I don't like you!'), on the other hand, uses *László* in the vocative case, to indicate that its function is to address the person called 'László'. English no longer has a vocative case, though the term *vocative* is still sometimes used to refer to proper nouns when they function as address **forms**.

voice onset time

When producing a **stop consonant** (i.e. a **plosive** sound), air is occluded (i.e. stopped or blocked) by the **articulators** before being released as a burst. Stop consonants can be **voiced** or **voiceless** (*see* the explanation of **voicing** below). Voice onset time (or VOT for short) can be used to determine the difference between voiced and voiceless stop consonants (e.g. /p/, /b/, /t/ and /d/). It is a measure of the amount of time between the initial release of air and the production of voicing (that is, the vibration of the **vocal folds**). In very basic terms, if the vocal folds start to vibrate *before* the occluded air is released, then what will be produced is a voiced stop consonant (e.g. the /d/ in /dɒg/). If, on the other hand, the vocal folds do not start to vibrate until the point at which the occluded air is released, then what will be produced is a voiceless stop consonant (e.g. the /k/ of /kɪl/). And if there is a delay between the release of the occluded air and the beginning of voicing (i.e. voice onset), then an aspirated plosive will be produced (e.g. the /p/ of /pat/). VOT is measured in milliseconds and can be used to explore various sociolinguistic phenomena. For example, the question of whether a person's first language (L1) affects their pronunciation of a second language (L2) can be investigated by measuring the VOTs of their stop consonants in both their L1 and L2 and comparing these to the VOTs of a **native speaker** of the L2.

voice quality

There are many definitions of the term *voice quality*, and how it is defined will largely depend on the context in which it is being used (e.g. in speech pathology, general *sociophonetic* research, **forensic speech science**) and an academic's own views on what constitutes voice quality. Very generally, voice quality describes a **suprasegmental** feature of speech that considers the habitual, anatomical settings an individual adopts when speaking. Voice quality is often described as capturing the characteristic sound of the voice, or the variations in the quality of what is being said over **phrases** or **utterances**, rather than individual **segments**. In order to produce speech, we require a source (the **vocal folds**) and a filter (the **vocal tract**). The source initiates sound, and the filter modifies that sound. Many experts will separate these two things when analysing voice quality, and consider only the tendencies of the source to determine voice quality – that is, they are interested in what is occurring in the **larynx** (and sometimes the **pharynx**). Following this definition, voice quality is defined by the vibration of the vocal folds. Voice quality would consider things like irregularities in vocal fold vibrations, overall muscular tension, and laryngeal frication. These elements would help us identify creaky voice (*see* **creak**), **tremor**/jittery voices, and even voices that have that Kermit the Frog-like quality where the larynx has been raised.

Voice quality can also be used not just to describe characteristics of the source, but also to take into consideration elements of the filter (in combination with the source). It is often the case that *supra-laryngeal* (above the larynx) articulators in the vocal tract also play a large role in the voice quality we perceive. This more encompassing view of voice quality may consider things like the **lips** (e.g. protrusion or spreading), jaw (e.g. open or closed), **tongue** tip/body (e.g. fronted or backed), and nasality. Regardless of the definition, voice quality can be examined both auditorily and acoustically. There is a limited amount of research that has been done on voice quality in comparison to other features of speech such as **vowels** and **consonants**. However, current research is starting to look at correlations of what we hear/perceive and what happens acoustically when we visualise speech – all of this is very important to increase our understanding of how individuals achieve different voice qualities. For example, even if Matt and Dan were from the same area and had the same **accent**, what specific elements of their voice quality would make them sound like them as individuals?

voiced

This refers to a sound that is produced with the **vocal folds** vibrating (*see* **voiceless** for when the vocal folds do not vibrate). **vowels** are usually voiced, though some **languages** (including English and Japanese) have voiceless vowels too. We also produce voiceless vowels when we whisper. **consonants** can also be voiced. On the **International Phonetic Alphabet** chart, when two consonants appear within the same box (i.e. they have the same **place** and **manner of articulation**), the symbol that appears on the right is the voiced version of the sound on the left. A very easy trick to see whether a sound is voiced is to put your fingers in your ears and produce the sound. You should notice a buzzing feeling in your fingers if the sound is voiced. Try it with /z/ and /s/. Which one is voiced?

voiceless

This refers to a sound that is produced when the **vocal folds** are not vibrating (*see* **voiced** for a description of what happens when the vocal folds do vibrate). Many **consonants** in English are voiceless, such as / s t f k p /. And whispered speech is entirely voiceless. It is also possible to produce some voiced consonants voicelessly. Such consonants are indicated with a special **diacritic**; for example, the **International Phonetic Alphabet** symbol [n̥] describes a typical **alveolar nasal** /n/ as actually being voiceless in its production. This happens in English when /n/ follows an initial /s/ in **words** like 'snow'. Try preparing to say this word and stopping before the **vowel**. You might find that the /sn/ part sounds whispered! You can check whether you are producing a voiceless sound by placing your thumb and forefinger against your Adam's apple. Try producing a voiceless alveolar **fricative**, /s/, out loud; unlike a /z/, you should not feel any buzzing in your fingers.

voicing

This is an articulatory process and refers to the vibration of the **vocal folds** during the production of speech sound. Air is expelled from the **lungs** and passes through the *trachea* (windpipe) to the **larynx**, where the vocal folds are located. If the vocal folds are open, and air passes through without setting them vibrating, then what will be produced is a **voiceless** sound (e.g. /s/ or /t/). If, however, the vocal folds are close together, then the **airflow** will make them vibrate and what will be produced is a **voiced** sound (e.g. /z/ or /d/). You can actually feel the difference if you rest two fingers against your Adam's apple and produce the sounds above. Try it with the /z/ of *zoo* and the /s/ of *sue*. With the former you should feel a vibration that you don't get with the latter.

vowel

You are perhaps used to the idea that English has just five vowels: <a>, <e>, <i>, <o> and <u>. Don't be misled! Vowels are not letters but speech sounds (the five letters referred to above are just convenient ways of representing vowel sounds in written English). In reality, a vowel is a sound that is produced with an open **vocal tract** and shaped by the **oral cavity**, with no restriction to the **airflow**. The particular vowel sound produced is determined by the height of the **tongue** (i.e. how close it is to the roof of the mouth, or palate), how far back the tongue is in the oral cavity, and whether the **lips** are rounded or **unrounded**. Try producing the sounds /iː/ (as in *eat*), /aː/ (as in *army*) and /uː/ (as in *ooh!*). You should be able to feel your tongue change position and the shape of your lips alter as you move from sound to sound. In English, all vowel sounds are normally **voiced**, but this is not necessarily the case in other **languages**.

waveform

In **phonetics**, a waveform is a graphical representation of the variations in air pressure due to speech sounds. Time is displayed on the horizontal axis, while the sound pressure level is displayed on the vertical axis. Waveforms allow you to see individual pulses that correspond to each vibration of the **vocal folds**. As a result, **voiced** sounds will appear **periodic** on the waveform, while a **voiceless** sound will appear **aperiodic**.

weak inflection

This term (and its opposite, *strong inflection*) relates to the Germanic **languages**, in which there may be two different sets of morphological endings (*declensions*) running in parallel. This distinction has carried over to English and is found in **verbs**, where the *strong verbs* are those that form the past tense by replacing the **vowel** at the centre of the stressed **syllable** (e.g. *take*/*took*; *run*/*ran*), and the *weak verbs* are those that form the past by addition of a **suffix** involving some kind of **alveolar** or **dental plosive** (e.g. *miss*/*missed*; *rain*/*rained*). The same terms were applied by extension to the two different sets of Germanic **nouns**, where the plural is formed in strong nouns by addition of a **sibilant** (e.g. *car*/*cars*), and in weak nouns by addition of a **nasal**, or vowel plus nasal, ending (*child*/*children*). There is nothing intrinsically weak or strong about these groups of **words**, and there is relatively little of the distinction left in **Present Day English**, compared to German or to **Old English**. Because of their ubiquity, what we now call the *regular forms* (i.e. strong nouns and weak verbs) are those that dominate in English. They have extended their reach compared with older forms of the language.

Wernicke's aphasia

This is a type of *fluent aphasia* and is characterised by speech that is structurally sound but lacking in sentence-level semantic **meaning**. This is in contrast to the speech of patients with **Broca's aphasia**, whose speech is non-fluent and composed of few **words** and short **sentences**. People with Wernicke's aphasia also have problems with **language** comprehension. The term comes from the work of the German physician Carl Wernicke, who was the first to discover that not all aphasia could be attributed to damage to the frontal lobe of the brain (which is the area affected in patients with Broca's aphasia). Wernicke's aphasia is instead caused by damage to the left posterior temporal lobe. *See also* **aphasia** and **jargon aphasia**.

wh-question

This term is named after the group of question **words** in English that happen to begin with *wh-* (e.g. *what*, *which*, *when*, *whose*, *why*), with *how* as an exception. These words usually introduce a question in which one specific part of the semantic content is missing and is the focus of the questioning behaviour. So, 'When is the train arriving?' would indicate with some certainty that there is a train and that it will be arriving, but asks the question when that will occur. Compare this to the other main type of question, known as **yes/no questions** or polar questions. If we ask 'Will you be at the party on Saturday?', there is again some content (there is a party on Saturday), but the answer to the question is not a time, a place or a person, as it would be in the case of wh-questions, but either *yes* or *no*. Note that these question words can be used as relative **pronouns** too (e.g. 'The car which I bought … '), so they have at least two jobs to do in English **syntax**. Only one of the wh-words is so general that it has the potential to be used recursively in interaction though, as parents will recognise. Small children delight in continually asking 'Why?' after they have been answered again and again. This game cannot work with *what* or *how*, for example. Note also that, although the core wh-words result in auxiliary-inversion/*do*-support (i.e. the first auxiliary is put before the **subject** after a wh-word, and if there is no auxiliary, the **verb** *do* is used), this is not the case for some phrasal wh-questions (e.g. 'How come Hazel isn't coming?'). *See also* **question forms**.

whisper

This is a type of **voice quality** that is produced when the **vocal folds** are narrowed, but do not vibrate. The narrowing of the vocal folds causes the **airflow** through the **glottis** to be more turbulent. Whispery, or whispered, voice is the type of speech you might expect to hear inside a library – it is quiet and hushed so as to not make much noise. This is because the vocal folds are not vibrating, and therefore not producing **voicing**, which is associated with louder, more sonorous sounds.

word

This appears to be such a simple everyday term, but in fact it is fraught with difficulty. When we say *word*, do we mean a word-form (such as *raspberries*) or a group of **forms** (such as *raspberry* plus its plural and possessive forms)? The latter, a group of related forms that differ only grammatically – and not semantically – are often referred to as a **lexeme** (or **lemma** in some fields, such as **corpus linguistics**). Another question that arises in relation to **texts** is whether we mean individual occurrences of a word (also known as *tokens*) or the number of different lexemes (*types*) that are involved. It would not make sense to say that Shakespeare has a large **vocabulary** just because he wrote a lot of words (tokens), unless there was also a large variety of different words (types). **Linguists** often avoid using the word *word* unless they have made it very clear at the outset which meaning they want it to have.

word class

There is a tendency even in contemporary **grammars** to use the relatively traditional grammatical term *word class* to refer to types of **words** according to their behaviour (the function that they have in the wider structure), their **form** (the kinds of morphological endings that they may take) and their **semantics** (whether they are arguments/**participants**, circumstances or processes). While it is convenient to behave as though all words belong to the content classes of **noun**, **verb**, **adjective**, **adverb**, or one of the grammatical word classes (such as **preposition** or **conjunction**), many words can act in the capacity of more than one of these types. Thus, the word *table* is seen as a prototypical noun (i.e. a particularly characteristic example of a noun) out of context, but in many contexts it is used verbally ('He tabled an amendment'), and most nouns and verbs can occur in places where we would prototypically expect adjectives, e.g. before the **head noun**, as in *the dancing bear* or *my photo choice*. There are complex arguments for when and whether these uses have actually caused the word to change from one type to another, but the important thing to note is that the tension between **category** membership and flexibility of behaviour is one of the strengths of human **language** and allows for its creativity and power. **part of speech** is sometimes used as an alternative term to *word class*. *See also* **open class** and **closed class**.

word form

This is often used, particularly in **corpus linguistics**, to refer to a single version of a **word**, as opposed to the **lemma** or **lexeme**, which represents all the **inflections** of a word. Thus, the following list represents four different word forms but only one lexeme or lemma: *play, played, playing, plays*.

word order

This refers to the typical ordering of the main elements of a **clause** in any **language**. In English and in many other languages (e.g. Indonesian, Spanish), the default order is **subject-verb-object** but there are languages (e.g. Japanese, Turkish) whose normal word order is subject-object-verb. Together these two patterns make up most of the world's languages, though a minority have a different word order (e.g. Malagasy has verb-object-subject, and there is an object-verb-subject language called Hixkaryana in Amazonia, as well as some evidence of an object-subject-verb language called Warao in Venezuela). Whilst this is one typological approach to the categorisation of human languages, it has also been questioned by some **linguists** who point out that the grammatical relations of subject and object are not universal, and that some highly morphological languages do not exhibit a stable ordering of these elements anyway.

wug

In 1958, the **linguist** Jean Berko Gleason carried out an experiment to find out how and when children learned the grammatical

morphemes (such as **noun** plurals, third person present **tense** and diminutive **suffixes**) of English. The experiment involved drawings of invented creatures and invented activities, so that the children could be asked to produce the inflected **forms** of these. The most famous of these creations was the little bird-like creature called a *wug*. Children were, for example, shown one wug and then another one, and prompted for the plural by being told 'There are two ____'. The elegance of this experiment was enhanced by its naturalistic nature – it was perfect for children, who are quite used to being taught new **words** for things and being asked to fill in gaps in **sentences** by their carers and teachers.

X-bar theory

This is a theory of ***phrase structure grammar*** first proposed by the American **linguist** Noam Chomsky. According to X-bar theory, the lexical **Categories** of **noun, verb, adjective** and **preposition** can each form the head of a structure made up of a phrasal node that is formed from the same category (the 'X' in *X-bar* stands for the lexical category in question, e.g. V for **verb**). Here, for instance, is a syntax **tree diagram** for the **noun phrase** *The Babel Lexicon of Language*, showing how the noun phrase is composed of a series of **phrases**:

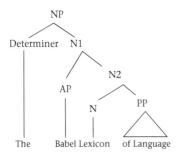

X-bar theory aims to provide an explanation of the internal structure of phrasal categories for **language** generally.

xenonym

This is the term given to the name of a **language**, place or group of people that is not used by the **native speakers** or inhabitants themselves. *Hungarian*, for instance, is a xenonym of *Magyar*, which is the Hungarian **word** for the Hungarian language. In the days of the British Empire, the British were notorious for using xenonyms in favour of native place names. Hence, *Mumbai* was changed to

Bombay, and *Chennai* to *Madras*. This latter example demonstrates how xenonyms can be used to subjugate a native language.

Xhosa

This is a Nguni Bantu **language**, and well known in **linguistics** for being a language that uses *clicks*. In fact, the first sound in *Xhosa* is actually a **lateral** click, as <x> in Xhosa is used orthographically to represent the lateral click sound. Xhosa is recognised as an official language in South Africa and Zimbabwe. There are over 8 million speakers that have Xhosa as a first language, and another 11 million speakers who use Xhosa as a second (or additional) language. Xhosa is comprised of a number of **dialects**, and the language is spoken across a relatively large geographical area. Linguistically, Xhosa is a **tonal language** with a relatively small **vowel** system (ten

X-BAR

Happy Hour:
2 Noun Phrases
for the price of 1

vowels). However, Xhosa is most famous for its complex **consonant** system. Xhosa contains the more common *pulmonic* **egressive** sounds, but it also includes eighteen clicks. These clicks are **dental**, lateral, and **alveolar**, and they are made in combination with pulmonic **egressive** consonant articulation. In addition to clicks, Xhosa also uses **ejectives** and **implosives**.

Y

Yakut

Yakut is a Turkish **language**, also known as Sakha, Saqa or Saxa. Yakut is spoken by over 400,000 speakers, and the majority of those speakers are also fluent in Russian. The word *Yakuts* is also used to describe the group of people who are a Turkic ethnic group from the Republic of Sakha located in the northeastern region of Russia. Yakut, like other Turkish languages, is an ***agglutinative*** language that has ***vowel harmony***. **word order** in Yakut is typically **subject-object-verb**, and the language does not exhibit grammatical **gender**.

yes/no questions

These are the kind of questions that in English are constructed by moving the first **auxiliary verb** in front of the **subject**, as in '*Could* you help me carry these cups?' In this case, the auxiliary is a **modal verb** (*could*) but the same mechanism works for the other auxiliaries too: '*Have* you got time to help me?'; '*Is* she coming to the party?'; '*Was* the window broken by those children?' Note that in English where there is no relevant auxiliary, the **dummy auxiliary** *do* is used instead: '*Did* Hazel make all those cakes?' Other **languages**, such as Spanish, front the main **verb** in such cases, instead of creating a dummy auxiliary: '¿*Hizo* Hazel todos los pasteles?' The semantic link between all these questions is that they invite one of two answers: *yes* or *no*. *See also* **wh-questions** and **question forms**.

Yiddish

This is an **Indo-European language** spoken by around 370,000 people across the world. The highest number of Yiddish speakers are in Israel, where there are 166,000 speakers. Yiddish combines elements of German and Hebrew and **loanwords** from some Slavic languages. Yiddish was traditionally the language of the Ashkenazi Jewish population in mainland Europe, particularly in Germany, and later in Eastern Europe. A huge percentage of the Jewish people killed in the Holocaust spoke Yiddish, and, as a result of the Holocaust, the number of Yiddish speakers drastically declined after the Second World War. Yiddish uses the Hebrew alphabet, and modern Yiddish is separated into two **varieties**. The more widely spoken variety of Yiddish is Eastern Yiddish, which is spoken in Eastern European countries such as Poland and Hungary, and the other is Western Yiddish, which is spoken in Western Europe in countries such as Germany. There are many **words** of Yiddish origin that have been borrowed into English, often with different Roman spellings. Such words include *schlep*, *schmuck*, *chutzpah* and *klutz*.

yod-coalescence

This describes the process whereby the /j/ **phoneme**, when part of a particular phoneme cluster, changes to become either an **affricate** or a **fricative**. For example, the /sj/ cluster in *issue* can coalesce to /ʃ/, resulting in /ɪʃuː/ rather than /ɪsjuː/, and the /tj/ cluster in *tune* can coalesce to /tʃuːn/. Contrary to **yod-dropping**, yod-coalescence can happen when the phoneme cluster spans a **syllable** boundary and before an unstressed **syllable**. Other clusters which can undergo yod-coalescence are /dj/ → /dʒ/ and /zj/ → /zʒ/.

yod-dropping

Have you dropped a yod recently? Yod-dropping is the process of eliding (i.e. omitting) the /j/ **phoneme** (i.e. the sound represented by <y> at the beginning of the **word** *yacht*) in English words like *tune*, *enthusiastic* and *pursuit*. Yod-dropping tends to occur at the beginning of **syllables** that contain the back **vowel** /uː/. By the end of the **Middle English** period, words such as *new* and *few* were pronounced with an /ɪu/ **diphthong**. However, in many **accents**, the /ɪu/ then developed into /juː/ as a result of a continued process of sound change. And once the cluster /juː/ is an option, so too is the possibility of eliding the /j/. Thus, *tune* can be pronounced with **yod-coalescence** as /tʃuːn/ or, after yod-dropping, as /tuːn/. You can hear these differences if you compare some British English accents with some American English accents. But yod-dropping doesn't happen in all accents. For example, Welsh English retains the /ɪu/ diphthong in words like *chew*, and so yod-dropping is not an option. And why *yod*? Because that's the name of the Hebrew letter *yodh* that has the sound /j/.

Zapotec

The **word** *Zapotec* is a **xenonym** which translates to 'inhabitants of the place of sapote', as the Zapotec civilisation (*c.* 700 BC – AD 1521) actually referred to themselves using the term *Be'ena'a*. While *Zapotec* is used to refer to the people that inhabited the area of what is now the modern-day Mexican state of Oaxaca, *Zapotec* also refers to a group of **languages**. The Zapotec languages are comprised of around fifty related Mesoamerican languages (spoken by over 400,000 speakers) that come from the Oto-Manguean language family. Zapotec languages are largely spoken in the state of Oaxaca, but many Zapotec speakers can also be found in California. There are many varieties of Zapotec that are mutually unintelligible from one another. However, there are some varieties that are mutually intelligible, and those tend to be geographically closer to one another. As a result of the **variation**, the Mexican government officially recognises a large number of different Zapotec languages. From a linguistic perspective, Zapotec languages are interesting in that some **varieties** contain **retroflex fricatives**, and all Zapotec languages display contrasts in **phonation** types in **vowels**.

zero anaphora

Alfred, Lord Tennyson's poem 'Now sleeps the crimson petal' begins: 'Now sleeps the crimson petal, now the white'. This line contains an example of zero **anaphora**, in that the **noun phrase** *the white* contains a zero-anaphoric reference back to the **noun** *petal*. That is, there is no noun after *the white*. Rather, there is a gap. In order to make sense of this part of the **sentence**, we infer that the gap must refer back to *petal*. The alternative to the zero anaphor would be to use an anaphoric **pronoun**, as in 'Now sleeps the crimson petal, now the white *one*'. This doesn't sound quite so effective, as Tennyson no doubt realised!

zero article

This refers to the use of a **noun** with no attached **determiner**. In 'Feminists campaigned against the decision', *feminists* is a zero-article **noun phrase** (sometimes known as an anarthrous noun phrase), while *the decision* is not, as the definite determiner *the* specifies that there is a particular decision, which is likely to be clear from context. Note the difference if we change the sentence to 'The feminists campaigned against the decision'. Here, the reader assumes that a particular, discrete group of feminists is being referred to, rather than feminists in general.

zero derivation

This is sometimes referred to as **conversion** and is the process of deriving a new **word** from an existing word, but without making any change to its **form**. For example, *gift* was originally a **noun** but can now be used as a **verb** (e.g. 'That present Hazel got me was awful – I'm *regifting* it'). You can sit on a *chair* whilst you *chair* a meeting. And if your colleague keeps talking over you while you're doing so, you can *eyeball* them until they shut up!

zero ending

In an inflectional **language**, a zero ending on a **noun** is, predictably, the lack of an **inflection**. For example, the nominative singular **form** of the Hungarian **word** *ház* (house) has no inflection. By contrast, the nominative plural (*házak*) does. The nominative singular, then, has a zero ending.

zeugma

This is when a single **word** modifies or governs two words grammatically but only fits one of the words semantically, resulting in a semantically incongruous **sentence** or **phrase**. An example of zeugma is 'He fell in love and down the stairs', where the **verb** *fell* can be used metaphorically (in the phrase *to fall in love*) and literally (e.g. *to fall over*), but, when used to refer to both literal and metaphorical falling, results in semantic incongruity. Zeugma is often used for comedic effect. The British humourist Douglas Adams

wrote of his time at university that he 'took a number of baths – and a degree in English'.

Zipf's Law

This law states that the most frequent **word** in a **corpus** will occur approximately twice as often as the second most frequent, which will occur approximately twice as often as the third most frequent, and so on. That is, the frequency of words in a corpus is inversely proportional to its rank position. Proposed by the **linguist** George Kingsley Zipf (1902–50), Zipf's Law was confirmed by Nelson Francis and Henry Kučera in their 1967 study of the Brown Corpus of 1960s American English. *See also* **corpus linguistics**.